The Palestine Yearbook 2015

The Palestine Yearbook 2015

The Ongoing Genocide the World Ignores

Compiled and edited by Diana Lodge

Copyright © Diana Lodge 2016

All rights reserved. Except for the quotation of short passages for the
purposes of criticism or review, no part of this publication may be reproduced,
stored in a retrieval system, or transmitted by any means, electronic,
mechanical, photocopying or otherwise, without the prior written permission
of the publisher.

First published in 2016 by
Stonebridge Publishing

thepalestineyearbook@gmx.co.uk

British Library Cataloguing in Publication Data
A CIP catalogue record for this book is available from the British Library
ISBN 978-1-909552-12-8

Cover photo: Ryan Roderick Beiler/Shutterstock
Designed by Rita Wüthrich

This edition printed and bound in the UK by
TJ International Ltd, Padstow, Cornwall

Every attempt has been made to check the facts contained in this book, but
please forgive the editor for any errors that have crept in. The essentials are
correct; in fact, this book barely scratches the surface of the wrongs done to
Palestinians in 2015, and at the time of writing, nothing has changed for the
better in 2016.

This book is dedicated to the Palestinian people,
who have endured so much undeserved injustice and horror.

Acknowledgements

This book has been compiled from a range of news items available online and much thanks is due to the journalists, mainly Palestinian, who have faced considerable danger, as described in the final section of this book, in carrying out their profession with integrity and courage. Particular thanks goes to Maan News, the International Middle East Media Centre, the Electronic Intifada, the Palestine Monitoring Group, and to Leslie Bravery, whose daily bulletins list the latest abuses inflicted on the Palestinians of the occupied territories (see www.palestine.org.nz).

Many thanks also go to David Halpin, for his help and encouragement, to Christa Mackinnon for reading the text and making insightful suggestions and corrections and to Abbas Shiblak, who also read the text with a knowledgeable eye and who added important data to Appendix I. Many thanks to Paul Matthews for his technical help and advice. Great thanks are due to Rita Wüthrich, who kindly contributed her design skills and experience in the hopes that this book may be of some use to the Palestinian cause.

Finally, my grateful thanks to Roy, who uncomplainingly kept the home fires burning while living with this present absentee.

Contents

Foreword

This book is an attempt to describe, factually, clearly and holistically, the systematic human rights abuses that continue to be inflicted on Palestinians in the occupied territories of the West Bank and Jerusalem, Gaza and in Israel itself.

Each of these examples given here represents a traumatic, and in some instances fatal, event in the life of an ordinary person or family in 2015. They are, however, only the tip of the iceberg. For every instance cited here, there are a hundred more that could have been included, if space permitted. What emerges from these accounts is a very deliberate genocide, organised by those in power in Israel while world leaders look the other way, or blame the victims rather than the perpetrators, or champion the Middle East's most powerful military state's right 'to defend itself', or talk about non-existent peace negotiations and a 'two-state' solution, or argue against the boycott movement. This empty talk continues even as Israeli leaders make it crystal clear that they intend to continue to gobble up vast tracts of the West Bank for illegal settlements, expel Palestinians from Jerusalem, continue the blockade of Gaza, demolish Bedouin villages in Israel's Negev, deny citizenship to Israel's internally-displaced 'refugees' and refuse to acknowledge the right of refugees outside Israel to return.

A terrible human price is being paid for this hypocrisy. Watching my grandsons pile out of their infant school with their friends, laughing and playing, it breaks my heart to think of Palestinian children in the occupied West Bank or Jerusalem. These children must face armed soldiers at checkpoints on their way to school; their schools may be tear-gassed; they risk being attacked by vicious illegal settlers; they lie in bed at night waiting for the next night-time raid, complete with stun grenades, tear gas and rubber-coated or live bullets; many suffer from nightmares, bed-wetting, listlessness and the other signs of trauma; their parents try to provide them with a 'normal' life while themselves facing the theft of their lands, the demolition of their homes, and the constant fear that their loved ones might be the next victims of the illegal occupation of their land. Those in Gaza can only wait, helplessly, for the next onslaught by one of the best-equipped armies in the world.

There are over 9 million Palestinians in Israel, the West Bank, Jerusalem, Gaza and refugee camps in Lebanon, Syria and Jordan. Israel's leaders are increasingly making it clear that they want to take over all the occupied territories for a purely Jewish state. Do the world's leaders intend to leave the Palestinians to rot in camps and ghettoes indefinitely (paid for by whom?), while Israel inexorably transforms itself into a deeply racist theocracy, ruling the Middle East through fear and division? The future, if this appalling state of affairs is allowed to continue and progress further, is tragic for the Palestinians, an indictment of all proclaimed Western values, and a betrayal and twisting of all that is best in Judaism and Christianity. It won't be wonderful to be Israeli either, unless you happen to be ultra-orthodox Jewish, male, heterosexual and, preferably, extremely rich.

While world leaders engage in an endless diplomatic dance of delay, dispossession, deflection and deceit, increasing numbers of people are waking up to the horror that the Palestinians have been facing for three generations. The Palestinians whose lives are described in this book are not terrorists; they are ordinary people who wish to lead peaceful, fulfilling, ordinary lives, and they have every right to do so.

As the clock strikes 12...

"[We] feel that we have nothing to lose. Life in the camp is intolerable. It cannot be even called life. We feel choked: no jobs, no hope, no breathing space."

Cousin of Muhammad Abu Latifa, Qalandiya reefugee camp, West Bank

This is hopefully the most appalling book you will read this year, and the worst thing about it is that it is not a work of fiction.

In these pages you will find brief details of land stolen from farmers who have owned it for generations, a wall over three times higher than the Berlin wall being built to steal yet more land and water resources, children killed by heavily-armed soldiers as a punishment for throwing stones, ancient trees hacked down by religious fanatics, houses destroyed leaving children homeless, tents donated by well-wishers to house those children subsequently destroyed, schools tear-gassed, churches and mosques vandalised, night-time raids on towns, villages and refugee camps by soldiers firing tear gas, stun grenades and rubber-coated steel bullets, communities denied fresh water and sewage disposal, families evicted from their homes because they are not Jewish, inhabitants of towns and villages trapped into ghettoes by an illegally occupying army, ambulances attacked, crops sprayed with herbicide, indigenous peoples denied citizenship because of their ethnicity, government ministers giving encouraging speeches to racist mobs, children being beaten by soldiers and bitten by police dogs, and individuals of all ages being humiliated, beaten up, pepper-sprayed, fired at and even burnt alive because they are Palestinian.

If you find this a hard read, too upsetting or indigestible, then reflect on this: Palestinians don't have to read this, they have to live it, and they have been living it for three generations and more while the world sits back and lets it happen to them.

31 December 2014

As midnight approaches, many Gazans are still suffering the results of the Israeli onslaught the previous summer.

According to the Gazan Ministry of Housing, approximately 124,000 homes were either destroyed or partially damaged. Families are living in tents, caravans, makeshift shelters, schools, or homes with damaged roofs, windows and walls, semi-open to the elements. Little four-month-old Rahaf Abu'Aasi, from the az-Zanna area in Khan Younis, lives with her family in one of the latter. They have tried to seal the windows with plastic bags and other materials, but it is getting desperately cold. As midnight strikes, she has just 9 days to live before she chokes to death from a bronchial inflammation.

Adel Maher al-Lahham is less than a month old. Is he suckling at his mother's breast, and is she dreaming that maybe Adel will one day escape the siege of Gaza, perhaps become a doctor or a lawyer? He has 10 days to live before he, too, dies of cold.

Meanwhile, in Qalandiya refugee camp in the occupied West Bank, young Muhammad Atta Abu Latifa is perhaps dreaming of Nour Taha. They have been in love for years and in June 2015 they will become engaged. He has 181 days to live before he will, allegedly, be shot in the leg and fall from a roof when Israelis attempt to arrest him during a raid on the camp. His family believe he was shot several times and that the Israelis came to assassinate him. When troops attack his camp he was often among those who try to defend their small patch, but around the time he died his energies have been going into planning his engagement party and building a house for him and his bride. Maryam, Muhammad's mother, reflecting on the life that lay ahead of him, comments "Muhammad is in a much better place right now."

The Dawabsha family, Saad and Riham and their two little ones, baby Ali and his brother Ahmad, have a few months more of family life ahead of them before a settler gang throws an incendiary into their small home in the West Bank village of Duma, south of Nablus.

Many more Palestinians and a much smaller number of Israelis will have died violently before the New Year ends. Well over 10,000 will have been injured.

January 1

The original intention was to describe the daily abuses faced by Palestinians in diary form, but it soon became clear that this would fill volumes. Take January 1st…

The previous day, Israel's Supreme Court gave approval for the demolition of three homes that had been lived in by four Palestinians from East Jerusalem who had attacked Jews in West Jerusalem. The families of those men are now waiting to be made homeless, in contravention of international law which forbids collective punishment.

'Stop work' notices have also been delivered on three buildings owned by Palestinians in the West Bank village of Idhna in Hebron on the grounds that building permission had not been granted (more of this later).

Over 5000 olive saplings have been uprooted in land east of the town of Turmusayya in the central West Bank. The vandals who did this most likely come from the illegal Jewish outpost of Adei Ad. This is attached to Shiloh settlement, which was built on lands confiscated/stolen from Palestinians.

5am: the IDF raid Ni'lin, invading three homes and abducting a 17-year-old.

7.15am: the army raids the Qalandya refugee camp, injuring one person and taking prisoner two others.

Between 08:55 and11:55am: the army raid Khirbeit Barza village, bulldozing crops and uprooting several olive trees.

9am: Jewish religious extremists, guarded by Israeli Defence Force soldiers, invade the Al Aqsa mosque compound in Jerusalem, one of the holiest sites in Islam and a World Heritage Site.

10am: the army destroy five livestock shelters in the Um al-Jamal area.

Around 11.10am: the army uproot several olive trees in Khirbeit Attuf village. Other troops raid al-Arqa village, seizing and holding captive for a time 17-year-old Ibrahim Yahya. Others, firing stun and tear gas grenades, occupy a home in Taquo and set up a military post on the roof.

Midday: illegal settlers throwing stones at Palestinian individuals and vehicles near the Za'tarah checkpoint, injure and hospitalise a Hebron resident, Ishaq Hamdan, damaging his vehicle.

4pm: settlers from Eiyash Qddush invade Jalloud village farmland and prevent local residents from ploughing.

4.40pm: Israeli forces open live fire at the entrance to Deir Nathim, near Ramallah.

9.30pm: troops raid al-Eisawiya village, abducting 17-year-old Mohammad Mustafa and taking three other prisoners. Others raid the Silwan neighbourhood of Jerusalem, firing stun and tear gas grenades.

In the evening, a gang of settlers invade farmland at al-Khadr, uprooting and plundering 80 olive trees.

In all, there are 23 raids, with night peace disruptions and/or home invasions in 9 towns and villages. Three people are beaten and one is injured and hospitalised. Some 25 Palestinians are taken prisoner, of whom 13 are detained. There are no arrests of Israeli settlers responsible for the attacks listed.

The Israeli navy continues to impose an arbitrary fishing limit off the shores of Gaza.

There are no Palestinian missile attacks today, nor throughout the next three months.

Welcome to Palestine 2015.

Is it genocide?

Convention on the Prevention and Punishment of the Crime of Genocide

Adopted by Resolution 260 (III) A of the United Nations General Assembly on 9 December 1948.

Article 1

The Contracting Parties confirm that genocide, whether committed in time of peace or in time of war, is a crime under international law which they undertake to prevent and to punish.

Article 2

In the present Convention, genocide means any of the following acts committed with intent to destroy, in whole or in part, a national, ethnical, racial or religious group, as such:

a. Killing members of the group;

b. Causing serious bodily or mental harm to members of the group;

c. Deliberately inflicting on the group conditions of life calculated to bring about its physical destruction in whole or in part;

d. Imposing measures intended to prevent births within the group;

e. Forcibly transferring children of the group to another group.

What you will read in the following pages amounts to genocide. This is very deliberate and arguably it started back in 1897 when Theodore Herzl, an Austrian Jew, held the first Zionist Congress, in Vienna. The aim declared at the congress was that the Jews would establish a safe homeland in Palestine – "Zionism aims at establishing for the Jewish people a publicly and legally assured home in Palestine."

From that day to this, the wishes and human rights of the indigenous peoples of that land have been ignored by Israel and her Zionist defenders. They have claimed that they, people of the Jewish religion, are the true inhabitants of the land, 'returning' after 2,000 years. They argue that they are the descendants of the Jews who fled after the sacking of Jerusalem by the Romans in AD 70 and the destruction of the temple built by King Herod.

They have tried to claim, firstly, that the land was uninhabited (which clearly it was not) and then, secondly, that the Palestinians are just Arabs, the descendants of Muslim invaders in the seventh century. This last is also nonsense: there is plenty of evidence showing that the Palestinians are the indigenous inhabitants of the region. They may have mixed with other races in the long course of history, changed their religion (though some remained Jewish and some Christian), and over time their language changed from Aramaic (the common language spoken in AD 70) to Arabic, but they are the indigenous people of the land. They are the descendants of peasants, fishermen, small traders, wandering herdsmen and others who did not flee in AD 70, because they loved their land and in any case had nowhere else to go.

In fact, modern DNA testing shows that it is the Ashkenazi Jews of Western Europe whose claim to be indigenous to what is now known as Israel and the occupied territories is somewhat dubious, as a high percentage of their DNA is showing itself to be northern European.

Be that as it may, the Zionist project that is modern Israel remains one of genocide, aimed at taking over the entire area, stealing the land from its owners, and declaring Israel to be a (solely) 'Jewish' state. In modern Israel, therefore, almost all the land is officially owned by the state and then leased, overwhelmingly, to Jews. Palestinians within present day Israel whose families fled their homes in the terrorist campaign known as the Nakba, led by Israel's first Prime Minister, David Ben-Gurion, are denied citizenship. Palestinians are referred to as 'Arabs', denying them their identity.

This is also the basis on which Israel and her illegal settlers steal land from Palestinians in the occupied territories, harass schoolchildren, hack down olive trees, drive to and fro on exclusive roads and lead very pleasant lives while the indigenous people suffer. In these pages, you will see that clauses a, b, and c of the definition of genocide are clearly being fulfilled. By starving mothers and children in Gaza, denying clean water and sanitation to Palestinian communities in Israel itself and in the occupied territories, and denying medical facilities to many Palestinian mothers in Israel, clause d is also being fulfilled. Only clause e is left, and the majority of Israelis have no use for Palestinian children;

in fact, they see their existence as a 'demographic threat'.

Palestinians in 2015

By the start of 2015, the Palestinians are scattered and cruelly divided into several groupings.

- There are the Palestinian 'Arab' inhabitants of Israel, approximately 20 per cent of the population of that state (around 1,700,000 souls).

- The Palestinian inhabitants of the West Bank and Jerusalem number approximately 2,750,000, some of whom live in refugee camps, denied the right to return the homes in Israel that they left as a result the Nakba/ the Disaster – Israel's terror campaign of 1948. The Palestinians here are constantly threatened and harassed by illegal Jewish settlers living on land stolen from the inhabitants, in contravention of international law.

- Gaza, a tiny enclave of just 362 square kilometres (about 225 square miles) squeezed between Israel, Egypt and the Mediterranean Sea is home to some 1.8 million Palestinians, many of whom are also refugees from modern Israel. It has one of the highest population densities in the world.

- Then there are those living in refugee camps in the adjoining Arab countries of Lebanon, Syria and Jordan. According to UNRWA, the United Nations Relief and Works Agency for Palestine Refugees in the Near East, there are some 526,744 registered refugees in Syria, 449,957 in Lebanon and 2,097,338 in Jordan. As the year unfolds, of course, many of those in Syria will face fresh horrors and renewed displacement. Although they have an absolutely clear right to return to their homeland, now known as Israel, the rulers of that country will not be offering any help, let alone entry, to these unfortunates.

- Finally, there are those who have made lives in various Arab states or elsewhere, outside the Middle East. Many of these have spent their lives trying to bring the plight of the fellow Palestinians to the attention of an uncaring world.

What has been done and is still being done to the Palestinians is a running sore on the face of humanity and a root cause of much of the turmoil that we see today in the Middle East, and by a knock-on effect in Europe. Thankfully, we are creatures of change. Nothing stays the same and the pervasively racist mindset that permeates the current Israeli government and people can and must change.

For this to happen, people need to wake up to what is being done to the Palestinians and stop making excuses for Israel. Robust measures must be taken at every level, including boycott and divestment, to bring the ongoing genocide to a halt and bring peace and justice to both sides.

It is hoped that this book will prove a useful handbook to people of conscience, whatever their race or religion.

Gaza ceasefire violations

"What I've seen is the attacks that take place on Israel and the indiscriminate nature of them. As PM, putting yourself in the shoes of the Israeli people, who want peace but have to put up with these indiscriminate attacks — that reinforces to me the importance of standing by Israel and Israel's right to defend itself."

PM David Cameron, Jewish Chronicle, April 2015

Before tackling the numerous human rights abuses that were being inflicted on Palestinians in 2015 (and still, in 2016), let's get one myth out of the way: that the blockade of Gaza, and Israel's regular all-out attacks on the enclave, are justified because"Israel has a right to defend itself".

In reality, there were **no** rockets fired into Israel from Gaza for the first three months of 2015. There were, however, **Israeli violations** of the ceasefire **almost daily**. While it is true that there may have been test rockets fired within Gaza or out to sea (within Gazan limits), these do not count as cease-fire violations. After all, Israelis are, *per capita*, the largest exporters of arms and military equipment in the world. In fact, they export many times more *per capita* than Americans, the largest arms exporters overall, and, thanks to their treatment of the Palestinians in Gaza and the occupied territories, they sell their equipment as 'battle tested'. Israel is free to test its arsenal whenever it chooses. The Palestinians are entitled under international law to defend themselves, and if test-firing were to make their rockets more accurate and therefore less likely to fall in civilian areas, this would surely be desirable.

To list all the ceasefire violations on both sides would take up most of this book, so hopefully readers will accept an abbreviated list of just two months' events – January and February 2015. You will find these in Appendix II, at the back of the book. Please show this to the next person who repeats the mantra "Israel has a right to defend itself."

We will briefly add some events from later in the year.

On 5 March, two fishermen were wounded when the Israeli navy opened fire on their boats which, according to the Palestinians, were within the six-mile limit. Four others were taken prisoner. On 6 March, fisherman Tawfiq Abu Riyala was shot and killed when, according to the Israelis, his boat deviated from the limit. Two fishing boats were taken by the Israelis. Eight days later the Israelis opened fire on fishing boats that were four miles off shore.

On 18 March, farmers east of al-Bureij refugee camp were forced to leave their land after they came under heavy fire from Israeli watchtowers along the border. On 20 March, Israeli forces shot and injured two men in the town of Abasan east of Khan Younis, within Gaza. On 31 March, in the first Palestinian violation of the year, the Israelis claimed that resistance fighters opened fire on an Israeli army jeep near al-Qarara. April's land violations are covered in Appendix III.

Attacks on the fishing fleet continued: on 7 April, Khalid Zayid was injured by a rubber-coated steel bullet while fishing off the coast of Beit Lahiya. On 23 April, a rocket was fired into Israel from the Gaza strip (no damage occurred). The Israeli air force attacked farmland causing widespread damage, while the army also attacked. On 24 April, 14-year-old Fadi Abu Mandil was wounded by long-range sniper fire while studying in his home in al-Mughazi refugee camp. On 25 April, two fishing boats were damaged by Israeli fire and the next day a farmer, Rami Matar, was wounded when an Israeli army position behind the Green Line opened fire on farmers in the east Jabaliya area.

On 8 May, Nael Salah, was critically wounded when an Israeli Army position behind the Green Line opened fire on people in north-west Beit Lahiya. A fisherman was wounded the same day. On 15 May, three people were wounded by Israeli army fire from behind the Green Line. On 26 May, 26-year-old Muhammad Ziad Bakr was wounded after the Israeli navy, claiming that his boat had deviated from the designated fishing zone, fired warning shots and then directly at the boat, according to their spokeswoman. The following day a rocket was fired from Gaza and Israeli planes fired missiles at three sites in addition to the navy firing on fishing boats. On 27 May, another fisherman was wounded.

On 2 June, the Israeli navy captured a fishing boat and took five people prisoner, including a 14-year-old, in addition to wounding three fishermen in a separate incident. The following day they hijacked another boat and took a further four men prisoner. A 22-year-old farmworker was shot in the stomach. A rocket was fired from Gaza but fell short; the Israeli air force responded with multiple air strikes. Another rocket was fired on 6 June. Hamas denied responsibility for the rockets fired to date in 2015, and it appears that they were the work of Salafist groups opposed to Hamas. The Israelis, however, blamed Hamas and directed their strikes at Hamas targets.

On 22 June, the Israeli army opened fire on four boys aged 16 to 17 as they were walking at the edge of Khuzaa village. It was Ramadan, and they had been told to fill in time before sunset, when they could break their fast and enjoy a family meal. Two boys were injured, one severely. Two bullets entered Ibrahim Abu Reda's right leg, one near the ankle and another below the knee, shattering his shinbone and severing veins and arteries. Ibrahim is the younger brother of Ahmed Abu Reda, 18, who was used as a human shield by Israeli soldiers for five days during last summer's war, as documented by the UN Human Rights Council's independent investigation of Israel's assault on Gaza as well as by other independent observers. The boys confirmed that there had been no warning shots. They had paused for a moment and then one of them fell to the ground wounded. Although the so-called buffer zone between Israel and Gaza was supposed to have been reduced to 100 metres after the 2014 ceasefire agreement, in practice it varies almost on a whim. A freedom of information request by Israeli human rights group Gisha concerning the buffer zone revealed that the army maintains a larger area than the officially agreed one. Israeli ceasefire violations on land and at sea continued regularly throughout the following months.

Between 1 January and 31 October, rockets were fired into Israel from Gaza on a total of 17 occasions (a small additional number were, according to the Israelis, intended to land in Israel, but fell within Gaza). No injuries were caused and most caused no damage to property. Additionally, on 2 September, two bullets were fired from Gaza and caused minor property damage. The Israeli Foreign Ministry also reports that there was "a number of incidents where hundreds of Palestinians approached the border security fence and threw stones and Molotov cocktails at IDF forces." They do not feel it worthwhile to mention that Israeli soldiers used live fire at demonstrators, killing 7 Palestinians, mainly youngsters, on 9 October alone, nor that by the end of that month they had killed 19 Gazans in October. The total includes Nour Rasmie Hassan, aged 30, who was five months pregnant, and her two-year-old girl, Rahaf. These two were killed in an airstrike on a residential property with no military connections – arguably not just a ceasefire violation but a war crime.

Israeli ceasefire violations continued to the end of the year. On 2 December, an elderly woman was struck in the neck by a live bullet while near al-Bureij refugee camp in central Gaza. On 4 December, 11 Palestinians were injured while demonstrating in the camp; two more were injured by shrapnel in the al-Fukhari area east of Khan Younis, and the navy fired on fishermen who were within the permitted limits. The following Monday, there were Israeli airstrikes after shots were fired at a military patrol vehicle. On 9 December, the Israelis entered Gaza and levelled agricultural land east of al-Bureij refugee camp. On 11 December, 58 demonstrators were injured and 41-year-old Sami Shawqi Mahdi was shot in the chest and died near the same camp. On 13 December, soldiers from Kerem Shalom military post opened fire on farmers at work on their land and injured one. The following day there were airstrikes after a rocket was fired (no injuries on either side). On 16 December, another farmer was shot in the leg and hand. The following day, four Israeli excavators entered Gaza near Deir al-Balah refugee camp and began levelling the land; three Palestinians were shot and injured. The day after, a Friday, 20-year-old Mahmoud Muhammad Saed al-Agha was killed; 31 others were injured by live fire, 9 by rubber-coated steel bullets, and 14 suffered from tear gas inhalation during clashes near Khan Younis. The same day, Israeli bulldozers entered the area on a search mission, it seems. On 22 December, 14 fishermen were detained. According to the Israelis, they had deviated from the fishing limit; a female farm worker was shot while working near the border fence.

Meanwhile, Israeli planes were busy between 6 and 9am spraying crops with herbicide. On 23 December, they did this for the third day in a row. Saleh al-Najjar, a farmer from al-Qarrara, lost 30 dunums (7.4 acres) of spinach and peas; Wael al-Shami lost crops of parsley and beans; an estimated 1500 dunums (371 acres) of land in central Gaza and 200 dunums (50 acres) of land in eastern Khan Younis were affected.

On 25 December, 22-year-old Hani Rafiq Wahdan, died after being shot in the head during a demonstration near the al-Shujayyia neighborhood east of Gaza City; 19 others were injured, one of whom, 48-year-old Yousif Abu Sbeikha al-Buheiri, died later.

No Israeli soldiers, sailors or civilians were injured by Gazans in 2015. All the death and destruction meted out to Gazans was due to the Israeli blockade.

The blockade of Gaza

"It is essential that the inhabitants of Gaza are able to exercise and enjoy the full range of fundamental human rights to which they are entitled. They must be able to live safe and secure lives free of the various forms of violence which afflict them at present; benefit from proper health care, education and housing; elect and hold accountable representatives of government; be subject to fair and impartial justice; and have ready access to the world beyond Gaza for religious, educational, medical, cultural, commercial and other purposes."

'Gaza in 2020 – a liveable place?' UN report 2012

Given half a chance (which of course they are not), Palestinians tend to be hard working and enterprising. Even before the Second World War, they were exporting oranges from Jaffa. Before the blockade of Gaza started after Hamas won the elections there and in the West Bank in June 2007, there were workshops and small businesses all over the strip that could by now be thriving.

In fact, Gaza, and with it the rest of Palestine, should indeed be thriving and even prosperous. There are substantial oil and gas reserves off the coast that belong to the Palestinians, not the Israelis – enough to make a considerable difference to the lives of many ordinary folk. But this can only happen if the Palestinians (via democratically elected representatives) are ever allowed their legal right to control the exploitation of those resources and thereby reap the full benefit.

In the 1990s, the PNA developed plans to build an airport and a modern maritime port in Gaza, as mentioned in Oslo 1 accord. The airport was completed first and flights to Egypt, Jordan and even Tunisia and Morocco started, with up to 700,000 passengers a year, both Palestinian and Israeli. The building of the port started later, in July 2000, but Israel reneged on its agreement not to halt the supply of construction materials. The port would have transformed the situation and boosted trade immeasurably.

The airport was destroyed by the Israelis and has been closed since 2001. The port site was destroyed by Israeli tanks in September of the same year and bombed in October.

Israel has, however, been firmly opposed to the idea of a Gaza port, since it might have rivalled Israeli ports. At the time of the 2014 ceasefire agreement, Ofir Akunis, then deputy minister in the Prime Minister's office, referring to demands that a date should be set for withdrawal from the occupied territories, said: "[the West Bank] is the cradle of the Jewish homeland... Returning to the 1967 border would be national suicide." He added that the likelihood of that happening "is similar to the chance that Israel will agree to a seaport and airport in Gaza."

The blockade

In 2007, angered by Hamas' electoral victory and refusal to accept terms dictated by Israel, which it is beyond the scope and time frame of this book to discuss, the Israeli authorities decided to blockade Gaza. In the words of Dov Weisglass, adviser to then Prime-Minister Ehud Olmert, they chose "to put the Palestinians on a diet, but not to make them die of hunger".

Documents revealed in 2012, following a legal battle between the authorities and Israeli human rights group GISHA[1], show that health ministry officials calculated the minimum amount of calories they needed to allow into Gaza to keep its citizens from actually starving. In reality, far fewer truckloads of food have been permitted to enter than would meet these basic requirements. Attacks on fishermen and farmers further restrict the amount of healthy, fresh food available to Gazans. Along with this, fuel and other necessities were also to be restricted. According to Gisha's director: "Israel banned glucose for biscuits and the fuel needed for regular supply of electricity – paralyzing normal life in Gaza and impairing the moral character of the State of Israel. I am sorry to say that major elements of this policy are still in place."

Fuel for the power plant was to be cut to a level that would disrupt the supply of electricity and water. Anything not on the list of permitted goods was to be banned, including cumin, basil, bay leaf, allspice, caraway, cardamom, chillies, chives, cilantro, cloves, garlic, sesame, tamarind, thyme, oregano and cayenne, along with tomatoes, potatoes, cucumbers, lettuce, toys (how mean!), glass-ware, paint and shoes.

Since the most recent onslaught on Gaza, in 2014, far fewer loads of building materials have been permitted to enter than are essential in order to repair the

1 www.gisha.org

damage. Not only this, but the list contains many 'dual use' items which are desperately needed for peaceful purposes, but could also have military uses. On 4 June, the Israeli authorities released five fishermen from the Bakr family who had been taken prisoner that morning. However, three fishermen remained in custody for the possession of fibreglass, which used to be permitted but had now been put on the list of banned goods, as it can be an ingredient in the making of rockets.

And if the ban on essential imports has had a catastrophic effect on life for ordinary people in Gaza, so too has the effectual ban on exports. Agricultural exports cannot thrive when arbitrary closures mean that perishable goods may be held up within Gaza until they rot. Manufactured exports are also subject to arbitrary delays and, in addition, may be reliant on imported materials that are simply not available. On 2 November 2015, GISHA posted an article that laid bare the cat-and-mouse game that is played by the Israeli authorities. The previous month, the authorities had announced that they would allow furniture made in Gaza to be imported into Israel. Wonderful news for Gaza's furniture makers, except that the same authorities had banned the import of wood planks more than 5cm thick into Gaza. As a result, Gazan furniture factories were laying off employees and facing closure. (The Israelis claimed that planks were being used to line smuggling tunnels, but there is evidence that tunnels were in fact being lined with clay bricks.)

The World Bank reported in May 2015 that the blockade has slashed Gaza's GDP by 50 percent since 2007. Commercial life has thus been brought to a virtual standstill and, with that, the possibility for youngsters to have optimistic dreams along the lines of 'when I grow up I'll…' For young people, the natural alternative to boundless optimism is all too often profound and dangerous despair…

Joint Statement

On 26 February 2015, a group of 30 NGOs issued a joint statement, appealing for an end to the blockade.

30 International Aid Agencies: "We must not fail in Gaza."

Six months have passed since a ceasefire on 26 August 2014 ended over seven weeks of fighting between Israeli forces and Palestinian armed groups in the Gaza Strip. As UN agencies and international NGOs operating in Gaza, we are alarmed by the limited progress in rebuilding the lives of those affected and tackling the root causes of the conflict.

The Israeli-imposed blockade continues, the political process, along with the economy, are paralyzed, and living conditions have worsened. Reconstruction and repairs to the tens of thousands of homes, hospitals, and schools damaged or destroyed in the fighting has been woefully slow. Sporadic rocket fire from Palestinian armed groups has resumed [editorial note: test firing, not rockets into Israel at this time]. Overall, the lack of progress has deepened levels of desperation and frustration among the population, more than two thirds of whom are Palestine refugees.

Living conditions in Gaza were already dire before the latest round of fighting. Most residents were unable to meet their food requirements and over seven years of blockade had severely compromised access to basic services, including to health, water and sanitation. But since July [2014], the situation has deteriorated dramatically.

Approximately 100,000 Palestinians remain displaced this winter, living in dire conditions in schools and makeshift shelters not designed for long-term stay. Scheduled power cuts persist for up to 18 hours a day. The continued non-payment of the salaries of public sector employees and the lack of progress in the national unity government further increases tensions. With severe restrictions on movement, most of the 1.8 million residents are trapped in the coastal enclave, with no hope for the future.

Bearing the brunt of this suffering are the most vulnerable, including the elderly, persons with disabilities, women and nearly one million children, who have experienced unimaginable suffering in three major conflicts in six short years. Children lack access to quality education, with over 400,000 of them in need of immediate psychosocial support.

Within this context, the international community is not providing Gaza with adequate assistance. Little of the US$ 5.4 billion pledged in Cairo has reached Gaza. Cash assistance to families who lost everything has been suspended and other crucial aid is unavailable due to lack of funds. A return to hostilities is inevitable if progress is not made and the root causes of conflict are not addressed.

Israel, as the occupying power, is the main duty bearer and must comply with its obligations under international law. In particular, it must fully lift the blockade, within the framework of UN Security Council Resolution 1860 (2009). The fragile ceasefire must be reinforced, and the parties must resume negotiations to achieve a comprehensive settlement of the Israeli-Palestinian issue. All parties must respect international law and those responsible for violations must be brought to justice. Accountability and adherence to international humanitarian law and international human rights law are essential pre-requisites for any lasting peace. Also imperative, Egypt needs to open the Rafah Crossing, most urgently for humanitarian cases, and donor pledges must be translated into disbursements.

We must not fail in Gaza. We must realize the vision of making Gaza a livable place and a cornerstone of peace and security for all in the region.

END

Signatories included ActionAid, Handicap International, Medical Aid for Palestinians (MAP), Médecins du Monde, Mennonite Central Committee, Oxfam, Save the Children International, UN OCHA oPt, UN OHCHR, UN Relief and Works Agency (UNRWA), UN Women, World Food Programme, World Health Organization and World Vision Jerusalem - West Bank – Gaza.

The situation in 2015

A fact sheet on the website of OCHA (the UN Office for the Coordination of Humanitarian Affairs), entitled 'Gaza one year on, The humanitarian impact of the blockade'[2] summarises the dire situation Gazans faced in 2015.

Key Facts

- In June 2007, following the takeover of Gaza by Hamas, Israel imposed a land, sea and air blockade on the Gaza Strip.

- The blockade has reduced Gaza's GDP by 50% (The World Bank, May 2015).

- The unemployment rate in Gaza during 2014 stood at 43% on average: the highest in the world. Youth unemployment exceeded 60% (PCBS).

- Nearly 80% of Gaza's population receives some form of international aid, the bulk of which is food assistance.

- The daily average of crossings by permit holders out of Gaza via the Israeli-controlled Erez Crossing in the first five months of 2015 stood at 449, more than double the same period of 2014, but less than 2% of the 26,000 daily crossings prior to September 2000 (second intifada).

- The Egyptian-controlled crossing (Rafah) has been continuously closed, including for humanitarian assistance, since 24 October 2014, except for 15 out of 219 days of partial openings, as of May 2015.

- Kerem Shalom is the only commercial crossing currently operating, out of four such crossings prior to the imposition of the blockade.

- Israel defines basic construction materials (gravel, steel bars, and cement), along with a wide range of spare parts, computer equipment, and vehicles, as "dual use" items, restricting their import.

- Less than 1% of the construction materials required to rebuild houses destroyed and damaged during hostilities, and to address natural population growth, have so far entered Gaza (Shelter Cluster, June

2 www.gaza.ochaopt.org/2015/07/
the-gaza-strip-the-humanitarian-impact-of-the-blockade/

2015).

- 408 truckloads of commercial goods exited Gaza via Israel in the first five months of 2015, an almost five-fold increase compared to the same period of 2014 (83), but only 7% of the volume in the equivalent period of 2007, prior to the imposition of the blockade (5,451 truckloads).

- Access to areas within several hundred metres from the Israeli fence surrounding Gaza is risky or prohibited, discouraging or preventing farming activities.

- Fishermen are allowed to access less than one third of the fishing areas allocated to them under the Oslo Accords: six out of 20 nautical miles.

•

1. **1.8 million Palestinians in Gaza are 'locked in', denied free access to the remainder of the occupied Palestinian territory and the outside world.** Movement restrictions imposed by Israel since the early 1990's and intensified in June 2007, citing security concerns, have undermined the living conditions in Gaza and fragmented the oPt and its economic and social fabric. In recent months the Israeli authorities have significantly increased the number of exit permits issued to Palestinians, however, those eligible for such permits still constitute a small minority, primarily patients, business people and staff of international organizations. The isolation of Gaza has been exacerbated by restrictions imposed by the Egyptian authorities on its single passengers crossing (Rafah).

2. **Longstanding access restrictions imposed by Israel have undermined Gaza's economy, resulting in high levels of unemployment, food insecurity and aid dependency.** These include restrictions on transfer of goods to the West Bank and Israel; on the import of "dual use items"; and on the access of people to agricultural land and fishing waters. The Israeli authorities have recently eased some of these restrictions, but

the basic constraints remain in place, preventing a significant improvement in the economy. This is compounded by the destruction of economic assets during hostilities, the severe electricity shortage and the inability of the Palestinian Government of National Consensus to assume effective government functions in Gaza, due to the ongoing internal divide.

3. **Israeli restrictions on the import of basic construction materials and equipment have significantly deteriorated the quality of basic services, and impede the reconstruction and repair of homes.** The limited access to these materials since 2007 has prevented or delayed the construction, repair and upgrade of homes and infrastructure, to address the rapid population growth and the devastation caused by recurrent rounds of hostilities. This has undermined the quality of health, education, and water and sanitation services available in Gaza, and prolonged the displacement of those who have lost their homes. While the import restrictions remain in place, following the August 2014 ceasefire, a temporary Gaza Reconstruction Mechanism (GRM) allowing for the controlled entry of the restricted materials was established, triggering a significant increase in the entry of such materials.

4. **Israel, as the occupying power, must lift the blockade, which prevents the realization of a broad range of human rights for Palestinians in Gaza.** The Secretary General of the United Nations has stated that the blockade and its related restrictions contravene article 33 of the Geneva Convention IV prohibiting collective penalties. **While Israel's recent relaxation measures are welcomed, a full lifting is paramount to stopping the continuing deterioration of the living conditions in Gaza and preventing a new cycle of violence.**

. END

Below, we will consider just some aspects of the situation, but it should be clear that the Gazans are facing an all-powerful, cruel, comprehensive, systematic and very deliberate system designed to make their lives insecure, miserable and highly dangerous.

Of farmers and fishermen

It is hardly surprising that the FAO assessed back in December 2014 that 80 per cent of the population were (and remain) food insecure, as Israel intends. About 19,000 Gazans rely on farming, a further 6,000 on livestock raising and some 3,600 on fishing, but all of these ways in which Gaza's meagre food imports might be supplemented are threatened by continuous Israeli attacks. The assaults on agriculture are discussed in greater depth later (see pages 207-10) because they are of a piece with attacks by the Israeli army and settlers on farmers and their land in the West Bank.

The Israelis would doubtless claim that the army's numerous violations of the ceasefire are necessary (and thus not violations?) to maintain the siege. Under the 2014 ceasefire agreement, however, the 'buffer zone' on Gaza's side of the Israeli security fence that surrounds the enclave was supposed to be reduced to 100 metres. In reality, on many occasions in 2015, farmers who were simply trying to work their land, and were not within 100 metres of the border fence, were fired upon and forced to retreat to avoid injury. Several individuals – farmers, bird hunters and just youngsters enjoying a stroll within the supposedly safe areas – were injured, some severely, in the course of the year.

Attacks on Gaza's fishing fleet are to some extent covered under Ceasefire Violations, so we will just give some basic facts here. According to a 2011 report by the Red Cross, 90 per cent of Gaza's fishermen are poor. Under the 2014 agreement, the fishing limit for Gaza was supposed to have been extended to 6 nautical miles from 3 (Gazan territorial waters should, of course, extend for 12 nautical miles according to maritime law, and under the Oslo accords Gaza fishermen were 'allowed' to fish up to 20 miles offshore).

Throughout 2015, Gaza's fishermen faced almost daily harassment by the Israeli navy. On some occasions, certain boats may have gone beyond the six-mile imposed limit, possibly following a shoal, but also possibly because they were attempting to smuggle goods, potentially arms, into Gaza. On many occasions, however, the boats were well within the limit and the naval attack on these unarmed men represented a clear ceasefire violation. It should be pointed out, though it is perhaps obvious enough, that on no occasion, as far as the editor is aware, did anyone from a fishing boat fire back.

By 3 September, when 11-year-old Bilal Abu Amro went out fishing with his father, three fishermen had been killed by the Israeli navy since the previous September. Bilal and his fisherman dad were near the shores of the Beit Lahiya village in the northern Gaza Strip when the Israelis attacked. He was shot in the thigh. Late in the year, the Egyptians joined the Israelis: on 5 November, 18-year-old Faris Meqdad was shot in the abdomen by fire from an Egyptian naval ship while fishing off the Gazan coast. He died in hospital.

Small wonder, then, that according to OCHA the number of fishermen in Gaza had dropped from around 10,000 in 2000 down to the current 3,600 by 2015. Boats and nets are frequently confiscated: on 2 June eight nets were confiscated; on 22 June, the Israelis returned 19 confiscated boats, but still retained some 60 boats, according to the head of the fishing union, Nizar Ayyash, and on July 7, three more boats were confiscated. By 5 October, according to the fishing union, the Israeli navy had conducted 1,370 attacks on Gaza's fishermen since the 2014 'ceasefire'.

Unexploded ordnance

To add to Gazans' miseries, the massive onslaughts on their densely-populated area enclave have left behind a lethal legacy. According to OCHA, around 7,000 items of unexploded ordnance remained after the 2014 fighting. Teams have been working to deal with the problem, but they are hampered by a lack of equipment. On 6 May, two children were injured in an explosion. On 14 May, bomb disposal units were at work dismantling an F16 rocket when it exploded, injuring some 70 people, 15 of whom were taken to hospital. On 6 August, four members of the Abu Naqira family were killed and 30 other people injured in an explosion when they were clearing rubble from their destroyed house in southern Gaza. A week later the 77-year-old matriarch of the family, Amina Abu Naqira, also died.

Even before the 2014 attacks, the problem was severe. According to a report published by the Office of the High Commissioner for Human Rights in 2012, 64 children and 47 adults were injured by unexploded ordnance between 2009 and 2012, reaching an average of four every month in 2012.

Healthcare

Some 17 hospitals, 56 primary healthcare facilities, and 45 ambulances were damaged or destroyed in 2014, and the total cost of the conflict to Gaza's healthcare system is estimated at $50m (£33m). In addition to those killed, some 11,000 people were injured, many of these very severely. A sizable proportion of these will remain handicapped for life and will need ongoing care that, in the current circumstances, it may prove impossible to provide. The Shams Al Amal School, Gaza's only school for disabled children, was destroyed towards the end of the 2014 offensive, though it is hopefully being rebuilt with help from outside Gaza. But with unemployment running at 43 to 44 per cent and basic education under threat, as described in the section on Children, what hope can there be for a youngster with prosthetic limbs?

A dispute between Hamas and the PLO over who is responsible for the salaries of healthcare (and other government) workers in Gaza led to workers going unpaid in 2015. There was also a chronic shortage of pharmaceutical supplies, again not helped by disputes between factions.

The main referral hospital for patients from Gaza and the West Bank is Makassed in East Jerusalem. On 27 and 28 October Israeli forces entered the hospital and demanded to see patient files, without permission from an Israeli court. (They had found a prescription from the hospital when searching a young suspect's home.) The head of the hospital, Rafis al-Hussieni, told *Maan News* that undercover, armed Israeli forces had been deployed throughout the hospital and had insulted staff and patients. On 29 October, troops fired tear gas canisters inside the hospital at staff peacefully protesting against this illegal and disgraceful intrusion.

Gaza's mental healthcare system is also overwhelmed. In September 2014, WHO estimated that 20 per cent of Gazans were suffering a range of mental-health challenges. Children, in particular (see pages 131-5) are suffering from PTSDs on a massive scale.

Another area showing the effects of Israel's blockage and periodic attacks on Gaza is maternity and neonatal healthcare. In August 2015, UNWRA published the results of a five-year survey, from 2008 to 2013, of infant mortality in Gaza. The results were horrifying: whereas mortality rates had been going down regularly across the Middle East and even in Gaza, the death rate in Gaza had now risen from 12 per 1,000 births in 2008 to 20.3 per 1,000 in 2013. So unusual is this, that the report was delayed so that the increased rate could be confirmed. At the last count, the rate had risen again and was now up to 22.4. On 7 July, the humanitarian coordinator for the UN in Gaza, Robert Piper, issued a press release about the ongoing humanitarian crisis. In this, he pointed out that the maternal mortality rate had doubled in the past 12 months.

Mr Piper also pointed out that by July 2015 only 28 per cent of the money pledged at the Cairo Reconstruction Conference of October 2014 had been forthcoming, leaving many homeless Gazans in desperate straights.

Fuel

As we have already said, the Israeli plan for Gaza's blockade was to keep the people 'on a diet' and restrict fuel so that the supply of electricity and water would be disrupted, the aim being to make life miserable. It appears that this objective has remained in force in 2015. For example, according to a report by the Palestine Centre for Human Rights, for the week of 23 to 28 April:

> The cooking gas crisis has fluctuated due to the closure of Karm Abu Salem for security claims. According to PCHR's follow-up, Israeli authorities only allow an average of 98 tons of cooking gas into Gaza per day. This limited quantity is less than half of the daily needs, which is 200 tons per day for the civilian population in the Gaza Strip during winter. The lack of diesel and benzene led to the aggravation of the crisis as a result of using the gas cylinder for cars or as an alternative for benzene to run generators. As a result, the demand for gas further increased.

Home generators are a necessity because the electrical supply is so erratic. Gaza receives electricity from the Israeli electricity grid, the Egyptian electric company, and from a power station inside Gaza. The total supply amounts to 230 MW of electricity, but the requirement is some 350 to 450 MW. Gaza's power station should be able to produce 140 MW of the total, but is unable to do so because of the restrictions on fuel imports and damage from Israeli attacks. In May, therefore, Gaza was suffering around 12 hours of power outages per day.

On 26 May, Gaza's electricity distributor complained that the Israeli military were refusing to give permits for technicians to enter Israeli territory in order to repair a 12 megawatt grid that had become disconnected on the Israeli side.

On 15 July, the Israelis opened the Kerem Shalom crossing, allowing diesel from Qatar to enter. By 24 August, health officials were warning that hospitals in Gaza might soon have to stop running their operating theatres due to lack of fuel for their generators.

In November 2014, the International Oil and Gas Conference was held in Israel. The Quartet representative's energy advisor, an Israeli named Ariel Ezrahi, gave a presentation entitled 'The Palestinian Dimension of the Regional Energy Landscape'. The rosy picture he painted suggested that Gazan gas resources could 'transform the Palestinian energy sector and boost the economy'. The plan apparently involves Gaza increasing its dependence on electricity from Israel and Egypt, with the West Bank taking electricity from Israel and Jordan. The Palestinian power sector would depend on Israel's Leviathan field.

In the light of the current restrictions on fuel into Gaza, Israel's determination not to allow a seaport or airport in Gaza, refusal to deal with Hamas, and their exploitation of Palestinian water resources to their own benefit (plus the fact that an Israeli, not a Palestinian representative, gave the presentation), it is hard to imagine that the Palestinians will truly benefit from their energy resources in the foreseeable future

---

UNCTAD/PRESS/PR/2015/026 Geneva, Switzerland, (01 September 2015)

UNCTAD's report on assistance to the Palestinian people states that Gaza could become uninhabitable by 2020 if current economic trends persist. In addition to eight years of economic blockade, in the past six years, Gaza has endured three military operations that have shattered its ability to export and produce for the domestic market, ravaged its already debilitated infrastructure, left no time for reconstruction and economic recovery, and accelerated the de-development of the Occupied Palestinian Territory, a process by which development is not merely hindered but reversed.

The report highlights the severe crises in Gaza related to water and electricity, as well as the destruction of vital infrastructure during the military operations in July and August 2014. For example, Gaza's 1.8 million inhabitants rely on coastal aquifers as their main source of freshwater, yet 95 per cent of this water is not safe to drink.

The report also estimates the direct losses (excluding people killed) of the three military operations that took place from 2008 to 2014 to be close to three times the size of Gaza's local gross domestic product. However, the total cost may be substantially higher once indirect economic losses are included and lost future income streams from destroyed productive capacities are added.

In addition to the 500,000 people who have been displaced in Gaza as a result of the most recent military operation, the report estimates significant economic losses, including the destruction or severe damage of more than 20,000 Palestinian homes, 148 schools and 15 hospitals and 45 primary health-care centres.

As many as 247 factories and 300 commercial centres were fully or partially destroyed. Serious damage was inflicted on Gaza's sole power plant. The agricultural sector alone suffered $550 million in losses.

It is estimated that, even before the military operations in July and August 2014, Gaza's electricity supply capacity was not enough to meet 40 per cent of the demand (2012 figures). **The electricity and energy crisis is exacerbated by the fact that the Palestinian National Authority is not permitted to develop and use the offshore natural gas fields discovered since the 1990s on Gaza's Mediterranean coast** [highlighted by the editor].

In 2014, unemployment in Gaza reached 44 per cent, the highest level on record. Joblessness was particularly severe among young women Palestinian refugees in Gaza, with more than eight out of 10 women out of work. The economic well-being of Palestinians living in Gaza is worse today than two decades ago. Per capita gross domestic product has shrunk by 30 per cent since 1994.

Food insecurity affects 72 per cent of households, and the number of Palestinian refugees solely reliant on food distribution from United Nations agencies had increased from 72,000 in 2000 to 868,000 by May 2015, representing half the population of Gaza.

The report maintains that even before the three military operations, the economic blockade in place since 2007 had already led to the large-scale cessation of productive operations and loss of employment. Exports from

> Gaza have been almost completely blocked, imports and transfers of cash severely restricted and the flow of all but the most basic humanitarian goods suspended.
>
> The report warns that donor support remains a necessary but insufficient condition for Gaza's recovery and reconstruction. Short of ending the blockade, donor aid will remain vitally important but will not reverse the ongoing de-development and impoverishment in Gaza.

For more, see also Children, Water and Ceasefire Violations.

Israel's attitude

Those working for relief agencies and NGOs bringing help to those in need in Gaza may feel great sympathy for the beleaguered people of Gaza, but this is apparently not shared by Israelis in general. On 28 July 2015, Yuli-Yoel Edelstein, Speaker of the Knesset and a member of Prime Minister Benjamin Netanyahu's right-wing Likud party, spoke of the withdrawal from (illegal) Gush Katif group of settlements in southern Gaza: "It was a desertion – unparalleled in its severity and cruelty [to Jewish illegal settlers] – on the part of a country that sent its citizens to settle a distant and sandy piece of land… a cynical and cruel plan whose drawbacks [greatly outweighed] its advantages." (Mr Edelstein was born in Russia, whereas most of the population of Gaza are descended from refugees who have never been allowed to return to their stolen homes and lands in modern-day Israel.)

A poll conducted the previous week revealed that 51 per cent of Israelis were in favour of reconstructing the illegal settlements in Gaza. It would seem that the Israeli 'man in the street' does not believe the people of Gaza have been forced to suffer enough.

Illegal settlers

"There is justification for killing babies if it is clear that they will grow up to harm us [the Jews], and in such a situation they may be harmed deliberately, and not only during combat with adults."

Rabbi Yitzhak Shapira, of the Yitzhar settlement

"Now go and smite the Amalek [seen by many West Bank rabbis as present day Palestinians], and utterly destroy all that they have, and spare them not, but slay both man and woman, infant and suckling, ox, sheep, camel and ass..."

The Torah

As of January 2015 there were 389,250 residents living illegally in Jewish-only settlements across the West Bank, and another 375,000 in occupied East Jerusalem, according to the Israeli Interior Ministry. They are crucial to Israel's long-term plan to take over and colonise the whole of former Palestine and their presence makes any rational two-state peace settlement an impossibility. Israel's rulers do everything they can to facilitate and augment their presence in the occupied territories. Whatever Benjamin Netanyahu says on the world stage about the possibility of handing the West Bank back to the Palestinians in a peace settlement, he has long ago committed to settlers that he would never do any such thing, now would they allow him to do this.

Their presence is illegal under international law. The Fourth Geneva Convention, Article 49, states "The Occupying Power shall not deport or transfer parts of its own civilian population into the territory it occupies." Under UN Security Council Resolution 242, dated 22 November 1967, Israel should have withdrawn from the territories occupied in 1967 long ago. Instead, it has chosen to regard those territories as part of 'Greater Israel'.

The Israelis now call the West Bank 'Judea and Samaria' and all Jews living there do so under Israeli law and have full Israeli citizenship, including the right to vote.

Religious thugs

Some settlers are there primarily because of economic incentives. However, there is a substantial and highly dangerous number of men and women with dysfunctional and violent religious views. Individually, they (and many Israelis, including key government figures) hold some or all of the following beliefs:

- The occupied territories belong solely to them because they are God's chosen people

- The Palestinians are interlopers – mere 'Arabs' (so not the descendants of the people who lived there in biblical times, which is what Palestinians truly are)

- The Palestinians are the descendants of the Amaleks who the Old Testament says should be eliminated from the face of the earth

- It is therefore a righteous act to kill them and their children and their livestock

- If Palestinians cannot all be killed, then it is righteous to take their lands, steal their crops, and destroy their livelihoods

- That the Jews are a holy and distinct human species and that all Gentiles are deeply inferior[1]

- That it is permitted to kill a child if he may grow up to harm a Jew, and that this applies to Palestinian children

- That Christians are idolaters (they have graven images of their god in their churches) and cannibals (holy communion) and that therefore their churches should be burnt and they should be driven out of Greater Israel[2]

- That they themselves should have as many children as possible in order to

[1] Rabbi Avraham Yitzhak ha-Kohen Kook, first chief rabbi of Palestine: "The difference between the Jewish soul... and that of all the nations, at all the levels, is greater and deeper than the difference between the human soul and the soul of an animal. Between the latter, there is merely a quantitative distinction; between the former, an essential qualitative distinction pertains."

[2] At a meeting of the so-called Nascent Sanhedrin in Jerusalem on 9 September, Rabbi Yisrael Ariel, founder of the Temple Movement (see page 113) stated Christians are idolaters and according to Maimonides, Jews should kill non-Jews who refused to abandon Christianity or Islam and follow Jewish religious law. See also Rabbi Ovadia Yosef "Why are gentiles needed? They will work, they will plow, they will reap. We will sit like an effendi and eat... That is why gentiles were created."

'go forth and multiply' and that Jewish women should be prevented from marrying Gentiles

- That the present secular Jewish state should be replaced, by violence if necessary, by a purely Jewish religious state (equivalent to the Islamic caliphate)

- That anyone who opposes them should be killed[3]

- That the mosques on the Al Aqsa compound should be destroyed and a new Jewish temple built in their place to bring about the arrival of the long-awaited Messiah and the world dominance of the Jews

- That settlers who attack Palestinian men, women and children are heroes; Palestinians who attack settlers are terrorists and they and their families and communities should be made to suffer.

In 2015, as in past years, these religious terrorists have attacked the Palestinians in many ways: destroying olive and other trees and crops, occupying (stealing) Palestinian land by setting up illegal outposts, shooting at civilians, pepper-spraying people, beating them up, driving cars into them, killing livestock, spraying land with toxic chemicals, releasing sewage onto Palestinian farmland, throwing stones at people and cars, spraying racist graffiti on walls, setting fire to houses, churches and mosques and, last but not least, murder.

While the Israeli government from time to time pays lip service to keeping them under control, in reality they are the invaluable storm troops of the Zionist colonial project. The Zionist state depends upon the settlers to colonise the occupied territories and create 'facts on the ground'. The settlers' activities are often coordinated with the army and, if they face a counter attack from Palestinians defending their property or themselves, the army frequently comes to their aid.

Rabbi Moshe Levinger – an Israeli hero and criminal

The life and death of Rabbi Moshe Levinger, buried with full honours in the West Bank's troubled Hebron on 17 May 2015, illustrates this relationship between the Israeli state and its settlers.

---

3 Yigal Amir assassinated Yitzhak Rabin in 1995 because the former was opposed to the peace process.

Lauded as a great Israeli hero, Levinger was a murderer and the man who, perhaps more than any other, bears responsibility for the violence and horror unleashed in Hebron in the final quarter of 2015. President Reuven Rivlin gave the official eulogy at Levinger's funeral, describing him as "one of Israel's most treasured sons". Netanyahu, in his letter of condolence to the family, said he was "an outstanding example of a generation that sought to realize the Zionist dream, in deed and in spirit, after the Six Day War".

The late rabbi was a founder of the Gush Emunim, a messianic religious settler movement and a follower of Rabbi Abraham Isaac Kook, chief rabbi of Palestine (died 1935) and his son, Rabbi Tzvi Yehuda Kook, who believed that reoccupation of the whole of what is euphemistically called 'Greater Israel' would bring about the arrival of the Messiah.

To Levinger and his followers every scrap of Palestinian territory and even the fruit of its olive trees belongs to the Jews, to whom 'God gave the land'.

This 'treasured son of Israel', established the first illegal outpost in the centre of occupied Hebron in 1968. Levinger made no secret of his intention to colonise the occupied territories. By international law, he should have been removed. Instead, the Israeli government eventually allowed him to establish the Kiryat Arba settlement on the outskirts of that city, on 25 hectares of land stolen from its Palestinian owner on the order of the military governor, for 'security reasons'.

In reality, Levinger was a violent religious fanatic of the type that belongs behind bars in any civilised society. In 1985 he carried out a three-month vigilante patrol of a Palestinian refugee camp near Bethlehem. A UN report[4] includes a witness statement detailing how "The settlers, with the help of the Israeli army and police, settled all around the camp. They constantly tried to harass the civilians living in the camp whenever they left or went back to the camp… The settlers then started to harass the inhabitants, provoking and humiliating them. Their objective was to force them to react to this humiliation and harassment and to defend themselves, and this is what happened. After this, the settlers attacked the camp, firing in the air but in the direction of the demonstrators, the inhabitants of the camp, who were protesting against the situation. They entered several houses near the edge of the camp, and one of

4 www.gaza.ochaopt.org/2015/07/
the-gaza-strip-the-humanitarian-impact-of-the-blockade/

these houses was where I lived with my family. In our house they destroyed the furniture, they mixed food, and treated us in an inhuman fashion, the inhabitants of the house ..."

The same year, Levinger entered a house in Hebron and assaulted a six-year-old. He was given a suspended sentence. Then, in 1988, after his car was stoned, Levinger got out and ran down the street in Hebron, firing indiscriminately. In the course of this rampage, he killed an innocent shopkeeper, Kayed Sallah, aged 42, and wounded a customer. He was given a five-month sentence for manslaughter and released after 92 days. In June 1991, he rioted in Hebron market, overturning stalls, firing his pistol and forcing traders to close their shops. He was not imprisoned for this until, in 1995, he caused trouble at the Tomb of the Patriarchs, during the course of which he assaulted an IDF officer. It's one thing to murder a Palestinian, it seems, but quite another to attack a fellow Jew.

Today, in Hebron, streets are blocked off by the army; some 800 settlers in the Old City are heavily protected as they attack and harass Palestinians; shopkeepers have their goods stolen; old people and children are forced out of their homes by ideological Jews and the city has become a battleground in which no Palestinian child can grow up in safety.

Virtual impunity

In May 2015, Israeli human rights organisation Yesh Din published 'Mock Enforcement'[5], a study into 'The failure to enforce the law on Israeli civilians in the West Bank'. The study found that only 7.4 per cent of police investigations into complaints made by Palestinian victims result in indictments, partly because of a routine failure to conduct proper investigations (witnesses are not examined and so on). An examination of 57 indictments found that, while some 58 per cent (of that 7.4 per cent) resulted in a guilty finding; over 40 per cent of those found guilty were not convicted (although those involved were responsible adults), and in 22.8 per cent of cases, the indictments were dropped. Overall, if a Palestinian in the West Bank or Jerusalem complains about an offence to the Israeli police, there is only a 1.9 per cent chance that this will result in an effective investigation, followed by indictment, trial and conviction.

---

5 www.yesh-din.org/infoitem.asp?infocatid=704

The report concludes that "… over the years of occupation, Israel's approach to ideological crime by its citizens against Palestinians has been quite different from its approach to criminality inside Israel. Perpetrators of such ideological crimes do not fit the usual 'offender profile', and their motives for committing these crimes are treated forgivingly, sometimes even empathetically."

By 'ideological crimes', the report means crimes committed by Jews (in this instance) who believe that God approves/commands the crime. The Zionist state condemns all Palestinian resistance to the theft of their land and ethnic cleansing as 'terrorism'. The rest of this section covers some of the terrorist crimes against Palestinians committed by settlers in 2015.

Stone throwing

Both sides, Palestinian and Israeli, throw stones at each other. Admittedly, some of the Palestinian stone throwers attack civilian settler vehicles as they pass along the Israeli-only roads to and from the illegal settlements of the West Bank and so on. On 13 September 2015, 64-year-old Alexander Levlovich died in a car crash probably due to stone throwing. Prime Minister Netanyahu, visiting the site, declared "war on those [Palestinians] who throw stones and bottles, and rioters."

The majority of stone-throwing youths, however, are responding to incursions by the Israeli army (an illegal army of occupation, remember) into their towns, villages and camps, in the course of which heavily-armoured soldiers fire stun grenades, tear gas and/or rubber-tipped or even live bullets and, on occasion, use skunk water (more of this later).

Most of the 500 to 700 children who are prosecuted in the Israeli military courts each year are charged with stone throwing. On 20 July 2015, the Knesset passed a law whereby adults convicted of throwing stones can be imprisoned for up to 20 years and minors for up to 10, even if no harmful intent is proven. Justice Minister Ayelet Shaked, of the religious zionist National Home party, which is strongly pro-settlement, said: "Today, justice was done. For years, terrorists avoided punishment and responsibility. Tolerance towards terrorists ends today."

She did not mean that this law would be applied to settlers.

Let's take a look at just a small sample of settler stone-throwing incidents in 2015:

2 January: settlers throw stones at American consular officials who have come to examine the land where settlers have uprooted some 5000 olive trees. Consular vehicles are damaged.

8.1.: militants from the Beit El settlement stone passing residents and vehicles on the way to the al-Jalazoun refugee camp

10.1.: as above

12.1.: settler militants stone a goatherd, Ghalib Al-Hamarah, as he tends his animals.

24.1.: militants from the Ni'lin Occupation settlement stone passing residents and vehicles on the main road between Ni'lin and Husan villages.

Some 27 more recorded instances in February and March, and below, for the sake of brevity, are just a few more examples.

Beit El's men are at it again on 8 April, when a windscreen is smashed as a driver is heading for al-Jalazoun refugee camp. On the 13th, stone-throwing militants damage a passing vehicle on the main road in Huwara. On the same day, an Israeli court accepts a plea bargain in the case of four Israeli teenagers who set fire to a café near Hebron, where they arrived with their faces covered and set fire to couches and armchairs. They caused heavy damage to the electrical system and spray-painted 'revenge' on the café door. They claim that they did it because they think a fire at the illegal West Bank settlement of Beit El was started by residents of the Palestinian town of Dura. Originally charged with incitement and destruction for racist motives, they are found guilty of arson and given three months' community service, a year's probation and a fine of 500 shekels (£83.75). It should be noted that fines for Palestinian youngsters found guilty of stone-throwing, even when no damage has resulted, are generally well over a thousand pounds.

More settler stone-throwing on April 17, 20, 23, 25 (two separate incidents), 26 (Beit El residents again), 27 (a settler mob stone a Palestinian home in the Old City of Jerusalem) again on 28 and 30.

On 4 May militants from Levinger's old stamping ground, Kiryat Arba, stone the home of a Hebron resident; stone-throwing militants from the Shiloh and Eli occupation settlements damage a passing vehicle on the Ramallah and Nablus main road on 7 May; the next day, militants from the Bitar Elit Occupation settlement stone passing residents and vehicles on the main Husan-Nahilin road; on 9 May a mob from the Pesagout occupation settlement stone several homes in the east of al-Bireh city and Ramat Yashi outpost settlers stone residents in Tel al-Rumeida; more stoning in Nablus the following day. On 12 May, a stone-throwing Israeli settler mob attack a home in the Tel al-Rumeida neighbourhood of Hebron, injuring and hospitalising a young girl. The following day, residents and homes are attacked in Kifl Hares village.

On 14 May, Yusef Dariya, a resident of Aqraba, is injured by a stone-throwing mob from the infamous the Yitzhar settlement. On 16 May, three people, Shaban Shakarneh, Abdel-Rahman Najjajreh and his wife, Jallilah, were injured and hospitalised by a stone-throwing settler mob near the main road between Nahalin and Jub'a. Several vehicle windscreens were smashed in the settler violence.

Also on 16 May, settler militants again invade the Hebron's Tel al-Rumeida neighbourhood and stone a house. ***The Israeli Army assist the settlers by detaining the householder, Mohammad Abu Eishe, while the settlers continue their attack.*** The next day, Kafr Itsiyon settlers stone and damage passing vehicles. On 20 May, Israeli settler militants raid the main bypass road in south Burin village, throwing stones and bottles at vehicles and residents. There are more stonings on May 22, 23, 29 (two separate incidents) and 30, when a Mexican tourist is injured in Hebron. The month ends with an attack in Jericho.

There's more of the same in June. Among the many incidents is one in Hebron, on 13 June, when an Israeli settler mob invades Sweissa village agricultural land in east Yatta, severs the branches off olive trees and stone a landowner as he tries to video the agricultural sabotage. The same day, the IDF keep a householder, Samer Zahada, captive while a gang of settlers stone his home in Hebron's Old City. A 60-year-old woman, Halimah Samhan, is injured and hospitalised when militants stone passing residents and vehicles between Ras Kar Kar and Deir Ibzi', near Ramallah. On 29 June, thugs from the Beit El Occupation settlement stone nearby passing residents and vehicles. ***The Israeli Army intervened on the side of the settlers when people being***

subjected to the assault attempted to stop the settlers.

In July there are 13 recorded instances. July ends with the arson attack by settlers in which 18-month-old Ali Saad Dawabsheh, is burned to death. The news, for once, reaches the outside world and Israel's rulers respond with suitable expressions of regret. But among other violence the following day, discussed later, settlers stone passing residents and vehicles on the main road between Nablus and Tulkarem and others invade Duma village and stone the home that was subjected to Friday's fatal settler terrorist attack. There are two incidents on 2 August and another on the 3rd, with two on the 4th. On 7 August, Israeli settlers set fire to a Bedouin family home near the al-Taybeh road junction and stone Palestinian Civil Defence personnel trying to extinguish the fire; a settler mob also stones fire-fighters trying to extinguish a fire in Arab al-Ramadin village.

We could continue throughout the rest of the year, but the pattern is the same. Palestinians who are caught throwing stones, most usually at Israeli soldiers who are invading their villages or camps, are treated with the utmost severity. Israeli religious fanatics, illegally occupying land with the nation's approval and support, are rarely punished. In fact, they are frequently aided or supported by the army.

Car violence

In recent years, there have been several cases in which Palestinians have deliberately driven their cars at Israelis. Sometimes, their families claim that the event was accidental; sometimes it is very clearly deliberate. The perpetrators are automatically either imprisoned or killed on the spot.

Not so when settlers injure Palestinians. There were over 20 cases of Palestinians injured by settlers' vehicles in 2015 up to the end of September, after which events became even more violent. While some may have been the result of bad driving, some were deliberate. For example, Hasan Abdul-Rahman Badran, 22, from al-Borj village, south of Hebron, was returning home on 23 February when a settler deliberately ran him down near a section of the (illegal) apartheid wall. He was bruised and cut; his pelvis was fractured and he was bleeding from his mouth. Witnesses related that the hit-and-run driver swerved towards Hasan.

The following day, a 10-year-old girl, Mariam Karim Dana, was hit by a jeep driven by a settlement security guard in the Ein al-Lawza area of the Silwan neighborhood, occupied East Jerusalem. She was taken to hospital with a broken left foot and bruises in her back and neck. Witnesses claimed that the car stopped after hitting her, then backed up and hit her leg. The police who arrived at the scene allowed the driver to leave without questioning him.

On 31 July (the same day that the toddler in Duma was burnt to death by settlers), a settler ran over a Civil Defence Force officer who was trying to extinguish a fire in the al-Khaliya district. The injured man was taken to hospital.

On 2 September, a settler deliberately ran into a flock of sheep in east Yatta, killing five of them.

We believe none of the drivers currently faces imprisonment and none have been shot out of hand.

Beatings, shootings, pepper-spraying and other attacks

Israel's illegal settlers in the West Bank and Jerusalem do not confine their violence to stone throwing or car 'accidents'. Other physical attacks occur on a regular basis; if Palestinian reinforcements arrive to protect the victims, the army frequently arrives to protect the settlers and, regularly, to join in the attack on Palestinians.

Any Palestinian, anywhere in the occupied territories, may at some stage in his or her life, if they happen to be in the wrong place at the wrong time, be subjected to settler violence (not that those in Israel itself are safe from racist attacks). On 7 March, a 63-year-old from Silwan in the Old City of Jerusalem was in Harat al-Sharaf square in the Old City walking home when four settlers obstructed his way and started to punch him in the face. He sustained bruises to his face and an eye injury. Fortunately for him, his attackers lost their courage when they saw a group of Palestinians approaching and ran away.

Fast forward to 8 July, and a mob from the Yitmar settlement invaded the area between Aqraba and Yanoun villages, and assaulted workers and engineers employed by the Ministry of Public Works and Housing at a construction site in the area. The settlers issued orders for a halt to construction and the Israeli Army forced the workers to leave the area. At 08:50 on 29 July, settlers forced

Yasser Abu Zeineh, a Palestinian man from Silwad, out of the truck he was driving, beat him up and then handed him over to the army.

There were more beatings (without army help) in August: for example, on 19 August, a man was beaten up by settlers in Jerusalem. On the same day, the UN Under-Secretary-General for Political Affairs, Jeffrey Feltman criticised Israel's decision to increase the penalty for [Palestinian] stone throwers and stated, "the past month has witnessed unconscionable crimes of hatred by extremist elements, reprehensible retaliatory violence, provocations at Jerusalem's holy sites, and a worrying increase in rockets launched from Gaza towards Israel." On 20 August, it was the turn of Hebron resident, Suhayeb Zahida, to be attacked near the Al-Ibrahimi Mosque, and the following day a Palestinian bus driver in Jerusalem, Mohammad Ghannam, was beaten up and his Zionist attackers threatened to burn him alive.

Children are a popular and easy target. Just to read the details of these regular attacks on little ones is stomach-turning. To give only a few examples: on 8 January, an armed terrorist from the Hadgi settlement in south Hebron opened fire on and wounded a 15-year-old boy, Ibrahim Al-Tubasi, as he was playing in the snow with his friends. On 16 February, an Israeli settler attempted to abduct a child in Jerusalem; the Israeli Army took prisoner three residents who came to protect the child. On the 22 February, 10-year-old Saleh Abu Shamsiyeh was playing in the snow in the Tel Rumeida area, in central Hebron, when he was attacked by settlers. Badly bruised all over, he was taken to hospital His father said that soldiers at a nearby checkpoint simply looked on. On 5 March, a 15-year-old girl, Aya Jaber, was admitted to hospital with a broken arm and other injuries after being beaten up on her way to school by a gang of settlers in Hebron's Old City. Again in Hebron, on 5 May, a 14-year-old boy, Mu'tasim Al-Muhtasib was admitted to hospital with severe burns after a gang of Israeli settlers in the Old City poured acid on him. And on and on it goes.

Pepper spray is a favoured weapon. On 4 April, 11-year-old Qammar Dafush, was admitted to hospital with burns to her eyes and bruises after being attacked by zionists in al-Shuhada Road, Hebron. In Jerusalem, on 27 April, Zakariya Sakafi was admitted to hospital with burns to the eyes and breathing difficulties after a pepper-spray assault. On 5 May, truck driver Rajih Nasr, from Halhul in the southern West Bank, had a lucky escape from a gang of settlers who had set up a road block on the main road between Nablus and Qalqiliya, but not before he had been beaten, stabbed and attacked with pepper spray.

On 27 July, bus driver, Mohammad Barakat, suffered severe burns to his eyes and upper body after being pepper-sprayed by two settler militants.

Many settlers, of course, carry firearms. Sometimes they just threaten farmers, shepherds, children and passers by. On 8 January, armed settlers threatened an ICU ambulance in east Yatta with an injured person on board. In Taquo, Bethlehem area, on 5 August an armed settler aimed his gun at a vehicle carrying three people, Hatem Qanibi, Oday Sharabati and Zaki Sharabati, while Israeli forces inspected their ID cards. On 19 September, a passing gang of armed Israeli settlers pushed their weapons into the faces of a Palestinian man, Amar Al-Saqraji, and his son, near the Beit Furiq village entrance.

However, these threats all too often turned into action. Sometimes the shot would fall wide of the mark, as when a settler opened fire towards a group of children in Beit Hanina in the evening of 8 May, but not always. On 4 January Hebron resident, Haytham Al-Rajjabi, was admitted to hospital with a leg wound after being shot by a settler from the Kiryat Arba settlement. On 24 January, a farmer, Mohammad Assad, was admitted to hospital with gunshot wounds after being shot by an Israeli settler while working on his land in the Khilat al-Nakhalah area of Irtas. From October onwards, fatal settler attacks on Palestinians became a frequent reality, with settlers generally claiming that they were 'defending themselves from a knife attacker', but often in cases where Palestinian witnesses assured journalists that no knife was involved (see pages 180 and 189).

Attacks on farmers and shepherds are a frequent occurrence and are covered later, in the section on olive trees and agricultural destruction (see pages 61-74).

IDF/IOF

"Inhabitants of Aida, we are the Israeli occupation forces. If you throw stones we will hit you with gas until you die. The children, the youth, and the old people, all of you – we won't spare any of you."

This chilling message was delivered over a speakerphone to the residents of Aida refugee camp, near Bethlehem, on the night of 29 October. After Qassan Abu Aker, aged 25, was taken, the speaker continued[1]:

"We have arrested one of you, he's with us now. We took him from his home, and we will kill him while you're watching as long as you throw stones. We will blind your eyes with gas until you die, your homes, your families, brothers, sons, everyone."

The night raid was apparently a response to local youths throwing stones at Israel's (illegal) separation wall, which runs close to the camp: mildly annoying, perhaps, but hardly a life-threatening terrorist attack. During the raid, the soldiers fired tear gas and stun grenades indiscriminately at houses and down the camp's narrow streets. So dense were the clouds of gas that children had to be rescued from the camp's community centres and neighbouring houses.

To those who survived or lost loved ones in the Holocaust, it may seem inconceivable that these words should come from an Israeli officer. To the Palestinians, who suffer such raids daily, what was most surprising was not the Nazi-style brutality, but that the Israeli called his army 'The Israeli occupation forces'. This entirely accurate description is how Palestinians refer to their persecutors, but Israelis prefer the euphemism 'the Israeli Defence Force'. In fact, the man was actually with the paramilitary Border Police, but to avoid going into too much pernickety detail, this section will include these and other armed forces whose job is to perpetuate the occupation. After all, if you are at the receiving end of tear gas, stun grenades, rubber or live bullets and so on, it doesn't much matter which Israeli ministry is paying for it.

Unfortunately for the officer responsible, his words were recorded and widely broadcast, so he was suspended from duty. The incident did not, however,

---

1   See www.middleeasteye.net/news/
watch-israeli-soldiers-threaten-bethlehem-refugee-camp-over-loudspeaker-1147215543

cause a sufficient stir to change matters for the residents of the camp. On 19 November, the troops detained a 6-year-old boy and held him for several hours because he tried to run away after they fired tear gas into a children's playground during clashes at the camp. Four days later, during another raid on the camp, tear gas was fired directly into a house holding 18 people, most of them children, but including an 87-year-old man, who was badly affected. The house may have been deliberately singled out, as the owner is currently in an Israeli jail. During the same raid, troops set up a sniper position on the roof of the camp's community centre. Salah Ajarma, director of the centre, told a *Maan News* reporter that this "will deprive Palestinian children from coming to the centre to join in on daily activities or from playing in the centre's garden and playground, because being there means that they may be sitting ducks for Israeli snipers."

Quis custodiet ipsos custodies?

We have noted the constant violent attacks by settlers on Palestinians and their property in other sections of this book, and pointed out that they are frequently aided and abetted by the military. The relationship between ultra-religious settlers and the military is a strange one. For many years, the former were not expected to do national service, as this might conflict with their religious beliefs[2]. Many Israelis resented this, and in 2014 a law was introduced that would have obliged almost all Haredi (ultra-Orthodox) to serve in the IDF. But as part of Netanyahu's bargaining efforts to create a coalition government, following the 2015 elections, this law was effectively dropped. However, just under 1,000 Haredi enlisted in the IDF in 2014 and efforts to recruit them have continued. Given their belief that Palestinians have no rights to their land and are the equivalent of the ancient Amalekites, whose total destruction is ordered in the Torah, their presence in the IDF represents a very real threat to Palestinian life.

But it is not just the Haredi in the military who are prejudiced against Palestinians. In June, a poll of Israeli schoolchildren found that only 28 per cent condemn 'price tag' attacks on Palestinians.[3] Two-thirds of Jewish Israeli

2 Men and women must work alongside each other, for example, and women wear 'men's' clothes. On one occasion, Haredi recruits walked out of a passing-out parade because women were singing the national anthem along with the men.

3 This is when settlers attack a Palestinian home, church or mosque, in retaliation either for a Palestinian attack on a settler or, more often, because the Israeli government has offended the settler movement in some way.

teenagers have never even met a Palestinian, although the latter form 20 per cent of the population; most Jewish children speak no Arabic and know nothing of Arab culture. They are certainly not taught the truth about the Nakba, and an increasingly large proportion go to religious rather than secular schools. Small wonder, then, that many Israelis arrive to do their military service with a racist and dangerous mind-set.

Agents provocateurs and assassins

The Israelis like to portray the Palestinians as unreasonable, murderous religious fanatics, suicide bombers and knife-wielding maniacs. Peaceful demonstrators do not fit with this image, so must be encouraged to stop behaving. This is where *agents provocateurs* come in. The first time they came to light was after an early demonstration, in 2005, at Bil'in, where the organisers had made it clear that no-one was to throw stones or indulge in any violence. But suddenly masked strangers, Arabic in appearance, started throwing stones at the soldiers, who responded with tear gas. At this point, the strangers produced guns and handcuffs and proceeded to make arrests.

On 4 October, 2015, undercover agents, disguised as Palestinians, raided al-Arabi Hospital in Nablus and arrested a patient, disabling surveillance cameras as they left. Three days later, masked men appeared to be joining a student protest heading towards Beit El. They then turned on the students, shooting three of them and then arresting them. On 11 October, they were at work during a raid in Bartaa, west of Jenin.

On 12 November, a group of agents disguised as a pregnant Palestinian woman and her relatives entered al-Ahli hospital, Hebron. There, they kidnapped 20-year-old Azzam Ezzat Shalaldah, who had been shot and seriously wounded after allegedly attempting to stab a settler the previous month. He had undergone three operations and was also having psychiatric treatment. During the arrest raid, a cousin who was visiting him was handcuffed to the bed. Another cousin, Abdullah Shalaldah, aged 28, was shot at least three times in the head and upper body as he came out of the bathroom, unarmed. He died instantly. The Israelis left with the patient in a wheelchair.

Non-violent demonstrations

As far as Israel is concerned, the right to hold peaceful demonstrations does not appear to exist for Palestinians in the occupied territories. This did not stop the latter from continuing to hold many such marches throughout the year in the hope of bringing their plight to the attention of the world. The Israeli response has been to attack demonstrators with tear gas and stun grenades and make arrests. On 8 March, for example, as several hundred women marched peacefully near Jerusalem's Qalandia terminal to mark International Women's Day, they were set upon by the IDF and nine of the women had to be treated for tear gas inhalation.

On Land Day, 30 March, Palestinians marched to commemorate the violent suppression of marches back in 1976, protesting against land seizures in Galilee, northern Israel. Hundreds of soldiers were present and demonstrators were attacked with tear gas in Huwwara, southern Nablus and Silwad.

On 29 April a small demonstration to protest against the Israeli siting of polluting chemical plants in the town of Tulkarem was violently dispersed with tear gas and rubber-coated steel bullets and a young man was shot in the abdomen. (Gushiri industries moved to Tulkarem after a court order banning their dangerous polluting activities in Israel.)

Regular peaceful protests are held against land theft, settlement building and the illegal occupation wall in Nabi Saleh village, Bil'in and Kafr Qaddum, and just as regularly demonstrators are met with unreasonable and unjustified force. The PCHR report on human rights violations in the occupied territories for the last week of April, for example, relates how the entrances to Nabi Saleh were blocked to prevent the Friday demonstration, one man suffered a fractured skull from a bullet, demonstrators were tear-gassed, and journalists and demonstrators were beaten, kicked and verbally insulted.

At Nabi Saleh, on 28 August, instead of blocking the progress of the protest march, soldiers encouraged marchers to descend a steep slope. Here, other soldiers, who had been lying in ambush, sprang out to try to arrest a local man and a foreign activist. As people ran to their aid, another soldier grabbed 11-year-old Mohammed Tamimi, who was lagging behind because his arm was in a cast. (A few days earlier, soldiers had fired tear gas into his house and a canister had broken his wrist.) The boy's head was caught in an arm lock and pressed against a rock as he struggled to escape, at which point his aunt and 14-year-old sister (both, of course, unarmed) rushed up and dragged the Israeli off the boy. The episode was caught on camera and widely seen.

The reaction of Miri Regev, Israel's 'Minister of Culture' was to call on the Defence Minister and Prime Minister to change the army's policy. In her Facebook statement she said, "We need to decide immediately that a soldier that is attacked is permitted to return fire. Period. I call on the minister of security to put an end to the humiliation and change the open fire regulations immediately!"

Night raids and other peace disruptions

Constant raids on Palestinian towns, villages and refugee camps in the illegally occupied territories formed a part of everyday life for many Palestinians in 2015, as in previous years. In fact, the number and intensity of raids increased throughout the year.

Israel justifies these as 'arrest raids', but the way such raids are carried out are an appalling violation of individuals', and particularly children's, rights to a peaceful life. While some raids take place in order to arrest adults and/or children who may have taken part in stone throwing or a more serious offence, on many occasions the aim is clearly punitive. On other occasions, raids appear to happen simply for training purposes, or because a new commander has taken over in a particular locality and wants to make his presence felt, or just to emphasize Israeli dominance. In the last week of March, for example, the Territorial Brigade raided Birzeit at night and searched the home of a university student as part of a training exercise. (Birzeit is in Area A of the West Bank and in theory is under full Palestinian control.) It should also be pointed out that many of those arrested are then held without trial, under military detention. Not only that, but captives are frequently beaten up and otherwise abused as a routine part of the arrest operation (see page 146).

By November 2015, it was estimated that there had been well over 80 raids per week throughout the year, and as many as 28 of these per week took place at the dead of night. To put this in perspective, it may help to bear in mind that the West Bank covers an area of around 2262 square miles (5,860 sq km), compared with Devon (2405 sq m/6629 sq km).

The raids mean that few Palestinians in the occupied West Bank or Jerusalem area can sleep peacefully; children may get caught up in the action on their way to and from school, or even in school itself, and youngsters, who have the natural desire of the young everywhere to rebel and be free are, of course, tempted to resist the illegal, harassing occupation forces that invade their privacy and threaten their homes, villages, towns and camps. The result is a senseless, brutal cycle of violence that causes far more problems than it could conceivably solve, unless the aim is to terrorise the captive population.

In the course of a 'normal' raid, masked and heavily-armed soldiers will arrive in force. The doors to houses where the wanted persons are believed to be living will be broken down without warning; furniture will be trashed; the soldiers may scrawl racist graffiti on the walls; clothes will be strewn around, and children terrorised by the yelling soldiers. Laser beams may be pointed in their eyes as they struggle to wake up. The soldiers may be accompanied by police dogs. Children may be shut up in a room away from their parents, but able to hear the banging, smashing and shouting. Young or old, in the over-crowded refugee camps, everybody is inevitably affected by a raid to some extent.

In response to the arrival of armoured vehicles bringing large numbers of soldiers, youngsters will often respond by throwing stones, bottles or Molotov cocktails. The soldiers, protected by body armour, will fire tear gas, stun grenades, rubber-coated steel bullets and live rounds at the protesters. They may also use skunk water (see below). They frequently break into houses and set up sniper positions on the roof. Injured Palestinians may be dragged to safety by their comrades, but ambulances may be held up by the military or even, on many occasions, attacked.

On 22 January, for example, soldiers used explosives to blow open the door to the home of the Abu Maria family, in Beit Ummar, looking for three brothers from the family. They attacked the mother, pulling her arms behind her back and tying them, and then beating her head, neck and arms. Her 18-year-old son was also beaten, as soldiers demanded to know where his brothers were. They also invaded the house of an uncle, where they stole his savings: 3,000 shekels (£513/$772). The following day, the family were allowed to visit their father, who had been in prison for four months. He told them that the previous morning, Israeli investigators had said: "Tonight we will go to your family's home. We will hit your wife, your daughter and your kids."

Occasionally, if the violence is caught on camera, the soldiers may be reprimanded. When soldiers fired tear gas into his home, Shadi al-Ghabbashy came out to protect his children by asking the soldiers to desist. Instead, they attacked him, beat him up, struck him on the head with their guns, yelled obscenities at him as he lay bleeding on the ground, cuffed him and took him to Beit El illegal settlement. In the course of the same raid, soldiers stopped several Palestinian cars and used them as shields. One driver was injured when a bullet struck his windscreen. Shadi's abusive treatment was videoed and widely shared, and two soldiers were later given 28 days' 'conditional imprisonment'. The army claimed that the father had tried to grab a soldier's gun (hardly surprising, given that they were hitting him with their rifle butts).

Frequently, houses are raided for no apparent reason except to terrorise the occupants, gather information on the internal layout (for future reference), and search, just in case there is anything to be found. Soldiers may go from house to house, gathering families into one room as they search. Money and jewellery often goes missing. During the most recent intifada, Israeli soldiers broke open the banks and stole all the cash, which may explain why many Palestinians prefer to keep their money in their own homes. On 15 March, for example, 5,000 shekels (£856/$1,200) and jewellery worth 12,000 shekels (£2,055/$3,000) were stolen from a house in Madama, south of Nablus, during a dawn raid. On 26 August, 21,000 shekels (£3600/$5412) and jewellery worth around 2,000 Jordanian Dinars (about £1875/$2,820) was allegedly taken from the home of a lieutenant colonel of the Palestinian Authority security services. (The Israelis found 'no conclusive evidence' of this.)

Tear gas

Tear gas may not be as dangerous as live bullets, but this doesn't mean it is harmless. It is particularly dangerous for the young and the elderly and, of course, those with breathing problems. The Israeli forces use tear gas far too liberally and often in circumstances where it need not and should not be used. For example, according to a video[4], tear gas was fired into the infants' playground of the Aida camp on Sunday, 8 February, at a time when there were no clashes happening. The firing of tear gas canisters frequently causes fires, as we have noted in the section on 'Olive trees and agricultural destruction'. In the course of raids, by day and by night, canisters are very often fired directly into houses, without any concern for the safety of those inside.

4 www.facebook.com/video.php?v=833091286734492

The chocking, horrible gas has caused many casualties in 2015 and at least four deaths. On 20 October, Huda Muhammad Darwish, aged 65, died as a result of tear gas inhalation. Relatives were trying to rush her to hospital, but soldiers at the checkpoint out of troubled al-Issawiya delayed the car and ignored the pleas of her relatives to let them through until it was too late.

The following day, Dr Hashem al-Azzeh felt unwell. A 54-year-old peace activist and medical doctor, who suffered from cardio-vascular disease, he lived in Tel Rumeida, in central Hebron. An ambulance was called but could not get through, so he was helped to the nearest checkpoint. The soldiers there refused to let him through and for 10 minutes he had to breathe air filled with tear gas. He collapsed and by the time he finally reached the hospital it was too late. Dr al-Azzeh was a brave man, of great integrity and compassion, who had remained in his house in Hebron despite numerous attacks by settlers and the military. He was determined not to be forced out. As a form of non-violent protest, he used to take foreigners on tours of the city, with its illegal settlers, streets closed off to Palestinians, and military checkpoints. His wife had suffered two miscarriages after being attacked by settlers, and his home had been invaded and trashed by them. On one occasion, his 9-year-old nephew was caught by settlers, who pushed a stone into his mouth and smashed his teeth.

On 30 October, 8-month-old Ramadan Thawabta died of suffocation after the military fired tear gas at protests in the village of Beit Fajjar, near Bethlehem. At 7.30am the following day, the army returned to raid the dead baby's home (presumably in the hope of finding something incriminating that could be used for 'damage limitation').

'Non-lethal' bullets

As with tear gas, the theory behind sponge-tipped rubber bullets is that they offer a non-lethal means of deterring rioters with a blunt shock. In July 2014, however, the Israelis introduced a new, black sponge-tipped bullet in place of the former blue variety. The new bullet was much harder and has proved very dangerous, causing many injuries. In March 2015, ACRI, the Association for Civil Rights in Israel, wrote to the Chief Police Commissioner and the Attorney General demanding that their use be suspended pending a full inquiry into their safety.

Their use continued, and so did casualties, just a few of which are mentioned here. On 15 April, 20-year-old Suleiman Mahmoud al-Tarbi was leaving home in al-Issawiyah when he was shot in the eye at close range. Although clearly severely injured, he was beaten by troops and arrested. On 12 July, 55-year-old Nafiz Dmeiri, who is deaf and mute, entered a grocery store to get away from clashes in Shufat refugee camp. He was shot in the face and lost an eye.

Even more lethal is the rubber-coated steel bullet used by the IDF and police in the occupied territories (its use is forbidden in Israel). These frequently cause severe injuries, accounting for most of over 6,000 injuries in 2014, and injuries continued to mount through 2015. Some 22 people were injured by rubber-coated bullets and tear gas at the funeral of Muhammad Jasser Karakra, on 12 April. In the same month, a 13-year-old girl was shot and injured close to Shufat checkpoint as she was walking home from school and a 24-year-old lost an eye after being shot while on a protest march. At the time of writing, there is no final count of injuries caused by 'non-lethal' means – tear gas, sponge- or rubber-tipped bullets and stun grenades – for 2015, but good reason to expect that the total will exceed last year's count.

Worse was to come, of course, when the government sanctioned the use of live rounds and soldiers were encouraged to use them even when there was no danger of harm to themselves or civilians (see Shoot to kill).

Skunk water

Developed by Israeli pesticide makers Ordotec, this vile chemical is sprayed by water cannon from the top of armoured trucks. Ordotec advertise this product as a harmless but effective way to control rioters. They claim that it is completely harmless and you can even drink it without suffering ill effects.

Skunk water smells of rotting flesh, faeces and sulphur. The smell is so repulsive that, according to activist Miriam Barghouti, as reported in *Electronic Intifada*, "the water lingers on your skin to a point when you want to rip your skin off." It is extremely hard to wash off (special soap is provided to official users) and lasts on furniture and other property, with the result that the contaminated objects have to be discarded.

It is used almost exclusively on Palestinians (though it has been used on Ethiopian Jews demonstrating against the racial prejudice from which they suffer in Israel). The Israeli forces have sprayed this humiliating, psychologically and physically disgusting chemical around entire neighbourhoods, into people's houses, into schools, at peaceful demonstrators and journalists, as well as at rioters. On 31 July, after the arson attack on the Dawabsha family (see page 166), skunk water was liberally sprayed in al-Issawiyah, choking Amna Mahmoud, 93, and Umm Fadi Mahmoud, 48. On 15 September, one of the village's mosques was sprayed, and on the same day the Silwan area, close to the Al Aqsa mosque, was also sprayed. On 2 October, the army fired rubber-coated steel bullets at the windows of houses in al-Issawiyah to break them before spraying them with skunk water. On 19 November, after soldiers said a Palestinian had thrown a tear gas grenade at a checkpoint in Hebron, soldiers responded by spraying the entire area around Tariq Ibn Zaid school, so children had to stay home.

As with so much else that has been used against Palestinians, Ordotec, who market skunk water as eco-friendly and low cost, claim that it "has been field tested and proven to disperse even the most determined of violent protests." In May, this field testing took the form of chasing 5-year-old Muhammad Riyad, who was at a weekly non-violent protest, until he tripped and fell and then spraying him.

Attacks on ambulances

We have already pointed out that ambulance crews attempting to reach those injured during disturbances are frequently blocked by the armed forces. As violence escalated in 2015, attacks on ambulances, their crews and their patients became increasingly frequent, as did raids on hospitals, already mentioned.

On 3 October, soldiers assaulted Fadi 'Obeidi, Hamza al-'Asali and Ahmad Shalloudi, Red Crescent medics, as they attempted to give first aid to wounded residents in the Bab al-'Amoud area. They also seized a wounded patient from an ambulance. The following day, the Red Crescent, which is a member of the International Red Cross (the name change is because of the crusader connotations of the red cross sign), announced a state of emergency after its staff and ambulances had suffered 14 attacks from soldiers and settlers in just three days. Two days later, there had been 27 attacks, with 10 ambulances damaged and 17 staff injured.

As the month wore on, it was clear that Red Crescent paramedics were being deliberately denied access to wounded (alleged) attackers. For example, on 17 October, 18-year-old Fadel al-Qawasmi lay bleeding after being shot by a settler. The army blocked medical personnel from attending him and then removed the body. The same thing happened when 16-year-old Ahmad Muhammad Said Kamil was shot at al Jalama military checkpoint on 24 October. (The Israelis claimed he had tried to stab a soldier, but Palestinian witnesses denied this.)

On 30 October, a medic was injured in the hand when soldiers shot at a Red Crescent ambulance in the al-Farrahin area in eastern Khan Younis, Gaza. On 27 November, an ambulance in Hebron had its windscreen shattered by a tear gas canister. On 4 December, another ambulance was directly targeted with a tear gas canister during the weekly protest at Kafr Qaddum. On 13 December, Red Crescent employee Muhamamd Abu Jumaiza was arrested at the Erez crossing between the Gaza Strip and Israel, despite having the appropriate permit to enter Israel. On 16 December, after soldiers had shot and injured 19-year-old Ayman Ameen Hassan al-Khatib, they prevented Red Crescent medics from treating him and seized their identity cards.

Note

Israelis who refuse to do military service must suffer economically: for example, they will not get support during their student years. Therefore, most young people will join the military for a while and will be expected to participate in these types of action. For many, it will contribute to their indoctrination and brutalisation – their sense of 'this is the way we do things around here'. It would be unfair to end this section without mentioning the courage and decency of over 60 former IDF soldiers who testified in 2015 to human rights group Breaking the Silence about their experiences during the 2014 assault on Gaza. For more, see www.breakingthesilence.org.il. The Israeli government is doing all it can to suppress this organisation.

Olive trees and agricultural destruction

"You must not destroy trees by wielding an axe against them. Although you may take food from them, you must not cut them down."

Deuteronomy 20.19

"Planting a tree in Israel is the perfect way to show you care. You can plant trees for many different reasons and help green the land of Israel while sending a special gift to a friend or loved one. For each order, a beautiful certificate of your choice is mailed to the recipient with your own personal message. Plant trees for all of these occasions: birth, Bar or Bat Mitzvah, graduation, wedding, birthday, get-well wish, or in memory of someone special. Over the last 100 years, JNF has planted over 250 million trees in the land of Israel."

Jewish National Fund website

Unfortunately, while good, 'pure', Jewish trees may deserve to live, nasty, Muslim or Christian, Palestinian trees, deserve to be destroyed. Olive and other fruit trees, grapevines, wheat, okra and a host of other crops grown by Palestinian farmers in the West Bank and Gaza are all, it seems, possessed of undesirable ethnicity and religious affiliations in the eyes of illegal settlers, the Israeli army and thus, presumably, Israel's rulers. The result is a vicious and apparently endless war on trees which strikes deep into the Palestinian heart as well as destroying their livelihood.

Carried out by people who claim to believe in and practise their religion to the letter, and indeed use it as a justification for ethnic cleansing, the wholesale war of destruction waged on trees in 2015 (and so many years prior), may seem bizarre. Trees ask nothing from us; they give so generously – fruits, shelter, beauty to delight our eyes, prunings for warmth and cooking fuel, and finally, when their allotted span is ended, material for furniture and buildings.

But alas for the 'Palestinian' trees, this bounty is their downfall. Olive trees are an essential part of the Palestinian economy today, as they have been for millennia. Some 100-80,000 or so of those living in the West Bank rely on olive trees for the bulk of their income, and olive trees contribute around £66 million

($100 million) to the economy of the West Bank. Palestinian olive oil is some of the best you can buy (go to Zaytoun's website, if you are interested in trying some). Trees are lovingly tended; some of them, with huge, broad, gnarled trunks, are called 'Roman' trees and are many hundreds of years old. The olive harvest is, or should be, a time of celebration, when the whole family joins together to collect the olives and then watch the rich, beautifully scented oil gush forth from the press.

Worse still, Palestinian farmers love their trees. They are an integral part of the land, part of their inheritance and their whole way of life. So, destroy a Palestinian's trees and, with luck, you may not only render him destitute, but also break his heart, his spirit. So that is exactly what the settlers and their military and governmental allies frequently do. We mentioned earlier on that the year started with the destruction of some 5,000 saplings east of the town of Turmusayya, near Ramallah. On 4 January, three people among a group planting olive trees near al-Far'un, including a 17-year-old youth, Hatem Badir, were wounded and hospitalised when Israeli troops attacked them, firing rubber-coated bullets and stun and tear gas grenades. On 9 January, settlers from a Jewish-only settlement, Susiya, came by night to an area south of Hebron and cut down some 300 trees belonging to the Shatat, Dawood, and Halabi families. On the 11 January, vandals from Tappuah settlement cut down over 170 of the treasured Roman trees in the village of Yasuf south of Nablus.

Who will protect the Palestinian farmers and their beloved trees? According to Yesh Din, the Israeli human rights organisation, out of 211 complaints filed with the 'Judea and Samaria' District police for cases of alleged olive tree vandalism documented by the organization between 2005 and 2013, only four investigations ended in indictment.

So the destruction continued throughout 2015. On 23 January, a settler mob, accompanied by the Israeli army, assaulted several workers planting olive trees on al-Sweissa village farmland in east Yatta. To give just a few more examples: on 5 February, settlers from Qadumim invaded Kafr Qaddum and sprayed toxic chemicals on a number of olive trees. On 17 February, the army came to the West Bank village of Tayasir with bulldozers and levelled an area of land belonging to Adnan Daraghmah, destroying his trees on the pretext that the area was a military zone and he had no right to plant or build there without permission from the (Israeli) civil administration. Metzad settlers destroyed 500 newly-planted trees near al-Shuyukh the following day (settlers returned to the village on 17 May to uproot trees for the fourth time).

Trees were destroyed in February and March in the Nablus area, Hebron, Burin village, Ein Qassis and Kahlah. On 18 March, the army was particularly busy, uprooting 150 trees near the Ma'allah area of al-Thahiriya and spraying toxic chemicals on the soil, as well as raiding the Kafr Atiya area of Aqraba, where they bulldozed crops, uprooted 300 olive trees and destroyed 5,000 metres of stone walls. On 2 April, settlers uprooted 100 trees in the Bethlehem area, while the army destroyed 150 in near Salfit. On 27 April, a gang of settlers invaded agricultural land in the Wadi al Amir area of Halhul and uprooted 85 olive and almond trees as well as grapevines, and on 29 April settlers raided Husan village, Bethlehem area, and chopped down 20 olive, almond and citrus trees.

On 6 May, the army came with bulldozers and razed farmland planted with almond and olive trees in Idhna, western Hebron, at the same time destroying a greenhouse, a support wall and several dry-stone walls, gardens and lands near residents' homes. One can hardly imagine how soul-destroying this must have been to the Ihreiz, al-Zaatari, al-Qawasmi and al-Tarturi families on whose lands this monstrous act of vandalism took place. While all this was happening, the army blocked off the area, firing tear-gas canisters and stun grenades. On 17 May, five young (aged around 16 to 20, according to witnesses) settlers from Bat Ayin set fire to land planted with 40-year-old olive trees in Hilet Ikdeis, north of Hebron, owned by the Hamdam family. Israeli troops arrived but refused the landowners' request for them to call for firefighters. Some six acres were destroyed by fire. An even greater acreage, some 80 acres in al-Shuyoukh, had been vandalised by settlers the previous day. On 22 May, soldiers firing tear gas canisters during the weekly protest march in Bil'in (against land theft/expropriation) set fire to land planted with olive trees (and again on 17 July).

On 4 June, the army came to Surif, northwest Hebron, with bulldozers and military vehicles and trashed five acres of Palestinian land, destroying trees, knocking down dry stone walls and then dumping the rubbish into three wells, making them unusable. The owners had been in dispute with the Israeli authorities, who were claiming the property as (Israeli) state land, but no court decision had been reached.

Overnight, on 20/21 June, settlers took a chainsaw to 60 trees near Jamaa'in village. The trees were said to have been over 150 years old. For the three brothers from the Zeiden family, to whom 40 of the trees belonged, the trees were not just their livelihood but also the witnesses and participants in a host of family memories, like dearly-loved friends.

July brought more of the same: either the army or settlers raiding and destroying at will. On 2 August, a settler mob raided al-Mugheir village, trying but thankfully failing to set fire to a home, but successfully burning 50 trees while the army supported them, firing stun and tear gas grenades at locals and wounding 17-year-old Foad Abu Aliya. Three more villagers were beaten and ended up in hospital.

Change.org petition, 16 September 2015, by National Coalition of Christian Organisations in Palestine and Palestine Israel Ecumenical Forum of the World Council of Churches

Your Excellencies,

Representatives of foreign governments to Israel and Palestine,

We, Palestinian Christians, along with people of goodwill in the global community, ask for your prompt intervention on a matter of utmost urgency.

Recently the shocking situation in the Cremisan valley and Bir Ouna has come to the attention of the world. Israeli forces have been uprooting hundreds of olive trees in order to clear space for a new section of the Separation Barrier. This new effort to annex occupied Palestinian territory directly affects Palestinian wellbeing. These developments have been distressing for the entire Palestinian community. It has a direct impact especially on Palestinian Christians, who are made more vulnerable by these actions from the Government of Israel. This is a clear violation of international law.

In its Advisory Opinion, *released in 2004, the International Court of Justice concluded "that Israel cannot rely on a right of self-defence ... or on a state of necessity in order to preclude the wrongfulness of the construction of the wall.... The Court accordingly finds that the construction of the wall, and its associated régime, are contrary to international law" (Para. 142).*

Fr. Aktham Hijazin, parish priest for Bir Ouna, has warned the world: "When you destroy the olive trees, you also kill the people here." And we remember the words of the Bible, "You must not destroy trees by wielding an axe against

---

*them. Although you may take food from them, you must not cut them down"
(Deuteronomy 20.19).*

*Just four months ago the High Court of Israel rejected the Israel-planned route
for the wall along the heart of the Cremisan Valley. It was acknowledged that
this route would bring great harm to the convent, monastery, and school
located there. The route would also directly impact privately-owned parcels of
land, destroying olive groves and with them the wellbeing of local communities.*

*Despite this previous judgment, under official Israeli pressure, the High Court
inexplicably allowed a new interpretation of its ruling to take force. As a result,
work began immediately on construction of the wall through the Cremisan
Valley.*

*We stand in solidarity with the people of Cremisan, remaining firmly
committed to non-violent struggle and prayer for the area. The Israeli legal
system appears to have been manipulated for the benefit of the occupation
régime; all options within the Israeli legal system have been exhausted. We
therefore call on international intervention to pressure Israel to return to the
original ruling of its High Court. Without such pressure, the State of Israel
will continue to act with impunity, humiliating the dignity of our people,
threatening the livelihood of Palestinian communities, and insulting any effort
toward building a just peace.*

*The construction of the wall on occupied land is a breach of international
law – the Cremisan Valley is only the latest victim. Local Palestinian Christian
communities urge you to put pressure on Israel to:*

a. immediately stop the illegal construction of the Separation Barrier on
   occupied land,

b. dismantle the sections already constructed on all occupied territory,
   and

c. replant the uprooted olive trees and compensate farmers who have lost
   their trees.

In hope,

National Coalition of Christian Organisations in Palestine

Palestine Israel Ecumenical Forum of the World Council of Churches

On 1 August, the Israeli Army raided the Bir Una area in West Beit Jala and bulldozed agricultural land to make way for the Separation Wall that is stealing up to 10 per cent of West Bank land. They destroyed 45 olive trees in the process, beating up and hospitalising the owner, Waleed al-Shatlah, when he objected to the loss of his land and livelihood. The urgent petition that went out on Change.org was totally ignored by the Israelis. Destruction of olive trees and the annexation of land belonging to local (mainly Christian) farmers and the ancient Cremisan monastery continued.

We could continue for much longer and the abbreviated details of further attacks on trees alone could easily fill many more pages. On 12 May, for example, the army raided Zif village in Hebron and felled some 300 trees in a nature reserve forest that had been planted with help from the Palestinian Ministry of Agriculture and several international aid organisations. But it's time to consider other attacks on farmers and agriculture, so for now let's just move to October and the olive harvest, that formerly joyful season. On 3 October, soldiers seized and for a while held captive an 11-year-old, Hatem Qulieb, as he was helping his family to harvest olives. On 9 October, dozens of settlers attempted an attack on Palestinian farmers who were picking olives on their land in the village of Yanun, Nablus area, but were stopped by local guarding committees. On 12 October, an armed mob from Yitzhar (again) opened fire on a woman and child who were harvesting olives.

On 14 October, 46-year-old Riyad Ibrahim Dar Youssef was returning to his home in al-Janiya village, western Ramallah, after a day spent harvesting olives. Israeli illegal settlements surround the village and access to villagers' lands is often blocked by troops. On this occasion, Riyad was set upon and beaten by soldiers. He died of a heart attack early the following day. On the same day, settlers attacked olive harvesters in the village of Burin, north of Nablus, injuring four Palestinians and a foreign volunteer called David Amos, aged 66. A stone thrown by a settler hit him on the back of the head and he was then kicked as he lay on the ground. He and one of the Palestinians were taken to hospital to be treated. On Tuesday 20 October, 14-year-old Saqir Mahmoud Hirzallah was picking olives with some friends on his family's land near Jenin when they were set upon by settlers. His friends managed to flee in time but Saqir was caught and beaten up. On the following Friday, Rabbi Arik Ascherman, of Rabbis for Human Rights, was attacked by a masked settler thug, who kicked, pushed and threatened him with a knife when he attempted to stop the man stealing olives. On the Sunday, a settler shot 22-year-old Azzam Ezzat

Shalalda in the neck, abdomen and legs. He and others had been picking olives in an orchard in troubled Hebron when they were set upon by settler paramilitaries. On the Monday, stone-throwing settlers from Elon Moreh prevented farmers in Azmut and Deir al-Hatab from harvesting olives. Attacks continued. On 9 November, a fanatic from Maale Levona settlement got out of his car and machine-gunned farmers harvesting olives near the village of al-Lubban al-Sharqiya. Fortunately, no one was hurt on this occasion.

On 24 November, a group of around 30 settlers from Yitzhar attacked a family from Burin as they were picking olives and then set fire to their trees. On the same day, US Secretary of State John Kerry, who was visiting PM Netanyahu, said: "Israel has every right in the world to defend itself. It has an obligation to defend itself. And it will and it is. Our thoughts and prayers are with innocent people who have been hurt in this process." He made no mention of the Palestinians' decades of abuse at Israeli hands. Netanyahu, who was pushing for recognition of the illegal settlement blocks, commented "It's not only our battle, it's everyone's battle. It's the battle of civilization against barbarism."

Attacks on farmers and shepherds

Farming, anywhere in the world, is hard work: long hours, often involving back-breaking labour, the risks of too little rain, or too much, or excess heat ruining crops, or extreme cold, and so on. No surprise that farmers tend to be a tough breed. What they should not have to deal with is a constant risk of physical attacks on them or their livestock, their workers and helpers, their crops, and the infrastructure and tools bought with their hard-earned money. But such is the fate of Palestinian farmers under Israeli occupation.

Attacks on farmers and shepherds like those already mentioned, whether by settlers or by the army, are a regular occurrence. Looking at a list of over 40 physical attacks between January and September alone (a list that is most probably far from complete), a clear picture emerges of a concerted effort to make the life of a farmer intolerably miserable. On 12 January, for example, troops in Ush al-Ghurab, Behtlehem area, fired stun and tear gas grenades at local goatherds tending their animals. That afternoon, settler militants stoned a goatherd, Ghalib Al-Hamarah, as he was tending his animals in the Hebron area. Two days later, a gang from the Alon Muriya settlement, positioned on the by-pass road to Salem village, assaulted several shepherds as they were herding their sheep in the area, while a settler vehicle drove into two sheep.

The settlers later withdrew, along with Israeli troops. The same day, settlers invaded Deir al-Hatab land, Nablus area, and used it to graze goats; men from the Kiryat Natavim settlement, meanwhile, assaulted several Palestinian shepherds at work in the Salfit area.

On 6 February, soldiers in the Khilat al-Miyah area of east Yatta assaulted two young goatherds, Ayad Al-Shawahin (13) and Hamza Shawahin (16), and held them captive for an hour. On 12 February, the army raided Assira al-Qibliya and assaulted two shepherds, Ahmad al-Bassat and Mohammad Abbaban, and on 19th, a gang of settler thugs beat up and hospitalised a Palestinian goatherd in the Aqweis area of east Yatta.

On 14 March, Israeli forces seized, and held captive for a time, six Palestinian minors – Mohammad Zied (13), Tariq Waqad (15), Baha Yahya (17), Awarah Awad (16), Ahmad Salah (16) and Qutaybah Hammad (17) – as they tried to work al-Arqa village farmland. Meanwhile, near Jerusalem, at 10.50am, a gang of settlers, supported by the Israeli army, raided the Aqabat area near Mukhmas and stoned several shepherds. Israeli soldiers then detained one shepherd, Abdel-Kareem Abu Ali, releasing him at 13:05.

Let's move on to 16 April, when settlers, with army support, again invaded Assira al-Qibliya agricultural land and forced Palestinian farmers off the land. The same day, Hebron area, Zionist fanatics from the Karmei Tsur settlement invaded Beit Ummar farmland and forced a farmer, Waleed Sabarnah, off his land. (The army returned to attack farmers on June 18.)

For the sake of brevity, we will just pick a few instances from the rest of the year. On 18 July, a mob from Magon settlement invaded Palestinian farmland, again with the support of the army, and beat up three men from the same family – Fadi, Mohammad and Baha al-Shawahin. The following day, settlers assaulted and hospitalised two Palestinian goatherds near Sussiya village. On 1 August, at two separate locations, settlers combined with the army invaded farmland and attacked farmers. Five people were injured in one of the attacks; in the other, a 17-year-old was injured by the army firing stun and tear gas grenades and three others were beaten up and hospitalised. Fifty olive trees were burnt. On 22 August, settlers from Esh Kudesh attacked Palestinian farmers while they were working on land east of Qusra village in southern Nablus. The farmers resisted and the settlers were forced to retreat, so the Israeli army then came to their rescue, firing tear gas canisters and rubber-coated steel bullets at

Palestinians, leaving a number of Palestinians injured. And on 2 September, a settler drove at a flock of sheep in east Yatta, killing five of them.

We hope you get the picture.

Property theft and destruction

We will cover the demolition of homes and other buildings, such as schools, in greater depth elsewhere, but demolitions are not restricted to housing. Israeli attacks on agriculture in the West Bank also feature the regular destruction of farm buildings and livestock shelters. Farmers living in area C, which covers a huge swathe, some 60 per cent, of the West Bank, must obtain building permits for livestock shelters and the like. The Israelis take great delight in refusing these, as we will discuss later. This gives them the excuse to indulge in the wholesale destruction of more recently built animal shelters, however necessary they may be.

On 14 January, the army destroyed a livestock shelter near Deir Jerir; on 19 January it was a shelter in the Khilat al-Warad area, Hebron, and two others in Barta'a al-Sharqiya village, Jenin, and two days later, a tent dwelling and two livestock shelters in Kafr Malik village, Ramallah, two more shelters in al-Jiftlik village and two in Ein Dweik al-Tahta village, Jericho. Four days later, they forced an Ithna resident, Musalim Abu Jahishah, to destroy his livestock shelter, plundered his herd of cows and made him to pay a financial penalty. The list continues throughout the year: farmers need shelters for their livestock; they have no choice but to take the risk of building them without permits; someone (settlers?) reports them, and the army comes and destroys the shelter. This is a clear attempt to harass the occupied community and equally clearly a breach of international law, but who will enforce this when governments in the west are far more concerned with blocking the BDS movement than in obliging Israel to comply with the rule of law?

It's not just livestock shelters, of course. Other farm buildings that are threatened include greenhouses. On 11 February, tent dwellings and greenhouses were destroyed in al-Jawiya village in east Yatta; on 24 February, the army, firing stun and tear gas grenades, set fire to a greenhouse in Azun Atma. The owner's son, Amar Ahmad, was overcome by tear gas. It was settlers who set fire to a greenhouse in Kafr al-Dik on 30 April, but the army carried out the raid on Ti'inik village the following month during which several greenhouses were destroyed and the destruction of a well was ordered (more about the use of water as a weapon against the Palestinians later).

After decades of a harsh and vindictive occupation, with severe travel restrictions making normal trade an impossibility, Palestinian farmers in the West Bank and Gaza are surely among the poorest in the world, so equipment costs a huge proportion of their meagre income. Israeli raids, whether by the illegally occupying army or their settler friends, are often accompanied by theft. At 2.30am on 23 January, the army stole a tractor during a raid on Bethlehem; two days later, six rolls of fencing wire and other equipment left with the army after a raid in the Safeh area, east of Tayasir village, Tubas. Another tractor went on 1 February when the army invaded Beit Ummar, Hebron, to deliver two house demolition orders. Two days later they got a good haul – not one but two tractors – this time from al-Samou', Hebron. On 7 February, it was the turn of the settlers, when a mob invaded agricultural land in al-Mazra'a al-Gharbiya, Ramallah, assaulted a farmer, Rasim Shartih, and stole several farm implements. More tractors went off with the army over the next few months: from Khirbeit Tanah village, Nablus, on 1 April; from Khirbeit Humsa, in the North Jordan Valley, on 12 May; from Jalloud village farmland on 4 June, and so on.

On 26 June, a water storage tank accompanied the tractor that was stolen by troops in the Wadi al-Malah area of the North Jordan Valley. On 11 July, the army raided Yasuf village in order to prevent the local village council from paving an agricultural road, on which occasion they seized a bulldozer, road-making equipment and a water storage tank. Eleven days later, they returned with several military vehicles and an armoured bulldozer in order to complete the damage by bulldozing the road. On 26 July, the army set up a checkpoint at the entrance to Qarawat Bani Hassan, raided an Islamic charity office, interrogated one person, and then made off with a plundered farm tractor (presumably it had dodgy connections?).

Crop destruction

Olives are not, of course, the only crop grown by Palestinian farmers. The healthy Mediterranean diet that Palestinians should be eating (not much chance of that for many in Gaza, or the refugee camps of Syria, or the impoverished Palestinian towns of Israel itself) includes plenty of wonderful vegetables, to be consumed with freshly-made pitta bread.

The sun-ripened crops of Palestinian farmers were another favourite target of the Israeli army and settlers in 2015. The excuses for this vandalism are varied: military necessity, which we will discuss below; too near a settlement; the land is needed for a road; the land is going to be stolen for a settlement; the troops had come under attack from stone throwers and set fire to crops while firing stun and tear gas grenades, or they are helping settlers. On one occasion, on 18 February, the army stormed farmland near west Deir Istiya and bulldozed an area simply in order to dig a grave for an Israeli settler from the Yaqar occupation settlement. The settlers, of course, don't bother about finding an excuse: they just know that (their concept of) God wants them to do it.

And so, on 19 January, troops invaded the area between Abboud and Wadi al-Zarqa and bulldozed crops. On the 26 January, they raided Immatin village and bulldozed crops in the al-Ramamin area near the Amanawil settlement. Not counting military exercises, the army bulldozed crops at Sarah village (5 February), the Khilat al-Nakhlah area (10 February), the Khirbeit Zunah area, Hebron (23 February); south Taquo, Bethlehem area (8 March), in Baten al-Ma'asi and Um Mohammad, al-Khadr, Bethlehem area (9 March), south Taquo again (the 10 March), and again the following day, Yatma village, on land near the Rahalim settlement (19 March) and farmland near the Kiryat Arba occupation settlement on the same day (they repeated this on 23 March). The devastation continued as the year wore on. On 4 August, the army raided the Izeima area and destroyed fields of planted vegetables and irrigation pipes belonging to Ahmad Barghash al-Shawahin.

But where would Palestinian farmers be without fanatical Israeli settlers? Very happy, one would imagine! As if the army's destructive efforts were not enough, 2015 saw numerous attacks on crops by settlers. As usual, these were frequently backed up by the army. On 15 January, settler militants bulldozed Irtas village crops. On 17 February, Kiryat Arba settlers bulldozed Palestinian crops in the Jabal Jalis area of Hebron. On 24 April, settlers from Eniv bulldozed crops on nearby Palestinian farmland, and on 14 June, men from the same settlement invaded agricultural land in the Ras al-Shumar area of Kafr al-Lebed village, setting fire to and destroying fields of wheat belonging to Rafiq Jbara. Civil and military authorities were called, but were too late to prevent the complete destruction of the crop. On the 27 June, militants from the Ihiya occupation settlement invaded Jallud village agricultural land and bulldozed crops in order to take the land for settlement expansion.

On 19 April, witnesses told Khaled Maali of *Maan News* that Israeli bulldozers had moved huge piles of the village's high quality fertile soil from Kafr al-Dik into the illegal Israeli settlement of Lishim, where it would now be used in settlers' gardens and also to grow trees on land bordering exclusive settler routes that Israeli military forces have seized from Palestinians as a 'buffer zone' for the roads. The greater part of the village's land has already been expropriated by the Israelis for settlement expansion, so this is a major loss.

On 26 June, settlers rolled burning tyres towards farmland in east Burin, and on 1 July, they set fire to crops in the same village. On 12 July, settlers building a road for themselves on Deir Istiya farmland bulldozed crops and uprooted 80 olive trees. On 18 July, settlers from Efrat invaded farmland in al-Khader, south of Bethlehem, where they uprooted hundreds of tomato and cauliflower plants and seedlings and destroyed an entire field planted with okra.

On 31 July, the same day that settler arsonists attacked the Dawabsha family in Duma with fatal consequences, arsonists from the Yitzhar settlement set fire to crops in the Jabal Suliman area, near Assira al-Qibliya and Orif villages.

On 9 August, the day after Saad Dawabsha died of his burns, settlers from Bracha set fire to land east and west of Burin village, which then spread to burn hundreds of acres of crops. In a separate (but possibly coordinated?) attack, settlers from Yitzhar set fire to land to the south of the village, the fire spreading across farmland to the southern village of Einabus. You might imagine that the farmers would at least on this occasion have received some support from the Israeli military, bearing in mind that Prime Minister Netanyahu had so recently assured the world that his government would deliver even-handed justice to Jewish and Palestinian terrorists alike. If fact, when the army arrived it was to clash with the Palestinians because settlers had accused them of throwing stones at settler cars on local roads.

Military exercises

These provide a convenient excuse for harassing the small farming communities of the West Bank. Please bear in mind that the Israeli army has no right to be in the West Bank and has the whole of Israel in which to conduct training exercises. But of course, if any army (including British and American troops) treated their own local farmers the way Palestinians were treated, their government would fall.

On 19 January, the Israeli army destroyed crops on al-Aqaba village farmland while conducting military exercises (they returned to do more damage to crops in the area on 3 and 6 May and 29 July). On the 29 January, they bulldozed Deir Nizam village crops on land taken for a new army observation tower and damaged crops at Bardala village during exercises. On 5 February, they returned to Bardala and ruined crops of wheat and chickpeas during exercises. Construction of another watch tower was the excuse for bulldozing crops between Rujeib and Awarta on 12 April. On 27 April, the army bulldozed land in the North Jordan Valley to make a road during exercises and on the same day set fire to grapevines and other crops in Hamsa village.

On 29 April, Bardala crops suffered again during exercises. On the same day, about 100 people in Ibziq village and another 80 in Hasmah Al-Foqa were evicted from their homes so the army could conduct exercises. Another 27 families, in al-Malah and al-Burj, North Jordan Valley, suffered the same fate the day after, as did families in Ras Al-Hamrah.

On 4 May, the Israeli army, while conducting 'military exercises', set fire to large areas of wheat and other crops in Ras Basilah, al-Sadoud, Ghabisha and al-Maksar, North Jordan Valley. When the Palestinian Civil Defence arrived to try to put out the fires, the army prevented them, claiming the land was a 'closed military area'.

Agricultural sabotage and destruction under the pretext of military exercises or construction continues. The destruction of olive and other fruit trees and crops, physical attacks and harassment of farmers, demolition of farm buildings and theft of farm vehicles, whether it is carried out by the army or by illegal settlers, are all intended to make life untenable and browbeat the local population into a hopeless submission. It is, as Archbishop Desmond Tutu has said, part of a system that is worse than apartheid.

Gaza farmland

Wherever Palestinians are farming their land, the Israelis will attack them. This is just as true for Gaza as for the West Bank. The attacks on agriculture discussed so far have taken place in the West Bank, but the same mentality that allows these to happen surely lies behind many of the Israeli violations of the ceasefire between Israel and Gaza in 2015. In Appendix III, ceasefire violations in the form of attacks on Gazan farmland in April are listed. The month was chosen at random. To have listed all such attacks throughout the year would simply have taken up too much space.

The ceasefire violations that are listed in the appendix are not, we suggest, any form of self defence, or indeed necessary for the maintenance of the siege of Gaza. The farmers involved were simply going about their business. The aim is to destroy Gazan agriculture and thus, even more sinister, stick to the plan to 'keep Gaza on a diet', as explained in the section on the blockade of Gaza.

Note

One final note, other forms of harassment and agricultural sabotage that have not been included here, but are discussed in other sections of this book, include water deprivation, road closures and restrictions, home demolitions and land seizure.

Land theft and settlement building

"We must not give anyone the sense that we are in any doubt about our right to our land. For me, the settlement of the land of Israel is an expression of that right, our historical right, our national right."

President Rivlin, talking with settlers on 24 August 2015

From its inception, Israel has consistently and relentlessly stolen land from its Palestinian owners. Governments of states friendly to Israel frequently complain about this, while doing virtually nothing to prevent it – and at the same time opposing any move to boycott Israel.

In Israel itself, some 93 per cent of the land is owned by the state and then leased out. It should come as no surprise that Palestinians have historically had great difficulty in leasing land from the state. Perhaps in order to avoid embarrassing its supporters too much, the Israeli government has invented various pretexts to offer a semblance of legality to its land theft in the occupied territories, some of which are listed below.

1. Sometimes the land is first declared a 'nature reserve' and is then fenced off.

2. Sometimes it is confiscated for 'military' or 'security' purposes, and is, after a while, converted to settlement use.

3. Sometimes it is ear-marked for local development (Jewish use only).

4. Sometimes the historic owners or users of the land – Bedouin herdsmen, for example – do not have title deeds, so their assumed but unwritten rights can be ignored.

5. Sometimes the Palestinian owners of the land are refugees who are not allowed back to claim their property, in which case the Absentee Property Law conveniently gives the land, buildings and so on to the Israeli state.

6. Various Jewish organisations and individuals with large sums at their

disposal may buy land (sometimes under elaborate cover names, so the owners do not realise to whom they are selling), which is then put into Zionist hands.

7. Illegal settlers may move onto privately owned Palestinian land. At first, the Israeli state declares their settlement 'illegal', but offers the land thieves protection from eviction and supplies electricity, water and other services. Eventually, the theft is officially 'legalised'.

8. What in Britain is called 'common land' was officially owned by the state under Ottoman rule, though recognised as common land. Under Israeli rule, all such land can be used by the state for whatever purposes it choses without reference to the land's traditional (Palestinian) users. It can therefore be used for settlement building.

All of this is colonisation, and it is not only completely illegal, but cruel and abusive. It should also be remembered that Israel already covers vastly more land than the United Nations ever allocated to it, having terrorised the inhabitants into fleeing and then occupied their towns and villages in 1948. The bulk of the Palestinian population in Israel is now confined to inadequately-funded townships. Israel exists, therefore, due to the wholesale theft of their land from Palestinians: it is the Israeli way of life and it should therefore come as no surprise that 2015 has seen more of the same.

Under the Oslo accords, which were only ever intended as a very temporary interim agreement, the West Bank is divided into three areas. Area A, which chiefly covers towns and cities, is supposed to be under full control of the Palestinian Authority (which does not prevent the Israeli army from raiding or blockading it at will). Area B is mainly rural and is under PA administration, but with security under joint PA/Israeli control. Area C is under Israeli control, though the Palestinians control education and healthcare. Area C constitutes about 60 per cent of the West Bank.

The Oslo accords make it clear that neither side is to take steps that would change the status quo in the occupied territories and make a final agreement more difficult. The Israeli government, however, choses to interpret the accords as giving them free reign to treat large areas of land in Area C as common land (and therefore for their own 'state' use – in other words for settlement building). They also feel free to take over Palestinian farm land for local government use for projects that might sound reasonable, until you realise that they all amount to stealing land from Palestinians and giving it to Jewish religious fanatics, often from abroad, who wish to take over the West Bank in its entirety: industrial zones (for settlements), landfill use, 'parks' (so farmers can no longer use their own land and the parks can be then allocated to settlements), road building (for settlers), military use and, of course, settlements themselves.

In January, the state announced that it would confiscate hundreds of dunums (there are approximately four dunums to an acre) of land in the al-Mekhath and Attus areas in Beit Ula, Area C. The land belonged mainly to members of the al-Emla family, who had lived and farmed there since the Ottoman era.

On 8 February, the Committee of Local Planning and Construction of the Jerusalem Municipality approved the construction of 64 new housing units in the Ramot settlement of occupied East Jerusalem, already home to some 50,000 settlers. On 16 February, the Jerusalem authorities announced their intention to use a huge area of land – some 546 square km – between the Palestinian villages of al-Issawiya and Anata for landfill. When the valley is full, the land will be converted to a public park. The Palestinians pointed out that the project was not intended to serve them, but was for settlement use. Bedouin families living on the land were not consulted.

Al-Issawiya is, of course, one of the most threatened of all Palestinian communities: perpetually suffering from road blocks to the extent of seeming, at times, almost like a mini Gaza; its inhabitants live in constant fear of the next army raid or the next abduction of a youngster. On 15 April, Israeli soldiers shot Suleiman Mahmoud al-Tarbi, aged 20, in the eye with a rubber-coated steel bullet by as he was leaving his home in the village during a raid. Three others were also injured. Some 86.4 per cent of the nearby Maale Adumim settlement is built on privately-owned Palestinian land already stolen from the inhabitants of al-Issawiya, Anata and other villages. On 27 May, Israeli civil administration officials left posters in al-Issawiya announcing that some 8,200 square metres of land on the eastern side of the town were to be confiscated 'for military purposes' for two-and-a-half years. Classically, such allegedly temporary confiscations are regularly renewed. On 8 June, more confiscation orders appeared, this time announcing that land to the south of the village, which the Israelis claimed had been deserted by its owners, would be taken to make a national park. The land had not, of course, been deserted, but was much needed for houses and schools.

By the end of October, al-Issawiya was being invaded on an almost daily basis and residents were being humiliated at checkpoints. Even elderly men might be expected to raise their shirts and pull their trousers down before being allowed to leave the village. Bags were simply emptied out onto the street. Houses were being regularly sprayed with skunk water. But there is more of this elsewhere in this book.

On 16 March, a group of settlers from the notoriously violent and dangerous Adei Ad settlement set up a cluster of mobile homes on private land belonging to farmers in Jalud, Nablus area, West Bank. This has often been the way in which a settlement begins life. The villagers have already lost 4,000 acres of their farmland to settlements and the local settlers are, as might be expected, a nasty lot. In February, a group of them attacked a 37-year-old villager and hit him over the head with an iron rod. Readers will not anticipate that the government of Netanyahu, who has openly boasted of the advance of settlements under his leadership, will remove the squatters.

A new threat appeared on 18 April, when Israel's Supreme Court gave its approval to a law extending the Absentee Property Law by allowing the state to grab property in East Jerusalem belonging to residents of the West Bank or Gaza. Property taken under the Absentee Property Law is then given to extreme right-wing/religious Jewish families whose aim is to make Jerusalem exclusively Jewish. This legal fig leaf to cover up the theft of land was approved under the contention that East Jerusalem is, as far as the Israelis are concerned, now part of Israel, while the state of the West Bank and Gaza is, well, hazy. In other words, the Israelis claim that the West Bank is now Judea and Samaria, but still, in order to placate other governments, play the game of pretending to be willing to reach a 'two state agreement'. (Every member of the cabinet has of course made it quite clear that this is not the case.) Under this ruling, Palestinians who are refused permission to return to live in property in East Jerusalem can now have it 'legally' stolen from them. As PLO Executive Committee Member Hanan Ashrawi said, "The Law constitutes a wilful and deliberate attempt by Israel to steal Palestinian property, expand the illegal settlement enterprise for the benefit of Jewish settlers and legalize the ethnic cleansing of the Jerusalem at the expense of the Palestinians, their homes and resources."

On 27 April, the Israeli government invited tenders for the construction of 77 new homes in occupied East Jerusalem. PM Netanyahu had already made an election promise to forge ahead with settlement construction there to pre-empt the possibility of concessions to the Palestinians in any 'peace' talks. And so, on 7 May, the government announced plans for the construction of 900 new housing units in ultra-Orthodox Ramat Shlomo settlement, East Jerusalem. A week later, tenders were invited for the construction of 85 settlement units in Givat Zeev, some 5km northwest of the occupied city, along with tenders for the construction of some 1500 hotel rooms.

All this settlement expansion comes at a huge human cost to individual Palestinians. Dozens of Bedouin families living in Abu Nuwwar were told in May that they were to be forced out in order to make way for the expansion of Maale Adumim. The EU envoy to the Palestinian Territories, John Gatt-Rutter, and UN Humanitarian Coordinator, James W. Rawley, visited the families accompanied by Palestinian officials to show support, but what can they really do to defend the defenceless? The Israeli aim is to create a band of settlements in the so-called E1 corridor, in order to divide up the West Bank, making a two-state settlement increasingly unrealistic.

At the end of May, Tzipi Hotovely, appointed to oversee the foreign ministry, told a group of leading diplomats that from now on they were to broadcast the message that, according to the rabbis, "All the land is ours." In other words, no more nonsense about Palestinians having rights.

And so, on 9 July, more bad news came to the Bedouin families of Abu Nuwwar, in the E1 corridor, when they were told by Civil Administration officials that they must move to the Jerusalem Gate area within the month. According to Bassab Bahar, chair of an East Jerusalem committee to protect Palestinian land, the area where they are to be forced to live is too close to a waste dump to be suitable for human habitation.

On 29 July, Netanyahu announced the immediate construction of 300 settler homes in the West Bank along with plans for additional groups of units elsewhere. The move was immediately condemned by the British government. But early in September, the Israeli government backed up its declared intention to promote settlement expansion by erasing around £113 million ($170 million) of debt owed by settlements to the government.

On 30 October, at a time of high tension throughout the occupied territories, the Israeli government chose to announce that it had 'legalised' houses in four illegal settlements: 377 homes in the Yakir settlement, 187 in Itamar and 94 in Shilo (the area where the murderers of the Dawabsha family probably live, see page 166) in the northern West Bank, and 97 in Sansana in the south. The announcement follows the regular pattern of 'legalising' settlement building retrospectively, ignoring Palestinian rights.

On Tuesday 17 November, Netanyahu approved the construction of 454 new settler homes in East Jerusalem. The previous Tuesday, the construction of 2,200 settlement units in Ma'ale Michmas settlement east of Ramallah had been given the go-ahead, followed the next day by the announcement that 891 units were to be built in the Gilo settlement, Bethlehem area. The move was condemned by the Japanese and German governments.

The separation barrier/the wall

The most blatant and, quite literally, divisive element in Israel's campaign to steal Palestinian land is, of course, the separation wall that, according to Israeli propaganda, exists and is still being extended to 'protect Israel' from Palestinians. In reality, the wall does not follow the 1967 dividing line between Israel and the West Bank and Gaza. Instead, it swallows vast tracts of Palestinian land into Israel, its pathway carefully drawn, in places, to syphon off Palestinian water resources.

In some places it is a strongly fortified wire fence; in others, it is a metres thick wall, infinitely higher than the notorious Berlin wall. Here, it casts a dark shadow: for example, over houses in ancient Bethlehem. Farmers face long delays if they want to pass through checkpoints to reach their land. Communities are separated from each other: the wall will, for example, separate the city of Beit Jala from the village of al-Walaja. Farmland is destroyed to build the wall and its buffer zones. It is a cruel symbol of Palestinian oppression.

As we have mentioned in the section on destroyed olive trees, 2015 saw bulldozers crashing their way through the Cremisan valley, with its ancient monastery, in order to continue the wall. A high court ruling had originally ordered that the wall be re-routed to save the valley, but this was overturned and, in any case, the military had made it clear that they intended to go ahead whatever the verdict. A different high court ruling, in January, saved the village of Battir, a World Heritage site, due to its ancient terraces and Roman-era irrigation system, from the wall. It remains to be seen for how long.

The wall and its accompanying land theft and destruction has claimed many victims. One 2015 victim was 22-year-old Lafi Awad whose home village of Budrus has lost much land to the separation wall, including land planted with olive trees belonging to Lafi's family. Lafi had fought against the wall and Israeli oppression by throwing stones at soldiers. In 2013, he had been arrested for his part in blowing up surveillance cameras installed in the wall. He was detained in the notorious Russian Compound for 17 months. When not resisting the occupation, he was a kind and helpful lad, who was happy to do the dishes and tidy up at home and who organised clean-up campaigns in his local village. In addition to feeling hemmed in and dispossessed by the wall, he was angered by the murder of Hadil Hashlamoun (see page 163) and also by the refusal of the Israelis to allow his uncle to travel to Jerusalem for chemotherapy for lung cancer. On 13 November, he went to the area of the village near the wall and threw stones or a stone at soldiers. According to a Palestinian witness, the soldiers had set up an ambush. Lafi was shot in the leg and then the soldiers grabbed him. When he resisted and tried to run away, a soldier fired two live bullets at him from close range. The Israelis claimed was shot when he tried to grab a weapon. The autopsy showed that the bullets had struck him in the back, confirming the Palestinian version. He died before his family could reach him. An angry young man, certainly (and with justification), but primarily a young man who wanted his freedom and a future, not a terrorist, and no threat to the man who killed him.

Continued land theft in Israel

As Israel continues to create 'facts on the ground' with impunity, many are now talking of the 'one state solution'. But what does this mean? No joy for Palestinians, unless the Israelis are forced, by some form of robust and effectual international pressure, to change their ways.

In 2012, a statement issued by the Jewish National Fund claimed: "The State of Israel does not steal Bedouin land. Negev land was state land from the time of Ottoman rule and Bedouins had no right of possession to this land." As we have already said, common land was, under Ottoman rule, officially state land, a piece of ancient imperial legislation that the state of Israel has adopted and adapted for its own convenience. What the JNF statement really means is that the nomadic Bedouin inhabitants of the Negev desert, who have lived there certainly since the 7th century, but are in all probability the direct descendants of the nomads who lived around that region in biblical times, have no rights.

Their land cannot be stolen because, in Israeli eyes, it's not their land; it rightfully belongs to Jews from Russia, America, Britain or wherever.

Today, around 70,000 Bedouin live in about 35 so-called 'unrecognised' villages, and the state regards the desert as state land and the Bedouin as trespassers. The state therefore denies them water, sewage, electricity, roads, healthcare and schools. In 2011, the Israeli government of the day formulated what became known as the Prawer plan. Under the plan, the Bedouin were to be forcibly relocated into townships and their lands developed for Jewish communities. The plan was officially shelved in December 2013, but stealth implementation continues.

The Bedouin villagers of Umm al-Hiran, in the Negev, were told in May that their village was to be destroyed in order to provide for a Jewish community, to be called Hiran. Justice Minister Ayelet Shaked, she who calls Palestinian children "little snakes", claimed that this was "not discriminatory" (after all, snakes aren't human). The villagers, some 700 in all, had been placed in the village by military decree in 1956, but a high court ruling on 5 May decreed that they had no right to the land. Civil and human rights group Adalah, which provided advocates for the Bedouin, pointed out that the ruling meant that it had been openly stated for the first time that Palestinians could be evicted from their homes and land to make way for Jews.

On 23 August, under military protection, the bulldozers moved in to start building the road for the new settlement. On the same day, protesters in Jaffa demonstrated against a new settlement plan, called Aovia. Before the Zionist terrorist operation that created modern Israel, Jaffa was home to some 80,000 Palestinians, with a further 40,000 in the surrounding area. Some 95 per cent of the city's inhabitants were sent into exile by the nascent IDF, but the city still has a sizable Palestinian population. Under the new plan, 'Arab' families will be removed to make way for a Jewish-only settlement.

It should not, therefore, be imagined that a 'one-state solution' will offer equal rights to Palestinians.

House demolitions

"The Civil Administration's planning committee examines and promotes construction plans equitably, dependent on the fact that these plans meet the relevant planning criteria and their promotion is approved by the political echelon."

The quotation above comes from a written response, dated May 2015, to AFP by COGAT, the (Israeli) Defence Ministry, which is in charge of the Civil Administration of Area C of the West Bank. This is the first time the Israeli government has openly admitted that political considerations govern the issue of planning permissions in the West Bank.

In reality, it has long been obvious that land theft for settlement building and the demolition of Palestinian homes go hand in hand. As we have seen in the previous section, land can be taken away from Palestinians for a whole host of reasons. When it comes to demolitions, the same inequalities apply. Settlers who want to build are usually given every help that the state can afford. Palestinians who need to build – homes, schools, industrial or farm buildings, shops, or a whole host of civic amenities - must apply for planning permission.

If they live in Area C (around 60 per cent of the West Bank), or Jerusalem, or indeed in Israel itself, they are likely to face insuperable difficulty in obtaining permission, however great the need. This applies to civic as well as more personal development. Common land/open spaces that are not privately owned are classified as state land and such areas are generally held for settlement development, not the development of Palestinian villages. It has been estimated that 70 per cent of Area C has been allocated for settlement development, compared with 1 per cent for Palestinian development. Private landowners generally need to hold onto what they have for future generations. The result is that overall plans for Palestinian areas are effectively non-existent or frozen. According to Israeli NGO BIMKOM[1], "The main goal of the partial special outline plans is to limit Palestinian building and to contain it within as small an area as possible."

The result is that Palestinians find themselves with a rising population and

---

[1] See Violations of Civil and Political Rights in the Realm of Planning and Building in Israel and the Occupied Territories, Shadow Report.

an antiquated housing stock desperately in need of up-grading, but unable to build legally, according to Israel's racially-biased system. The Zionist view is that Israel exists for the Jews. The current government, with a high proportion of ministers from ultra-religious settler parties, has made it very clear that they intend to take over the occupied territories permanently as part of Israel and that there will be no Palestinian state. From the skewed viewpoint of Israel's illegal settlers (and key government ministers) it is not they who are establishing 'facts on the ground', but the Palestinians, who have no right to be there, yet have the effrontery to build 'illegally'.

So rarely is permission to build given to Palestinians living in Area C of the West Bank or in Jerusalem that they have no choice but to build without permission and hope for the best, relying on international support for help in fighting a grossly unjust system. This means that in 2015, as in previous years, many families lived under permanent threat that their home would be demolished. It surely takes very little imagination to appreciate the stress that this uncertainty places on fathers, mothers and their children. Most of the families living in fear for their homes are already living in great hardship. Their resources are limited, their employment often insecure, arrogant and violent settlers constantly threatening them, opportunities to better themselves blocked (often all too literally, in the form of road blocks and checkpoints that restrict everyday life). To know on top of this that your home – the place above all else where you and your children should feel safe and secure – may be bulldozed at a moment's notice is a stress factor that no one should have to suffer.

Do not imagine that people whose homes are destroyed in this manner are generally offered any alternative accommodation (the exception being Israel's Bedouin, whom the state wishes to shove, against their will, into townships). Palestinians whose homes are destroyed by 'the only democracy in the Middle East' are lucky if they are allowed to remove their belongings before their home is bulldozed. They may also have to pay, often crippling sums, for the privilege. Below are just a few examples of house and other destruction in the occupied territories in 2015.

In the third week of January, the homes of 77 people were destroyed in east Jerusalem, Ramallah, Jericho and Hebron. The average temperature at that time of year is around 8 degrees centigrade. Over half of the newly home-less were children. Over 500 rabbis from Israel, Britain, the US and Canada protested against this and the injustice of the entire system in an open letter, organised by Rabbis for Human Rights, in February, but the heartless demolitions continued throughout.

In February, a two-storey house in the village of al-Jarushiyya, belonging to Palestinian Judge Kifah Abd al-Rahim Sholi, was destroyed. The following month, a temporary shelter on Mount Scopus, erected to house homeless Bedouin, was destroyed. It had been provided with EU funding. The excuse was that it was on land designated as a 'state park'. This designation is often used to prevent Palestinian communities from expanding or to exclude Palestinians from common land. In practice, such land is often handed over to settler organisations for their own use.

In April, over 100 soldiers, accompanied by dogs and bulldozers, arrived at a house in east Jerusalem shared by two blind brothers and their families (12 people in all). The soldiers admitted that they didn't have a destruction permit with them, but they continued anyway, leaving just two rooms. According to a neighbour, they beat one of the brothers, knocked down the children's play room, deliberately soiled and destroyed feed for the families' horses, cut the Internet, phone and water connections and damaged the sewage system. Opposite the Amro families' vandalised home is a field where local lads used to play football. This has now been fenced off by the Israelis. A week later, the bulldozers returned to demolish a house still under construction.

The cost of fighting unjust planning decisions is huge. The houses mentioned above are in the Wadi al-Joz neighbourhood, much of which has been designated part of the Tzurim Valley National Park. A lawyer fighting to have 12 houses in the neighbourhood re-zoned (and therefore not demolished) told *Electronic Intifada*'s Jesse Rubin that simply hiring an engineer to make a report to submit to the court would cost around £33,000 ($50,000).

On 28 April, one of 13 houses threatened with destruction in the village of Nabi Saleh, West Bank, was demolished. Soldiers fired live rounds and tear gas at nearby houses. On 6 May, a house in al-Deirat-Rifaiyya, home to 17 people, was reduced to rubble. This West Bank village, in the notorious Area C, is home to around 1,800 people and over half the houses there have been built without permission. A local taxi driver told a *Maan* reporter that everyone over 45 in the village has had at least one home demolished.

In Silwan, where the aggressive settler organisation Ateret Cohanim buys or simply takes over residential properties and fills them with settlers, throwing out Palestinians, in order to 'Judaise' the area, the Israeli authorities regularly destroy Palestinian homes. On 27 May, a newly-built apartment was demolished. The previous week it had been a three-storey building and three stores. Three more Silwan homes were destroyed on 2 June. The family of one were assaulted as they evacuated their home and a 70-year-old woman was injured when a tear gas canister was fired into the house.

When a wedding hall, print shop, carpentry workshop, builders' yard and small gas station in Beit Hanina were demolished, the owner was order to pay a fine of £10,000 (60,000 shekels). In October, a family in Jerusalem destroyed their own home in order to avoid the fine. They still received a fine of £42,600 (250,000 shekels) for building in the first place. The Tawtah and al-Tawatnji families were told they could postpone the destruction of their three-storey block on payment of £94,000 (550,000 shekels). They could not afford the fine, so the building was destroyed on 19 August.

The village of Khirbet Susiya, Hebron, home to around 450 people, is under threat of total demolition. The residents had already been forced out of their original village in 1986, on the grounds that there was an ancient synogue there and it was this an archeological site. They had therefore had been obliged to rebuild on their farmland. The villagers had applied for approval of an outline plan for the 'new' village, but the civil administration claimed there was no infrastructure. In May, the court (the judge is himself a settler) refused to allow an interim injunction pending a court hearing for 3 August (later postponed). The plan is to expel the villagers to make room for the expansion of an illegal settlement, also called Susiya. So often have the houses of Susiya been demolished, that the inhabitants are now mainly living in tents and other temporary shelters. They are denied access to their wells, while dwellers in Jewish Susiya enjoy all the necessary facilities and infrastructure, including swimming pools.

On 16 July, the residents received a list of structures they were ordered to demolish, which included ten residential homes, the clinic, eight animal shelters, and twelve storerooms and outhouses. International pressure was, for once, brought to bear, with the US State Department spokesman, John Kirby, asking for the demolition notices to be rescinded. In late September, Senator Dianne Feinstein also became an advocate for the village and met with a group of villagers who were brought to Washington by Rabbis for Human Rights. Naima, a villager, described one of the occasions when the demolition men had come to the village. She had heard the bad news and rushed home to find her mother's house wrecked. Her little pre-school daughter, who was being looked after by her granny, was lying on the ground, wet from urine, paralysed with terror. She took months to recover.

In contrast to the inhumane and unjust treatment of Susiya villagers, when the courts ordered the demolition of just two illegally built structures in the settlement of Beit El in July 2015, Netanyahu responded by authorising the construction of 300 new homes in the settlement.

On 6 October, a groups of settlers held a protest rally outside the Prime Minister's house, demanding the building of more settlements 'to combat terrorism'. Social Affairs Minister Haim Katz told protesters "we must start building kindergartens and schools, expand existing settlements and build new ones…" and Minister of Tourism Yariv Levin stated "We're here to strengthen the government to do the things we all believe in."

In November, demolition orders were issued for houses in the village of Fasayil, in the Jordan valley. The demolitions will leave 46 people homeless, including 31 children. On 4 December, as temperatures dropped, the European Union missions in Jerusalem and Ramallah called for a halt to demolitions and asked that confiscated materials, including human and livestock shelters, should be returned. The previous day, the Israelis had seized 10 tents donated to the inhabitants of al-Hadidiya village by the International Committee of the Red Cross, following earlier demolitions.

On 7 December, the army delivered demolition notices to 12 families in Qalqilya, despite the fact that the families had all the correct permissions.

In Israel

Palestinians in Israel also suffer from the unequal application of planning laws. According to Human Rights group Adalah, only 4.6 percent of new homes built in Israel are in Palestinian towns and villages, despite the fact that Palestinians make up over 20 percent of the population. No Palestinian citizen holds a professional position on any of Israel's planning committees that oversee and approve community master plans. None of the 74 staff of the interior ministry's Planning Authority is Palestinian. Of 1,765 advisers in the Planning Authority's database, only 65 are Arab. There are six district planning committees, none of which has ever had a Palestinian district planner or legal adviser, and only 6 out of 164 employees are Palestinian. There are no Palestinians in the planning and engineering departments of Haifa, Lod, Ramle and Tel Aviv-Jaffa.

On 10 February, the home in Lydd of Hana al-Naqib and her four children was demolished, although it had been built on land owned by the family for generations and licensed for building. The house had been built with generous donations from family, neighbours and other well-wishers, and they had only moved in three months earlier. The children, aged 7, 8, 14 and 15, had been thrilled to have a home of their own at last. Hana, as a single parent, lacked the money to fight in the courts. Instead, she and her children had to stand in the house of a neighbour and watch their dreams turned to rubble.

Maha al-Naqib, a neighbour, told *Electronic Intifada,* "These are people who have been living on this land way before 1948 but when they want to build or expand, the municipality refuses to give them permits on a racist basis."

In Ramle, about 11 miles from Tel Aviv, 11 families received demolition notices in mid-April. Five apartments were demolished in the nearby village of Dahmash on 15 April.

In Kafr Kana (ancient Cana, where Jesus turned water into wine), the bulldozers also arrived in April and destroyed the house of Arfan Khatib. Friends rallied round and the house was rebuilt, to be destroyed two months later, just as the house was about to be connected to water and the family move in. Despite the increase in population, the local authority has refused to expand the town's residential area for some 15 years.

The plight of Bedouin in the Negev desert, where Israel plans to build luxurious Jewish-only settlements while forcing the Bedu into cramped townships, destroying their ancient way of life, has been mentioned in the previous section. The Prawer plan has officially been shelved, but this does not mean that it will remain so. Needless to say, demolitions in 'unrecognised' villages are part of the scheme. On 20 April, bulldozers demolished homes in the Bedouin village of al-Araqib village in the Negev (Israel) for the 83rd time, even though the court had ruled that the village was not built on state land. On 5 May, the Supreme Court gave the authorities permission to demolish another Negev village: Atir, also know as Umm al-Hiran. On 28 May, bulldozers came to demolish the home of Ali Hammad Abu Rabia in the Makhul village, Negev.

As with the West Bank, demolitions are often given the green light because a town or village has no local master plan and so permits are not given. Umm al-Fahm, population 50,000, is the second largest Palestinian town in Israel after Nazareth, but it has no master plan so all its homes illegal. It is estimated that there may be as many as 30,000 Palestinian homes – one in 10 homes – in Israel that lack the required permits. It is also estimated that around 100,000 new homes are needed to solve the Palestinian housing crisis.

Three times more Palestinian homes are demolished in Israel than in the occupied territories.

Punitive demolitions

In November 2014, Israel also resumed its policy, halted in 2009, of punitive demolitions – destroying the homes of those involved in attacks, regardless of who is living there. This policy of collective punishment is illegal under international law and has been widely condemned. An army investigation in 2005 had concluded that the practice has little deterrence value.

On 19 January, soldiers arrived at two adjoining houses in Shuhada Street, Hebron, belonging to Amal Hashem Dundeis and welded the doors shut. The justification for this was that a Molotov cocktail had been thrown from nearby. The elderly Mrs Dundeis, who suffers from diabetes, collapsed and was taken to hospital. Settlers taunted the crowd that gathered to try to help.

On 1 July, the home of Uday Abu Jamal, who carried out a terrorist attack in November 2014, was sealed with steel boards. The Red Cross provided the homeless family with a tent, but less than a week later soldiers returned and demolished it. On 19 August, the family of Mahir Hashlamoun, who carried out a stabbing attack, were told that their apartment would be destroyed. On 6 October, PM Netanyahu called for punitive home demolitions to be speeded up. The same day, two homes in East Jerusalem were demolished with explosives, which also damaged neighbouring houses, and the apartment of another attacker was filled with concrete. On 14 October, four more families were given 72 hours' notice to evacuate their homes. On 14 November, four more homes were destroyed, in Nablus and Silwad.

On 7 December, it was the home of Ibrahim al-Akkari, who carried out a car attack in Jerusalem in 2014, killing one Israeli and injuring others. On 10

December, troops arrived at the Hebron homes of Taher Fannoun (shot dead after he stabbed a soldier) and Abdul-Rahman Maswada (stabbed a soldier and settler), where they took measurements and gave warnings of intended demolition. The family of Muhammad Abd al-Rahman Ayyad, in Silwad, were told on 21 December that their home would be demolished; three families in Qalandiya refugee camp suffered the same fate on 24 December.

Bear in mind that if the so-called terrorist has been shot on the spot, and Palestinian witnesses deny that an attack was taking place, there will be no official investigation, but the 'attacker's' home may still be demolished.

Water deprivation

"And when I talk about the importance to Israel's security... It means that a housewife in Tel Aviv can open the tap and there's water running in it, and it's not been dried up because of a rash decision that handed control of our [sic] aquifers to the wrong hands."

Benjamin Netanyahu, 1998

The area that encompasses Israel, the Golan Heights, the West Bank, Jerusalem and Gaza has a typical Mediterranean climate, with hot, dry summers and relatively mild, wet winters, and an annual rainfall slightly less than half that of Britain. Its water needs are met partly by the river Jordan and its major tributary, the Yarmouk, and partly by aquifers (water that has sunk down through the permeable rock and is stored underground). The chief aquifer is the mountain aquifer, which is divided into three areas: two of these, the Northern and Western basins, are shared between the West Bank and Israel, while the Eastern basin lies under the West Bank.

Throughout 2015 Israel continued its established policy of exploiting the water resources of the occupied territories to its own advantage and that of the illegal settler population and to the extreme disadvantage of the Palestinians. It is impossible to do justice here to the deliberate injustice of Israel's criminal water policies, but below is just a very brief summary.

Before 1967, Israel covered approximately 3 per cent of the Jordan basin area. With the capture of Syria's Golan Heights, it gained control of the headwaters of the Jordan and use of the waters of the Yarmouk, from which it draws between 70 and 100 million cubic metres annually. The Jordan has now been diverted upstream to flow into Lake Tiberias/Sea of Galilee, in Israel, and has been reduced by the time it reaches the Allenby Bridge (between Jordan and the West Bank) from an average flow of 1250 mcm per year in the early 1950s to between a mere 152 and 203 mcm per year (1994 figure).

In 1967 Israel also gained control of the crucial mountain aquifer, 80 per cent of which lies under the West Bank. Israel now channels approximately 73 per cent of the water drawn from the mountain aquifer into Israel, where it serves 50 per cent of Israel's personal water needs; it takes another 10 per cent for use by illegal settlers, and just 17 per cent is drawn by Palestinians.

In Israel

The Jewish citizens in Israel enjoy plentiful clean water and excellent sewage facilities, thanks in no small part to water stolen from the occupied territories (though in fairness Israel has now invested heavily in desalination plants and other water technology).

Israel's Palestinian citizens have not been so fortunate. In Arab/Palestinian towns, the infrastructure has long lagged behind that of Jewish townships. This is partly because of much lower budget allocations and lower municipal taxes. Israeli sources have accused 'Arabs' of failing to collect taxes owed. However, the state has invested heavily in industrial areas (which pay higher rates) in Jewish towns, but scarcely at all in the over-crowded and impoverished towns in which Israel's Palestinian population is chiefly crammed. Whereas in most countries urban and local authority improvement schemes concentrate on the most deprived areas, which in Israel are preponderantly Arab/Palestinian, in Israel money has been preferentially allocated to Jewish areas, and especially to the illegal Jewish settlements in the West Bank and Jerusalem. In Palestinian townships, therefore, pipes leak and the systems are antiquated and desperately in need of improvement schemes.

For the 90,000 or so Bedouin living in the unrecognised villages in Israel's Negev, the situation is even worse, for they have no piped water or sewage. Born in present day Israel of parents, grandparents and countless earlier generations stretching back in time, they enjoy no citizenship rights in the Middle East's much vaunted 'only democracy'. They are, perhaps, a sign of the terrible future that awaits Palestinians of the West Bank and Jerusalem, regardless of whether the final solution is one or two states. Jerusalem Palestinians have 'residency', which Netanyahu threatens to take away, but no citizenship, unlike the Jewish inhabitants of the city. So, like the Bedouin, they will become stateless sub-humans, unless Israel is made to follow international law.

West Bank

Under the Oslo accords of 1995, every water project in the West Bank was to be approved by the Joint Water Committee, composed of equal numbers of Palestinians and Israelis. In Area C (60 per cent of the West Bank) the Israeli

Civil Administration also has to give approval. This situation was supposed to apply for only five years, pending a full peace settlement. It has now been in force for 20 years.

- Israel vetoes all Palestinian applications for schemes involving water drawn from the Western Basin.

- Permits are rarely granted for schemes in Area C.

- Permits for sewage treatment plants are blocked because Israel demands that the plants also treat sewage from the illegal settlements, which would amount to *de facto* recognition.

- The separation Wall meanders away from the 'Green Line' between Israel and the West Bank in order to incorporate many the West Bank's underground wellsprings and existing wells and cisterns.

- The Wall also blocks several water run-offs, resulting in flooding during winter rains.

- Each of Israel's illegal settlers consumes approximately four times as much water as each Palestinian.

- The settlements have either stolen or drained many wells crucial to Palestinian agriculture.

- Palestinian wells and water pipes are routinely destroyed by the Israelis.

- Many Palestinians, in the absence of a regular water supply, are forced to buy back water (taken from their own mountain aquifer) at highly inflated prices from the Israeli water company Mekorot.

- At times of water shortage, supplies to Palestinian areas are cut off, while settlers suffer no restrictions.

- The illegal settlements frequently discharge their sewage onto Palestinian land, contaminating it and causing major health problems.

- Some 10 per cent of Palestinian communities in the West Bank are not connected to a drinkable water supply.

Israel claims that Palestinian inefficiency and corruption are entirely to blame for their water problems. While it is true that there is a high leakage rate in Palestinian towns, Israel's stranglehold on the Palestinian economy is largely to blame for failings in the Palestinian infrastructure.

Israelis are themselves profligate users of water. Around 70 per cent of Israel's water is used for agriculture, which accounts for just 5 per cent of their GNP. Much of the agriculture is water intensive (for example, melons and cotton), requiring irrigation and thus unsuitable for a relatively arid climate. Their forest plantings (to conceal villages abandoned by fleeing Palestinians during Israel's first phase of ethnic cleansing) have historically often been of trees with a high water uptake, again unsuited to a Mediterranean climate. The illegal settlers continue to fill their swimming pools and irrigate parks even during times of drought, when Palestinians are denied water for essential purposes.

Here a few examples of Israel's water policies in action in 2015. In early January, Israel announced that it would withhold taxes collected on behalf of the Palestine Authority in retaliation for the latter's application to join the International Criminal Court. In April, when the withheld funds were returned, Israel announced that it would keep a third of the money in return for services, including water, electricity and hospital bills.

On 29 January, Israeli bulldozers destroyed a 1,000-metre water pipeline donated by the Palestinian Agricultural Relief Committee to supply the residents of Yezra village in the northern Jordan valley with water. On 13 April, demolition orders were issued to destroy an electricity grid in Qasra, near Nablus, as well as a home and a water well. On 25 April a demolition order was delivered for an electricity grid and a water well in the western Hebron village of al-Kum. On 4 June, Israeli forces filled three water wells in Surif village, Hebron area, with rubble. On 22 July, they destroyed a Roman era water well in Beit Ula, Hebron area, and on 26 July settlers filled an ancient well in Deir Istiya, west of Salfit, with earth and rocks.

And then, as temperatures soared up to 40°C in August, Mekorot started to cut off water supplies to Palestinians. As a result, thousands of chickens as well as cattle in the village of Kafr Qaddum, Qalqiliya, died. (The village has lost much of its land to settlers, who continued to be supplied, without restriction.) A protest on 5 August was ignored, and the following week the villages of Qarawat Bani Hassan, Biddya and Sarta also found their supply severely restricted. On 16 August, the main water pipe supplying Kafr Qaddum was broken by a military bulldozer.

Jerusalem

The Palestinian inhabitants of Jerusalem suffer from the same restrictions and biased planning as their fellows in the rest of the West Bank. For example, on 10 June, Israeli forces demolished a water well in the al-Issawiya neighbourhood of East Jerusalem, without giving prior notice to allow an appeal. And just as many villages in Area C of the West Bank do not have a piped water supply, so many of the 'unlicensed' houses in Palestinian areas of Jerusalem (where Palestinians cannot get licences to build), have no water supply.

The neighbourhoods of Ras Khamis, Ras Shahada, Dahyat a-Salam, and the Shu'afat Refugee Camp, which lie beyond the separation wall but within the city area, have petitioned, so far in vain, for a proper water supply. The existing supply is sufficient for 15,000 people, but expected to supply 80,000.

Nevertheless, the Israeli water authority announced in July that it intended to collect water charges even from those homes without any water supply.

Houses in East Jerusalem that are connected to a water supply may often find themselves cut off, sometimes for weeks at a time. The city authorities responsible for ensuring that the population receives a reliable, clean and drinkable supply, deliberately fails to ensure such a supply to Palestinians.

Gaza

In densely-populated Gaza, the situation is dire. About 90 to 95 per cent of Gaza's water supply is thus unsafe to drink, and is the cause of high rates of cramp and colic among children, skin infections and other health problems.

The coastal aquifer, which is the only local source of fresh water, is now heavily polluted with sea water and sewage. The infrastructure in Gaza was already suffering from decades of neglect since the 1967 occupation. Since the siege started back in 2007, there have been several major Israeli assaults on Gaza: Operation Cast Lead in 2008, Operation Pillar of Defence in 2012, Operation Protective Edge in 2014. All of these have combined to damage Gaza's already inadequate water infrastructure.

The heavy bombardment of 2014 caused an estimated £23,677,000 ($34,000,000) in damages to the water infrastructure. Approximately half a million people were directly affected by damage to water facilities and one million were affected due to damage to the wastewater plant and wastewater pumping stations. Over 100,000 remain unconnected to the water infrastructure. Some 14 technicians from the water and energy sector were killed. The infrastructure was already heavily compromised by the economic effects and restrictions of the blockade, combined with damage from previous assaults.

Damage to wastewater treatment facilities may also be partly responsible for the high levels of chlorides and nitrates in the water – particularly dangerous during pregnancy as a cause of blue baby syndrome (nitrates diminish the oxygen-carrying capacity of the mother's haemoglobin). Many other factors are doubtless involved, but this may be one reason why the infant mortality rate in Gaza has risen, according to figures released in August 2015 by UNRWA, from 20.2 per 1,000 in 2008, to 22.4 in 2013. It is expected to rise further.

In March 2015, however, Israel finally began to fulfil its obligation under the Oslo agreement by supplying an additional 5 million cubic metres of water. However, Israel had destroyed the al-Muntar reservoir, constructed to hold the increase, in 2014 – surely not a legitimate target. When water began to flow through the badly damaged pipes a huge percentage was inevitably lost. It should be noted that Gaza must pay Israel for the increased supply.

The Israeli blockade also prohibits the mobile pumps required to counter large-scale flooding. Israel's ally, the Egyptian government, is busy flooding the smuggling tunnels which formerly brought arms, along with much-needed supplies, into Gaza. They are also digging ditches along the Gaza/Egypt border and flooding these with seawater and sewage, causing land subsidence and massive additional pollution. (Following the coup by General Sisi against the government of Mohammed Morsi, the United States resumed its approximately $1.3 billion of military aid to Egypt, designed to keep Israeli/Egyptian relations sweet.)

Clearly, a massive programme of repair and new construction is required, but with the ongoing blockade and Israel's control of the Palestinian oil and gas resources which should be able to finance this, there seems to be very little hope that this will happen. The flow of repair materials into Gaza, as we have seen, is severely restricted and international promises of finance remain largely unfulfilled. Under international humanitarian law, Israel holds responsibility for the people of the Gaza strip, but it refuses to acknowledge this.

Prisoners in their own land

"Currently, freedom of movement and access for Palestinians within the West Bank is the exception rather than the norm... [Palestinians] are barred from freely accessing large segments of the West Bank. These restricted areas include all areas within the municipal boundaries of settlements, the 'seam zone', much of the Jordan Valley, East Jerusalem, restricted roads and other 'closed' areas... [estimated] to be in excess of 50 percent of the total area of the West Bank."

World Bank report, 2007

It is not only Gaza that is under a crippling siege: the occupied territories of the West Bank and Jerusalem are carved up by a tortuous system of permanent and temporary road blocks, permanent and 'flying' checkpoints, roads for settlers only, settlements blocking easy access between villages and towns, closed off 'military zones' and, last but not least, the infamous separation wall.

The Israelis claim that these restrictions are necessary for 'security reasons'. In practice, this means that the occupation army's primary aim is to maintain the occupation while protecting Israel's colonising settlers and nurturing the growth of illegal settlements on Palestinian land. To this end, settlers are allowed with virtual impunity to attack Palestinians on a daily basis, often with the support and protection of the army. If, on the other hand, Palestinians attack settlers – for example, by throwing stones at settler cars – then retaliation is swift and ruthless. This will not just take the form of mass arrests and large-scale punitive raids, but collective punishment through the total isolation and blocking-off of whole communities.

Meanwhile, the growth of settlements and fragmentation of Palestinian areas continues. The West Bank and Jerusalem are thus becoming parts of Greater Israel, peppered with increasingly smaller Palestinian enclaves, making any realistic Palestinian state an impossibility.

To recap: the West Bank should not be occupied, but belongs by international law to the Palestinians. Whether you choose to believe in a 'two-state solution' or the so-called 'one state solution', a lasting peace between Palestinians and Israelis cannot entail the Palestinians having all, or almost all, their land stolen from them (as has happened in Israel) and being locked up in economically non-viable ghettos.

Settler roads

In order to facilitate the colonisation of the occupied territories, Israel has created a network of roads in the area C, which is under Israeli control, linking the illegal settlements with each other and with Israel[1] - roads that are accessible only to settlers. As settlements grow and new ones become 'recognised' as legal by Israel, so too does the exclusive/excluding network. Checkpoints exist to allow Palestinians, with permission, to cross these roads in order to get to work, access their lands, visit families, reach their schools and so on.

The building of these roads not only separates Palestinians from their lands and from each other, is also causes massive destruction of farmland and therefore of livelihoods. It has been estimated that 10 per cent of Palestine's olive trees have been destroyed for road building and settlements since 2001 – over 2 million trees. In 2015, for example, Hiyam Mousa witnessed the tragic loss of a section of her family's ancient olive grove in order to construct a bypass road linking West Bank settlements to West Jerusalem.

The resulting system means that, while Jews can freely drive to and fro along an integrated road system designed to make their life easy, Palestinians are hemmed in and blocked at every turn by a system not designed by or for them. Road construction can be a contentious issue in any society, but under the Israeli colonial system it entails no local consultation (with Palestinians), no community benefit (for Palestinians), and no compensation.

This is apartheid, and who can deny it?

Permanent checkpoints

There are some 96 of these in the West Bank, 57 of which are internal, cutting communities apart. Israeli civil rights group B'Tselem points out, with regard to the latter: "In light of the unlawfulness of the settlements, the restrictions pile one illegal action on top of another: sweeping, disproportionate impairment of freedom of movement of an entire population to realize and perpetuate a policy that is illegal from the start..."

1   See www.visualizingpalestine.org/visuals/segregated-roads-west-bank

For example, the city of Nablus and the surrounding area, containing some 15 villages and three refugee camps is home to some 200,000 Palestinians and is under Palestinian Authority control. The governorate is, however, surrounded by settlements and movement is therefore severely restricted, with entry and exit only allowed at four checkpoints. Israeli rights groups have asked that this 'siege' be lifted, but the authorities claim is it necessary for security reasons. Palestinians, however, believe that it is to facilitate settlement expansion. Meanwhile Nablus villages that lie close to settlements suffer constant harassment.

At any time, a permanent checkpoint may be closed, forcing residents to take even longer and more circuitous routes. Nablus' Huwwara checkpoint was closed several times in July, for example, and drivers were diverted to the Awarta checkpoint. Occasionally, restrictions may be eased. In September, a road linking Ramallah and the village of Beitin was opened to private vehicles after 15 years' closure. Taxis, buses and trucks, however, must still make a 20-kilometre journey instead of using the 3km road.

At other times, checkpoints are 'improved' as talks aimed at reducing them fail. On 25 February, the Israelis installed iron gates at the container checkpoint in Wad Nar in spite of ongoing negotiations aimed at removing the checkpoint altogether. The checkpoint, which is permanently manned, controls the flow of traffic between the northern and southern districts of the West Bank, so its continuation is seen by Palestinians as part of the Israeli plan to isolate Bethlehem and the southern West Bank.

Hebron, where settlers' leader Moshe Levinger (see page 40) first started the settler movement, suffers particularly acutely. Here, settlers wage a non-stop war aimed at taking over the city, making it a centre of violence against Palestinians (see page 42) and punitive measures to protect the settlers from counter attacks. As a result, 77 per cent of residents live below the poverty line; 1,829 shops have closed down in the past 15 years, and there are over 18 military checkpoints in the Old City alone, making Hebron a ghetto within a ghetto.

Flying checkpoints

In addition to the permanent checkpoints, there are at any given time hundreds more so-called 'flying checkpoints', adding to the confusion, frustration and general difficulties of life for Palestinians. The Palestine Centre for Human Rights report for 10 to 16 September 2015, a time period chosen at random, but before the escalation of violence in October, gives a flavour of this:

West Bank

Israel has imposed a tightened closure on the West Bank. During the reporting period, Israeli forces imposed additional restrictions on the movement of Palestinian civilians:

Hebron: Israeli forces established 11 checkpoints in various areas in the governorate.

On Thursday, 10 September 2015, Israeli forces established 2 checkpoints at the northern entrance of Halhoul village, north of Hebron, and at the entrance of Samou' village, south of Hebron. At approximately 07:30 on Friday, 11 September 2015, Israeli forces established a checkpoint at the northern entrance of Athana village, west of Hebron.

At approximately 16:00 on Saturday, 12 September 2015, Israeli forces established a checkpoint at the entrance of Beit Awaa village, south of Dura, southwest of Hebron.

On Sunday, 13 September 2015, Israeli forces established 2 checkpoints at the entrance of al-'Aroub refugee camp, south of Hebron, and at the entrance of Abdu village, southeast of Dura village, southwest of Hebron.

On Monday, 14 September 2015, Israeli forces established 2 checkpoints at the entrance of al-Daheriya village, south of Hebron, and at the northern entrance of Yatta village, south of Hebron.

On Tuesday, 15 September 2015, Israeli forces established 2 checkpoints at the northern entrance of Yatta village and at the entrance of al-Koum village, southwest of Dura, southwest of Hebron.

At approximately 15:00 on Wednesday, 16 September 2015, Israeli forces established a checkpoint at the southern entrance of Halhoul village, north of Hebron.

Qalqilya: Israeli forces established 7 checkpoints in various areas in the city.

On Saturday, 12 September 2015, Israeli forces established 3 checkpoints at the entrance of 'zoun village, east of Qalqilya, the second checkpoint between Jayous and Kafor Jamal villages, northeast of the city, and the third checkpoint were established at the eastern entrance of Qalqilya.

On 14 September 2015, Israeli forces established 3 checkpoints at the entrance of Hejaa village, at the entrance of 'azoun village, east of Qalqilya, and at the eastern entrance of Qalqilya.

At approximately 03:00 on Tuesday, 15 September 2015, Israeli forces established a checkpoint between Jayous and Kafor Jamal villages, northeast of Qalqilya.

Tulkarm: At approximately 20:00 on Thursday, 10 September 2015, Israeli forces established a checkpoint at the entrance of Shoufa village, southeast of Tulkarim.

At approximately 21:30 on Monday, 14 September 2015, Israeli forces established a checkpoint on the main road between Tulkarm and other villages located in the north of Tulkram, which called (al-Sha'rawiya), near the intersection of 'alar and 'Ateel villages, north Tulkram.

At approximately 21:00 on Tuesday, 15 September 2015, Israeli forces stationed at 'nab military checkpoint on the main road between Tulkram and Nablus, stressed their arbitrary measures against Palestinian civilians and restricted their movement.

Jenin: On Monday, 14 September 2015, Israeli forces stationed at al-Jalama checkpoint separating between Jenin and Israel, northeast of Jenin, closed the checkpoint against the Palestinian civilians movement , who have a permit allowing them to travel into Israel on the occasion of Jewish holidays.

The report finishes by stating that no arrests were made as a result of these checkpoints.

The effects – poverty, fear and humiliation

The effects of this complex system of internal checkpoints and settler roads are many. A 2013 World Bank Report[2] concluded that checkpoints were reducing chances of employment and, with that, hourly wages and costing some 6 per

---

2 The Labour Market Impact of Mobility Retrictions, World Bank cent of GDP. Obviously, another result is that a day's work takes longer, as there are frequently long delays at checkpoints and long detours are necessary to get from A to B. Checkpoints or closed off roads may also mean that goods must be unloaded on one side and then reloaded on another. Farmers and others often have to resort to donkeys instead of more practical transport.

Only some 30,000 Palestinians now have permits to work in Israel, and only married men over 22 can apply for work permits for Jerusalem. On many occasions, only elderly men and women are allowed to enter Jerusalem without permits. And work permits, for example to work in the North Jordan Valley, are severely restricted. As one soldier, a contributor to Breaking the Silence, put it: "We were told there is a very clear definition. If any family relation – fourth degree down – has ever been charged with an act of violence against Israel, no work permit will be issued… We're at war with them for over fifty years now, clearly someone somewhere back on the family tree had thrown something sometime, you see?"

Other accounts from Breaking the Silence tell of yelling and aggression towards Palestinians at checkpoints, drivers' keys being taken and then thrown away, bribes being extorted, looting, and deliberate humiliations. One (Palestinian) account from February 2015 gives the picture: 17-year-old Muhammad Asri Fayyad was with a busload of school kids on an organised trip to Israel. Like the others, he had the necessary permit. At the al-Jalama checkpoint, north of Jenin, they were all told to put their mobile phones in a particular place when they went through, which he did. His was not returned, however. Instead, he was taken to a room and ordered to strip. A ceiling fan was then turned on and it became freezing cold. When the boy knocked it to try and stop it, soldiers entered the room and rifle-butted him. He was then painfully tied hand and foot to a chair and left from 9am till 2pm, when a female soldier came in, took a silver necklace he was wearing and ordered him to dress. He was told he could not enter Israel; he was given a bag containing the broken pieces of his mobile, and was allowed to leave.

By late October, residents of al-Issawiya, East Jerusalem, were suffering humiliating inspections every time they wanted to leave the area, with men, including the elderly, being forced to raise their shirts and sometimes lower their trousers. Queues were interminable, as schoolchildren and workers among the 19,000 residents waited at the single pedestrian exit. Some 3,400 children exit every school day, while 3,200 (including children attending the disabled school) must enter to reach schools inside the area. They were having to get off a bus on one side and get onto another bus on the other side. Sometimes, soldiers would empty their bags onto the ground instead of bothering to search. At a time when rumours abounded of soldiers shooting youngsters and then throwing a knife on the ground beside them, the stress levels among parents can easily be imagined.

And the delays can have fatal consequences when seriously ill people are held up at checkpoints. Casualties in 2015 included a middle-aged man, an elderly women and a baby (see page 57).

The separation wall

Israel's separation wall was promoted as a justifiable response to suicide attacks in Israel. But it does not run between the occupied territories and Israel – the so-called 1967 Green Line. Instead, it carves off and incorporates large and crucial slices of Palestinian land into Israel; it is thus another form of land theft – and on a massive scale. Some 85 per cent of the Wall runs inside the West Bank and when complete it will have appropriated 10 per cent of the West Bank's land

In places, it is 8 metres/25 feet high (compared with the Berlin wall's 3.6 metres/11.8 feet), with a buffer zone of between 30 and 100 metres; in other places it is formed of razor wire, fencing 6 metres/20 feet high, trenches 2 metres/7 feet deep, sand paths to show footprints, roads for patrol vehicles, watch towers, drones and surveillance cameras.

- The 200,000 Palestinians of Jerusalem will be totally cut off from their brethren in the West Bank.

- Palestinians in the closed military zone of the Jordan Valley will be isolated on all sides and cut off from lands and means of making a living – they will be in a ghetto.

- Salfit, the West Bank's most fertile area, will lose more than 50 per cent of its land.

- Bethlehem is encircled by a high concrete wall, casting a permanent shadow over nearby houses, menacing the inhabitants, and leaving just 13 per cent of the district's land.

- Gaza, as we have seen, is surrounded at land and sea.

- The West Bank's biggest aquifer has been stolen by the Wall.

Palestinians who peacefully oppose the existence of the Wall and annexation of their lands at regular demonstrations at the villages of Bil'in and Ni'lin, west of Ramallah, and al-Nabi Saleh have faced Israeli soldiers firing live and rubber-coated bullets, tear gas and stun grenades, attempts by undercover agents to lure them into stone throwing, ambush attempts, arrests, injuries and attacks on their homes.

An advisory opinion issued by the International Court of Justice in 2004 ruled the barrier illegal and said that the stolen lands should be returned and Palestinians compensated for their losses, but construction continued in 2015. We have mentioned (see page 64) that work started in August 2015 on the section running through the Cremisan Valley. Here, opponents thought that they had won a legal battle to save the valley when, in April, the Israeli High Court ordered the military to re-plan their route. Alas, they were to find that the Wall was still to be built, with only minor adjustments, when the bulldozers arrived in and started uprooting 1,500-year-old olive trees. The valley lies between two illegal settlements, Har Gilo and Gilo, and the Wall neatly steals some 3,500 dunums/865 acres of land from the largely Christian farmers of Beit Jala and gives them to Gilo.

Collective punishments

The army at times places concrete blocks at the entrances to certain towns and villages as a collective punishment. On 5 April, parts of the eastern end of al-Issawiya village were sealed off. On 15 April, all entrances to the town of Hizma, in the Jerusalem district, were blocked and a notice read: "To the area's residents: Only a few are responsible for disturbing the peace - because of them, this barrier was placed. You must not cooperate with them! Stop these actions that harm your lives." The town, home to 7,000 people, is separated from East Jerusalem by the Wall and from the West Bank by illegal settlements and land has been stolen from the town for both the Wall and the settlements. When B'Tselem complained that this collective punishment was illegal under international law, the sign was removed.

Also in late April, the al-Zaayyem neighbourhood of East Jerusalem suffered when an iron gate set up at the main entrance was kept shut for ten days, so that residents were forced to take a long detour on a dirt road to reach schools and workplaces.

Al-Buera, in the Hebron district, has had its main road blocked for 15 years, so residents have to park their cars outside and carry goods in on foot. In October, al-Issawiya was similarly sealed off, with residents not allowed to enter in vehicles and non-residents barred. Journalists were told that the border police 'felt like' closing the town.

In November, Israel's security cabinet gave the military the power to seal off any town or village it chose in order to 'search for suspected terrorists' without first getting approval. In December, the town of Tulkarem, with over 50,000 residents, was sealed off with cement blocks and mounds of earth. Surrounding areas, including a refugee camp and several villages, were also sealed off.

These are only a few examples of the many closures imposed on Palestinian towns and villages in 2015. In spite of the numerous settler attacks on Palestinians, no settlements have suffered from flying checkpoints and road blocks in 2015, however many times the settlers may have attacked Palestinians.

Christians

"We the Palestinian Christians suffer along with the rest of Palestinians from occupation and hardships of our economic situation. Muslims and Christians suffer equally, as there is no difference in suffering for any of us. We are all living in the same complicated circumstances, and overcoming the same difficulties."

Archbishop Sebastia Theodosios (Atallah Hanna)

In 2009, a group of Patriarchs and Heads of the churches in Jerusalem, including representatives of the Roman Catholic, Greek, Armenian and Syrian Orthodox, Lutheran, Anglican, Maronite, Ethiopian and Coptic churches, signed the Kairos document – an appeal for help for all Palestinians, whatever their faith. The document lists their sufferings, outlined in this book:

- The talk of peace when the reality is a brutal occupation

- The separation wall, which confiscates Palestinian land and turns communities into prisons

- The settlements which "ravage our land in the name of God and in the name of force, controlling our natural resources, including water and agricultural land"

- The humiliating checkpoints

- The splitting of families

- The refugees waiting to be allowed to return to their homes

- The huge numbers of Palestinian prisoners

- And Jerusalem, where Palestinians face having their right to reside there removed and their homes demolished – a "city of discrimination and exclusion".

It points out that the Palestinians are the true inhabitants of the Holy Land, and have been there from the most ancient times. It asks for support for the Boycott and Divestment movement as a peaceful means of exerting pressure on Israel to respect their human rights. The state of Israel claims that all these hideous acts are needful for 'self defence', but, as the writers point out, "if there were no occupation, there would be no resistance, no fear and no insecurity."

The document is beautifully and eloquently worded, expressing the hope that one day peoples of all faiths will be able to treat each other with genuine love and respect in the Holy Land:

> In this historic document, we Palestinian Christians declare that the military occupation of our land is a sin against God and humanity, and that any theology that legitimizes the occupation is far from Christian teachings because true Christian theology is a theology of love and solidarity with the oppressed, a call to justice and equality among peoples.

Slowly – far too slowly – some of the world's Christians are beginning to listen to this call, but 2015 was to prove, once more, a terrible year for Palestinian Christians, as for all Palestinians. The attempt to destroy the church schools which provide an excellent education to so many Christians and Muslims in Israel and the destruction of the olive trees in the West Bank's Cremisan valley in order to build the separation wall through it, splitting off Christian farmers from their land and isolating the ancient monastery are covered elsewhere (see pages 139-41 and 64). Here, we will note a few more events of 2015.

At dawn on 26 February, Jewish fanatics broke into the Church of the Dormition, in Jerusalem, scrawled racist graffiti, and started a fire which damaged a study room and other facilities. The attack came a day after fanatics had burnt a mosque in al-Jaba'aa, west of Bethlehem. This was not the first time the church, built allegedly on the site of the death of the Virgin Mary, had been attacked. On an earlier occasion, in 2013, "Jesus is a monkey" was scrawled on the walls, together with the name of an illegal settlement that had been dismantled, and there was another attack in 2014. The church is home to 22 Benedictine monks. In an interview with Judith Sudilovsky of the *Catholic News Service*, in 2014, one of the monks pointed out that he had already been spat at three times that day. (Some extreme Orthodox Jews are encouraged to spit every time they pass a church.)

On 14 April, vandals smashed gravestones in a Maronite Christian cemetery in northern Israel, in the village of Kufr Birim. The villagers were driven out in 1948 and never allowed to return; the Israeli army raised most of the village to the ground in 1953. On 29 June, another depopulated Christian village suffered vandalism, this time by the state, when Israeli police and Land Administration officials, broke into the church in Eqreth in Akka (Acre) and stole all the furniture. They even uprooted and destroyed plants in the church compound. This was presumably done because the former inhabitants continue to demand their right to return to their stolen lands and village and hold summer camps to teach their children about their history, culture and rights. The priest, Father Suheil Khoury, told Al-Arab News Agency: "We grew accustomed to these violations, but they cannot terrorize us. We will continue our activities; their attacks will never deter us… Our hope is in our youths in Eqreth to remain steadfast and determined in this blessed land. One day, we will return to our village, our land."

In the early hours of the morning of Thursday, 18 June, arsonists broke into the Church of the Multiplication, in Israel, the supposed site of the miracle of the loaves and fishes. The present church incorporates the remains of a fifth-century Byzantine church and its mosaics. The offices and store rooms were badly damaged and there was considerable smoke damage inside the church itself. As usual in these cases, the arsonists left graffiti: "False idols will be smashed" and "Pagans". Palestinian spokeswoman Dr Hanan Ashrawi commented that the attack, and others like it, were the "outcome of racist ideologies, and constant incitement, as well as the discriminatory laws of Israel" and pointed out the Israeli government's legal, financial and political support for extremist settler groups. Suspects were eventually arrested, but have not yet been tried and convicted at the time of writing.

Meanwhile, the theft of Christian lands continued as the separation wall snaked its illegal pathway across the Cremisan valley, cutting farmers off from their lands (see page 64). In late May, Christians discovered that a Swedish company had been set up in 2007 by American Zionist Irving Moskowitz in order to conceal the true, settler, purchasers of a church compound near al-Arrub refugee camp, between Bethlehem and Hebron. The sellers had believed that the hospital compound, known as Beit al-Baraka, was being refurbished for Christian use, but now learned that it was to become yet another settlement. Once the Swedish company had registered the purchase with the Israeli civil administration, it appeared that the company had been dissolved and ownership had passed to American Friends of the Everest Foundation, funded by Moskowitz for ethnic cleansing purposes. A protest march on 5 June was prevented by the army from reaching the site and protesters were assaulted by troops. Another march, on 27 June, was also attacked and Orthodox Archbishop Atallah Hanna was detained by troops and prevented from joining the marchers. The fraudulent sale is illegal under international and canonical law, but the Israelis, who proclaim their religious tolerance, are covertly (with security guards disguised as workers, for example) allowing the sale. The new settlement will further divide up the West Bank and threaten the nearby refugee camp.

For Palestinian Christians, one of the most heart-breaking aspects of their on-going sufferings is the active support given by certain influential evangelical groups to their Zionist oppressors. There is no space here to delve into the bizarre and dysfunctional depths of fundamentalist Christian theories linking the second coming of Christ with the return of Jews to Israel and the modern state of that name. Suffice it to say that if you believe that God is love, and that anything that is not loving is therefore not of God, then is it madness to support the abuse of the Palestinian people, as detailed in this book.

One means whereby the Israeli government lures visiting Christians into a deceptively rosy picture of the situation is through its total control of tourism. Not only does the state and/or its supporter agencies fund visits by people of influence, American senators and congress members and the like, during which they are relentlessly subjected to Israeli propaganda, but so too are more ordinary visitors controlled. As Rifat Kassis, of Kairos Palestine, says, "millions of tourists come to Bethlehem, Palestine, every year and, without talking to a single Palestinian, return home as enemies of Palestine and ambassadors of Israel." Israeli tourist enterprises are given advantageous loans, whereas Palestinian ones are starved of funds. Palestinian hotels are denied building permits and very few Palestinian tour operators receive permits to operate in Israel. Only 25 Palestinian tour guides have permission to guide in Israel, compared with 8,000 licensed Israeli guides. Palestinian tour operators face unnecessary obstacles when applying for visas for their clients. The numerous checkpoints are also used to delay and frustrate Palestinian tour operators and any visitors who might wish to look beneath the bland surface to see the reality beneath.

All of this leaves the Israelis free to project an image to Christian visitors that is far from reality and also to cash in lucratively on the tourist trade. Bethlehem is besieged by the separation wall and checkpoints and its Christian inhabitants see the tourist trade, on which so many families rely, diminishing year on year. The Israelis, meanwhile, are promoting their own Christian tourist routes, in which significant areas of the occupied territories are marketed as part of Israel, Nazareth is an alternative Christmas destination to Bethlehem, and visits to areas controlled by the Palestinian Authority are discouraged.

But we will end this section with the final sentences of the Kairos document:

> In the absence of all hope, we cry out our cry of hope. We believe in God, good and just. We believe that God's goodness will finally triumph over the evil of hate and of death that still persist in our land. We will see here "a new land" and "a new human being", capable of rising up in the spirit to love each one of his or her brothers and sisters.

Al Aqsa under Threat

"I think it's the center of Israeli sovereignty, the capital of Israel, the holiest place for the Jewish people… It's my dream to see the Israeli flag flying on the Temple Mount."

Deputy Foreign Minister Tzipi Hotovely

The beautiful Al-Haram Al-Sharif, the Noble Sanctuary, site of the Al Aqsa mosque and the stunning golden Dome of the Rock, is considered to be the third holiest site in the Islamic world and is central to Palestinian Muslim (and to some extent Christian) identity. On the UNESCO world heritage website you will find it listed as endangered, partly because, in the ongoing troubles in the area, funding for its maintenance and repair has not been readily available. But it faces a far greater threat, for it is believed to be built on the site of the first (built by Solomon) and second (built by Herod) Jewish temples. Powerful groups in Israel want the entire site, which they call Temple Mount, to be razed and the mosques replaced with a third temple. To Muslims, it the same as planning to demolish Westminster Abbey and St Paul's in order to build a mosque or a synagogue would be to British Christians.

The present agreement regarding the site is that Jews may not pray or perform religious rites in the compound, but instead use the Western Wall compound, where there is what is thought to be the only remaining section of wall belonging to Solomon's temple. In order to clear this area for Jewish worship, the Israeli authorities demolished a treasured medieval area of the city known as the Moroccan quarter in an act of vandalism deplored by those who love history. This entailed a wholesale eviction of Palestinian families, many of whom had lived there for generations. The event happened long before 2015, but is mentioned here because it helps to explain why many, indeed most, Palestinians do not take Netanyahu's word regarding Al Aqsa mosque that his government will not change the status quo at face value.

The orthodox Jewish belief is that Jews should not enter the Temple Mount/Al Aqsa compound because they might be walking over graves and thus become impure and also because they might unwittingly tread on the site of the original Holy of Holies. On 22 October 2015, Ashkenazi Chief Rabbi of Israel, David Lau, and the Sephardi Chief Rabbi, Yitzhak Yosef, together with 100 other leading Israeli rabbis issued a joint statement reiterating the ban and the reason behind it: "With time, we have become unaware of the exact location of the Temple, and anyone entering the premises may unknowingly enter the holiest of holies, potentially risking kareth [the extinction of the soul]."

Not all Jews, however, hold to this, and Jews are allowed to visit the Al Aqsa compound, but without praying or performing rituals, at certain hours. The arrangement might work well enough if it were done with the respect and decency which people of different religions should show one another. This is not what has been happening in 2015 (and previous years). Almost daily, Jewish religious extremists have visited the sacred compound, escorted by heavily-armed Israeli soldiers, with the aim of making their presence felt and, if possible, conducting rituals.

At the same time, the Israeli authorities have employed a cat-and-mouse game with Muslim worshippers. Sometimes women are allowed in; sometimes not. Sometimes only men over 50 are allowed to worship there; sometimes this is relaxed. Occasionally, old folk from Gaza are allowed out of the besieged enclave to visit the mosque. Frequently, certain people – men and women – are banished for specified periods of time. There appear to have been no restrictions on which Jews might visit the compound visit until 7 October, when PM Netanyahu banned all Knesset MPs, Muslim as well as Jewish, from visiting the mosque.

Jewish infringements on the Al Aqsa site have frequently been the cause of trouble. In 1990, 21 Palestinians were killed and 150 were injured in clashes with members of the Temple Mount Movement (see below) who attempted to enter Al Aqsa and place the foundation stone for the Temple. In 1996, Israeli archaeological excavations and the digging of tunnels near Al Aqsa, sparked violence that resulted in the killing of 70 Palestinians and 15 Israeli soldiers. The mosque was central to the Second Intifada, which started after Ariel Sharon, then Israeli opposition leader, forced his way into the compound, accompanied by a delegation of Likud members (the same party as Netanyahu) and hundreds of fully-armed Israeli riot police. In the ensuing clashes between Muslim worshippers and the police, 7 Palestinians were killed and 250 wounded.

Jewish extremists

The Jewish extremists who almost daily visit the mosque belong to groups that want to destroy the mosque and, indeed, take over the whole of Jerusalem for the Jews. They are the same people who are buying up or expropriating properties in Silwan and throwing out the Muslim tenants. Like the Israeli government, which consistently refuses planning permission to Palestinians who wish to build housing and so on in Jerusalem, they want Jerusalem to be the capital of an exclusively Jewish state. They have no respect for the Palestinian population of the city, or for the Muslim and Christian religions.

Foremost among the groups planning the destruction of the mosque is the Temple Institute, which has detailed blueprints for the new temple/synagogue it plans to build on the Al Aqsa site. A leading figure is American-born Rabbi Yehuda Glick, who was shot and wounded by a Palestinian in October 2014 while at a conference entitled 'The Jewish People Return to Temple Mount' (his assailant was shot on the spot).

An example of the extremist attitude towards Palestinians was witnessed on 18 May 2015, Jerusalem Day, a holiday to celebrate the capture of the city in the 1967 war. On this occasion, mobs of young Israelis rampaged/marched through the streets of the Old City chanting 'death to Arabs' and other familiar slogans, such as 'a Jew is a soul, an Arab is a son of a whore', 'may their [Palestinians] memory be erased', and Mohammad was 'a homo'. Leaflets were handed out demanding that the government should demolish the "mosques on Temple Mount so that we can build the Temple and renew the offering of sacrifices".[1] The march culminated in a mass rally at the Western Wall, attended by Naftali Bennett, Minister for Education.[2] On that occasion, some 160 Jewish extremists stormed the Al Aqsa in groups. Two men tore their clothing (signifying grief), while others danced and chanted religious songs by the Chain Gate.

Among other prominent Israeli politicians who want to destroy Al Aqsa is Agriculture Minister, Uri Ariel: "We've built many little, little temples, but we need to build a real Temple on the Temple Mount."

---

1 The Temple Institute is devoting much effort to breeding a 'perfect' red heifer. Only nine were discovered from the time of Moses until the destruction of the Second Temple. The tenth will mark the coming of the Messiah. Its ashes will be burnt with crimson thread, hyssop and cedar wood to produce a special purifying water.

2 See www.electronicintifada.net/blogs/ali-abunimah/ video-israeli-mobs-celebrate-jerusalem-day-anti-palestinian-rampage-old-city

According to Benjamin Netanyahu, as we have mentioned, the government no intention of changing the status quo as far as Al Aqsa is concerned, and Palestinian and other leaders who have voiced concern are simply stirring up trouble. However, on 8 April 2013, the *Jerusalem Post* revealed that the Education, Culture and Sport ministries had already given somewhere between NIS 300,000 and 700,000 to the Temple Institute. As the institute's website proclaims: "The rebuilding of the Holy Temple, called by the prophet Isaiah a 'house of prayer for all nations,' is a positive commandment, and the vision of the Temple's rebuilding, which will usher in an unparalleled era of world peace and harmony, is the central theme of the entire Torah. The Temple Institute is proud to represent the concept which has been heartfelt prayer of the Jewish people for two millennia."

Not surprisingly, in view of the above and not forgetting the treatment of Palestinians in all other areas of life, the Al Aqsa has remained a flashpoint in 2015. Not only that, but the Israeli has government done very little to dampen the flames.

From the start of the year, the Jewish extremists were being urged by their leaders to visit the mosque. When there, they frequently behaved aggressively, trying to break the existing rules. On 18 February, for example, according to *Maan News*, 58 settlers entered the compound through the Moroccan Gate, accompanied by police, at the same time as a 'military tour' of some 20 soldiers. One of the police pushed a Palestinian girl to the ground in the course of the tour. The following day, 78 settlers came and tried to perform rituals but were prevented by Muslim worshippers. Another group allegedly performed rituals by the Chain Gate. On 4 March, settlers again attempted to perform rituals by the Chain Gate, but were stopped by mosque guards. Palestinian women and youngsters had to leave their ID cards at the gates of the mosque and a worshipper was detained by Israeli police and taken for questioning.

Provocations continued as the year wore on, at times reinforced by events in the surrounding area. On 31 March, for example, bulldozers demolished part of a house belonging to the Amr family. The family were kept in a small room while their home was attacked and two youngsters were beaten by soldiers. There was no legal reason or justification for the damage, which included a room, balcony, storehouse, toilets, surrounding walls and trees. The house, however, lies a few metres from the mosque and the demolished room had been used by bus drivers as a convenient place in which to perform the necessary ablutions.

On 26 June, one of the rare trips from Gaza was cancelled after a rocket landed on open ground in Israel. The day before, six women, including a journalist, had been banned from the compound. On 3 July, a 10-year-old girl was attacked by an Israeli policeman in the compound after chanting "Allahu Akhbar" (God is Great). On 3 July, the Gazans were at last allowed to worship there, and on the 13 July some 800 Gazans were permitted to travel to join in the Laylat Al-Qadar, to celebrate the night when the first verses of the Koran were revealed.

But Jewish visits resumed after the end of Ramadan (20 July). On 26 July, Israeli forces entered the compound through the Moroccan, Chain and Hutta gates, firing stun grenades and rubber-coated steel bullets at Muslim worshipers to clear the way for Jewish visitors. They entered the mosque itself, firing rubber-coated bullets, and attacked the security guards. Some 19 guards suffered bruises, fractures and cuts. A carpet was burnt and there was damage to walls and doors. The Israelis later claimed that they were responding to stones thrown at them. More unwelcome visitors the following day. On 29 July, Yehuda Glick visited the compound with 63 other fanatics, all heavily guarded. Glick had been banned from the compound in August 2014, after attacking a 67-year-old woman, Ziva Badarna. On 30 July, a group of Palestinian schoolchildren on a summer camp activity were prevented from entering the Al Aqsa while right-wing Jews toured the site. Daily visits continued throughout August, with Jewish extremists being encouraged by their leaders to visit the mosque in force.

On 16 August, inspectors from the Israeli Nature and Parks Authority, accompanied by troops, confiscated 1.7 acres of land belonging to the al-Husseini and the al-Ansari families. The land, now encircled by a barbed wire fence, is adjacent to the eastern wall of Al-Aqsa Mosque, near the Golden gate. No prior warning was given.

On 26 August, Isra Ghazzawi and Baraa Ghazzawias were arrested as they attempted to enter the mosque to attend religious school. According to their headmistress, "The occupation soldiers tore the birth certificates of the two claiming they weren't original copies." (The girls have to show these because they are too young to have Israeli ID cards.) Two journalists who tried to record the incident were also detained and two cameramen fined for causing an obstruction. By now, Israeli soldiers at entrances to the mosque were routinely preventing or delaying the entry of schoolchildren.

The following day, Palestinian women were told that they would not be allowed access the mosque before 11 a.m. because entry from 7 a.m. to 11 a.m. was for Jews only. On 31 August, six of the mosque's guards were told that they had been banned from the site for two months.

Muslim defenders

Groups prepared to defend the mosque against its would-be destroyers include the Murabiteen (men) and Murabitat (women). The latter have been prominent in holding teachings within the grounds of the compound and attempting to prevent Jewish extremists from praying or conducting rituals there. Both groups have demonstrated against the increasingly oppressive Israeli control over the mosque. On 9 September, they were banned by Israeli Defense Minister Moshe Ya'alon, whose office declared that they "engage in inciteful and dangerous activity against tourists, visitors and worshipers at the site, which leads to violence, and strive to undermine Israeli sovereignty [sic] on the Temple Mount." Sheikh Azzam al-Khatib, head of the Islamic Waqf which runs Al Aqsa, replied that "The occupation regime has no right to intervene in Al Aqsa's matters… Any Muslim who enters Al Aqsa mosque and prays is a protector of the mosque. Nobody has a right to prevent a Muslim from entering their holy site and praying."

By Sunday, 13 September, the mosque was effectively under siege, as young men had barricaded themselves inside to protect it, while Israeli forces stormed the compound through the Chain and Moroccan gates, firing rubber-coated steel bullets and stun grenades and injuring several worshipers. Some 600 Jews then visited the compound and over 500 the following day. The same day, PLO official Hanan Ashrawi (a Christian, as it happens), issued a statement in which she said, "By imposing its own version of its concept of the Temple Mount on the third holiest Islamic site, Israel is not only provoking the Palestinians, but the entire Muslim world. We call on the international community, including Arab countries and Muslim states, to intervene immediately before Israel succeeds in launching a global holy war." But the heavy-handed military behaviour continued the next day, when a fire broke out, allegedly caused by stun grenades, after soldiers had entered the southern mosque. Another tour by Yehuda Glick followed the next day, during the course of which two guards, Mowafak al-Hamami, 50, and Hamza Nimer, 35, were assaulted by Israeli forces and taken to hospital and a woman was pushed and sworn at by an extremist.

By 20 September, settler groups had organized a demonstration at the Bab Al-Silsila Gate and were calling on more people to perform Talmudic rituals inside the mosque. Settlers were being urged to visit the mosque and a group calling itself 'women for the temple' was promoting an education day concerning the proposed new temple. Restrictions on Palestinian entry continued and, as the Eid al-Adha holiday approached, main entrances to East Jerusalem (Palestinian) neighbourhoods were barred with cement blocks, making it difficult for residents to shop and prepare for the feast. By 27 September, settler groups were allegedly urging their followers to celebrate the Jewish Feast of Tabernacles inside the compound. The following day, dozens of Israeli forces raided the compound, firing stun grenades and rubber-coated steel bullets. Snipers were positioned on the roof of the southern mosque, the doors of which were closed with chains. Several windows were removed.

By 30 September, Sheikh Azzam al-Khatib was informing a journalist from *Maan News* that "Al-Aqsa has become a detention centre and not a mosque. It has been turned into a military barrack; it has been surrounded by soldiers for four days." The Israelis were imposing a 'new reality'. (An all too familiar form of reality to Palestinians.)

Thus, by the end of September, the Israelis had set the scene for the upsurge of violence that was to follow, fuelled not just by the constant attacks on this Muslim holy site, but by land theft, road blocks, house demolitions, water deprivation, settler attacks, agricultural and economic deprivation, the Gaza siege, and a wholesale disregard for the rights of the Palestinian people.

Note: on 26 October, following an agreement reached at a meeting in Amman between Israel, Jordan and the US to install surveillance cameras across the mosque compound, the Islamic Endowment that runs the compound began installing surveillance cameras around the site. The idea was that cameras would help both sides to identify trouble-makers and breaches of the existing arrangements, thus reducing tension. The Israeli police intervened and removed the cameras that had been installed on the grounds that the details of the agreement had not been finalised.

Desecrated cemeteries

Further angering and alarming Palestinians have been the encroachments on ancient cemeteries of huge historical and cultural importance. The Ma'man Allah/Mamilla cemetery is thought to be the burial site of some of the Prophet's close companions and also of many who fought the crusaders. It now lies within West Jerusalem's 'Independence Park' (we have pointed out elsewhere that declaring an area 'a national park' is one of the means by which Palestinian land is stolen). The Israelis have progressively been invading the cemetery boundaries over recent years, even though the land supposedly comes under the jurisdiction of the Islamic Waqf and as such should not be seized. On 14 July, planning permission was approved for 192 settlement units, a hotel and a shopping centre on the site. In August, in a sign of complete contempt for the religious and cultural sensibilities of others, the Israelis opened a new pub on the cemetery site.

The Bab al-Rahma (Door of Compassion) cemetery lies outside the eastern walls of Jerusalem's Old City and has been in use for over a thousand years. On 2 September, Israeli officials ('nature authority') cordoned off a large area of the cemetery with a barbed wire fence. Palestinian activists removed it the same day.

Dangerous precedent

Another reason why Palestinians distrust PM Netanyahu's reassurances that Al Aqsa will not be harmed nor the status quo changed are the treatment of other mosques, in particular, the Ibrahimi Mosque in Hebron. Just as settlers are now pushing relentlessly, with covert or explicit government support, to change the status quo at Al Aqsa (in fact, destroy it altogether), so too has the Ibrahimi Mosque been a centre of dispute. And here, the status quo has very definitely been changed. Hebron is in occupied territory and the mosque, also known as the Cave of the Patriarchs, is thought to be the site of the tombs of Abraham and Sara and their successors and is therefore also sacred to Jews as well as to Muslims.

After Jewish settlers, led by Moshe Levinger, started to occupy Hebron, the mosque became a centre for trouble, with Muslims reacting against Jewish incursions. A climax was reached in February 1994, when Baruch Goldstein, one of the settlers, killed 29 Muslims at prayer in the mosque. The attack was formally condemned by the Israeli government, but the same government continues, as we have seen, to encourage and support the settlers who revere Goldstein as a martyr.

An area of the mosque was subsequently cordoned off for Jewish worship. In February 2010, the Israeli government included the mosque in a national heritage site protection and rehabilitation plan – in effect, claiming it as part of Israel, to protests from the UN, Arab states and even the US. Pressure on Muslim worshippers continues: on 3 June, the army, with no explanation, chained al-Yusifiya door of the mosque, opening it again on the following Sunday after strong protests. The next Saturday, masked settlers attempted to attack the mosque at the time of dawn prayers, but were foiled and ran off. The army frequently bans the traditional call to prayer, at the behest of illegal settlers (some 49 times in May alone, and 51 times in August).

Israeli officials who wish to visit the mosque often give little warning and refuse to remove their shoes when doing so. The mosque guardians now have to keep plastic covers to spread when this happens. In September, when tensions were already escalating to dangerous levels, the Israelis announced that the mosque would be closed to Muslim worshippers for six entire days for Jewish religious celebrations. As with Al Aqsa, soldiers guard the entrances and inspect (Muslim) worshippers.

Other mosques that came under attack in 2015 included the al-Huda mosque in the West Bank village of al-Jaba'aa, near Bethlehem. A settler gang set fire to the mosque in the early hours of 24 February, causing extensive damage. They also spray-painted "Death to Arabs" and other hate messages. And in constantly-threatened Silwan, the al-Qaaqaa Mosque, which serves some 5,000 worshippers, received a demolition notice on 21 August.

Islamic Movement ban

On 16 November, the Israeli cabinet outlawed the northern branch of the Islamic Movement, led by Sheikh Raed Salah, on the grounds that "For years, the northern branch of the Islamic Movement has led a mendacious campaign of incitement under the heading 'Al Aqsa is in danger' that falsely accuses Israel of intending to harm the Al Aqsa Mosque and violate the status-quo."

The timing of the ban – so soon after the Paris massacre – gave the Israelis the chance to imply that the movement, numbering some 10,000 members but very widely supported among Palestinian Muslims and even Christians, could be equated with ISIS. However, while it is true that the sheikh had constantly maintained that Al Aqsa was under threat (with considerable justification) and had encouraged supporters to defend the mosque, he had always condemned violence. Salah had been sentenced to 11 months in October for inciting violence at the mosque in a speech back in 2007.

The movement's offices were immediately raided and computers, files and cash taken. It should be pointed out that the Islamic Movement has, or had, a sizable charitable section, which offered much-needed help to Palestinians suffering from Israel's discriminatory policies, such as the 'Present Absentees', who receive no social services or access to normal amenities.

Three days after the announcement of the ban, Netanyahu told a meeting of foreign diplomats that Israel stood with France against terrorism. In a speech linking stabbing attacks on occupation soldiers and settlers with international terrorism, he said "It's difficult for civilized men and women to recognize that our cities, our airways, sometimes our waterways are prowled by beasts that devour the innocent in their way… The beasts increasingly have a name: it is radical Islam. That is what is doing the killing, the murder, the rape, the burning, the beheadings. We must stand together and fight together militant Islam. The people of Israel grieve with you, the people of Israel stand with you. Now and always," he added.

Palestinians now fear that the attack on the movement may presage an all-out attack on Palestinian political parties. Meanwhile, Jewish groups that wish to destroy the Al Aqsa mosque continue to promote their plans, with active support from many within the Israeli government.

Military injustice and prisoners

"The only thing that could deter a suicide bomber is knowing that if caught, his sister or his mother would be raped…"

Mordechai Kedar, Bar-Ilan University, July 2014

Palestinians in the occupied territories are subjected to a system of military justice which they have now endured for well over fifty years. The system is designed to maintain the military occupation, facilitate colonisation, and criminalise any resistance. The bulk of the population has never known a democratic justice system..

The prisoners' rights and support group Addameer has estimated that 40 per cent of the male population has been arrested at some point. Prisoners from the occupied territories are held in jails in Israel, in contravention of international law. Their families are often denied visiting rights for long periods and must obtain special permits to travel to see them. It is, of course, particularly difficult for relatives of Gazan prisoners to visit.

As we have seen, arrests often happen in the 'wee small hours', when a large force of soldiers arrives in a town, village or refugee camp, batters down the door of a house and grabs the victim. If the intended victim has fled, the family may be handed an order demanding that he or she is produced at a military outpost or illegal settlement the next day.

Prisoners are routinely beaten up, held in excruciatingly painful positions, the safety of their families is threatened (see above and also page 55), they are subjected to solitary confinement in appalling conditions, and denied adequate medical treatment.

Accused prisoners know that any charge made against them is likely to be upheld by the military courts, which have an estimated conviction rate of up to 99 per cent. Among a population terrorised by decades of brutal occupation, it is scarcely surprising that the Israelis can usually find informers to testify against a chosen suspect. Information resulting from 'extreme' interrogation measures/torture is routinely accepted. 'Secret evidence' is often with held from the defence.

Military orders

The 'only democracy in the Middle East' uses a raft of military orders to make any resistance to the colonisation process, peaceful or otherwise, illegal.

- Military order 101, in place since 1967, criminalises organizing and participating in protests, taking part in assemblies or vigils, waving flags and other political symbols, and printing and distributing political material. In addition, the order deems any acts of influencing public opinion as prohibited 'political incitement'. Any assembly deemed political requires a military permit. The order provides the excuse with which to suppress and harass human rights activists.

- Military order 378 established the military courts. Defining 'security offences', the order makes it possible for the courts to deem any act of resistance to the occupation to be 'terrorism'.

- Military order 1644 concerns children. As you will see in the section on children, Palestinian minors continued to be terrorised and appallingly treated throughout 2015.

- Military order 1650, dated 2010, broadened the definition of who could be deemed an 'infiltrator'. It replaced order 329, designed to prevent Palestinian refugees from ever returning to their homes. Under the new order, Palestinians who came from Gaza or have an address there may be forcibly returned to the ghetto. Israeli human rights group Hamoked estimate that this order threatens some 35,000 individuals.

- Military order 1651, dated 2010, defined and codified several previous orders. Notably, it defines the process of 'administrative detention', under which so many Palestinians are detained without trial. Detention orders are initially for up to 6 months, but are frequently renewed repeatedly at the request of the military.

The judges are officers who do not necessarily have a full legal training. Prisoners may be held for interrogation for up to 90 days; trials must be completed within 18 months (9 months for Israeli civil courts). The age of majority in the military courts is 16 (18 in the civil system in Israel, though this may change). Palestinian prisoners are supposed to be interrogated in Arabic and their confessions should be in Arabic, but they are often made to sign confessions in Hebrew, which the majority of them do not understand. These confessions are, however, routinely accepted in court.

The evidence presented in court may be heard in secret by the judge and not divulged to the defence. For example, 19-year-old media and journalism student, Jureen Qadah, was arrested in her home on 29 October 2015 and subsequently sentenced to three months' administrative detention. At the time of her arrest, she was shackled and blindfolded and thrown to the ground, injuring her leg. She then spent 18 hours in a military jeep. At her court hearing, where she was charged with Facebook incitement, the judge refused to release the secret information on which her arrest was based.

In addition to military orders, the 'Unlawful Combatants Law' of 2002, amended in 2008, classifies Palestinian detainees from Gaza as 'unlawful combatants'. This law, which contravenes the UN definition of the Gaza strip as occupied territory, means that Gazans are protected neither as prisoners of war, by the third Geneva Convention, nor as civilians, under the fourth Geneva Convention. Instead, the regular Israeli courts can detain Gazans without trial, evidence or legal representation for unlimited periods.

By the end of December 2015, there were 6,800 political prisoners, including 470 children, 60 women, 500 from East Jerusalem and 355 from Gaza.

Detained leaders and activists

Among the political prisoners there is a significant number of leaders, human rights campaigners, peace activists and lawyers – the natural leaders of the Palestinian community. This serves several purposes for the Israelis: obviously, it helps Israel to leave the Palestinians without charismatic leaders; many of those who are imprisoned are highly articulate and well educated, so removing them from circulation helps Israel to promote the notion that Palestinians are mere stone-throwing hooligans without a just cause; treating peace activists and human rights leaders harshly may deter others from following their course; imprisoning natural leaders allows Israel's supporters to imply that there must be a good reason for their detention, and any state wants to see terrorists behind bars, doesn't it?

Five current prisoners are members of the Palestinian Legislative Council. Among them is PFLP member and lawyer Khalida Jarrar, an outspoken feminist, the vice chairperson of prisoners' rights NGO Addameer, head of prisoners' issues in the Palestinian Legislative Council and a member of the National Palestinian Committee for the follow-up of the International Criminal Court. She was arrested at 3am on 2 April and was immediately given a 6-month detention order. It is surely no coincidence that her arrest followed one day after the ICC treaty officially went into effect for Palestine. Israel, for very obvious reasons, had been bitterly opposed to Palestine's becoming a member of the ICC

As a fellow member of the Legislative Council, Jamil al-Majdalawi, commented: "Israel does not lose a chance to attempt to break the resistance's will, the people's resistance and their leadership symbols, and Khalida Jarrar is one of those symbols of resistance."

At a hearing on 8 April, the military prosecution stated that it did not intend to issue a list of charges against Jarrar because it was not convinced that the information was enough to detain her until the end of the legal procedures. The following week, however, she was indicted on 12 charges of security-related crimes. These included visiting a released prisoner, campaigning for the release of a political leader, giving speeches and lectures, participating in a book fair and suggesting that Israeli soldiers should be kidnapped in order to exchange them for political prisoners (she agreed to accept this last charge in a final plea bargain, while denying it was true).

In May, she was due to be released on bail, but the military judge accepted a prosecutor's appeal, based on a secret file, not shown to the defence. (Another judge had previously deemed the secret evidence insufficient to keep her in jail.) At the end of August, two witnesses told the court their confessions were the result "pressure and ill-treatment during interrogation including sleep deprivation, being tied in painful stress positions for long hours, being threatened with further torture and with the arrest of family members." They had also been denied access to lawyers. Finally, after several more court appearances, Jarrar agreed to a plea bargain and was sentenced to 15 months on 6 December. She had previously defied an order banishing her from her home in Ramallah, where she lives with her devoted husband, Ghassan, whom she met at university, to Jericho, where she has no family. Ghassan has spent 11 years of their 30-year marriage in administrative detention.

Administrative detainees

Jarrar was initially held as an 'administrative detainee'. Introduced under British colonial rule, this system of imprisonment without trial has been continued by the Israelis to subjugate Palestinians who resist the occupation in any way, however peaceful. By the end of December 2015, there were 660 Palestinian administrative detainees.

In a relatively novel move, Israel has now imprisoned a small number of Jewish administrative detainees (there were over 300 officially registered attacks by settlers on Palestinian persons and property in 2015, though the true number is probably much higher). At the time of writing, there are fewer than 10 Jewish administrative detainees.

A prominent Palestinian detainee in 2015 was 31-year-old lawyer Khader Adnan, affiliated to the Islamic Jihad movement and, like Jarrar, an advocate for prisoners' rights. Arrested in June 2014, he was held without trial in Hadarim prison, Israel, where his wife was not allowed to visit him until late March 2015. He was sentenced to two weeks' solitary confinement after giving a sermon highlighting the ill-treatment of sick prisoners. In early May, he went on hunger strike, ingesting only water, in protest at his 'administrative detention' and that of so many others. He was held in a very small room with no ventilation but was finally taken to hospital, when he went into a coma and there were fears that there might be permanent brain damage. Even when nearly blind and deaf and vomiting blood, Adnan was kept shackled hand and foot to his hospital bed.

On 14 June, Israeli ministers approved a bill allowing hunger strikers to be force fed. Please note that force feeding is extremely painful and can cause severe injury or even death. The prisoner is stripped and tied down and a tube is then inserted through his nose and down to his stomach. In a previous mass hunger strike, in 1980, two prisoners died as a result of force feeding and a further two died later from medical complications. To his credit, Leonid Edelman, chairman of the Israeli Medical Association, immediately condemned the bill as unethical. Adnan ended his hunger strike on 29 June (without being force fed), after an agreement was reached which the Israeli authorities that he would be released on 12 July.

In a statement issued on 8 August, UN representatives Robert Piper, James

Turpin and Dr Gerald Rockenschaub, condemned force feeding and reaffirmed that hunger striking was a legitimate means of peaceful protest and a fundamental human right:

> We emphasize the importance of working towards improving health and human rights conditions of Palestinian prisoners in line with international standards. The practice of administrative detention is incompatible with international human rights law and should be ended. All detainees should be promptly charged or released.

One aspect of administrative detention that amounts to psychological torture is the fact that the detention order can be renewed repeatedly, so detainees can never know when they will be released. Prisoners' rights group Addameer have documented many instances when a detainee has been walking out of prison to meet his family, only to be handed another detention order and told to turn back.

In August 2015, the Prisoners' Centre for Studies claimed that out of 480 then held under the system, 75 had had their sentences renewed four times in a row and 135 for three times.

Torture and CIDT

There is no specific crime of torture in the Israeli penal code, nor any framework for the mental and physical rehabilitation of victims or right to compensation.

A so-called 'temporary' Israeli law permits the security services to interrogate (Palestinian) 'security suspects' without making an audio-visual recording of the interview. This law, initially introduced in 2002 and regularly extended ever since, was once more extended on 4 July 2015, this time for a year and a half. The law enables interrogators to use various forms of torture, or 'extreme measures' to extract confessions. Equally, it makes it very difficult to prove that false confessions were the result of these methods.

In addition, Israeli law permits security detainees to be held for 21 days before meeting their lawyer. They may be kept in solitary confinement during this period, with no contact with any person other than their interrogator(s).

In 2014, eight official complaints of torture were filed against Shin Bet, Israel's security service, in the first half of the year and 51 in the second half, after there had been an escalation of violence. The figures are not in for 2015 at the time of writing, but a similar increase may be expected following the escalation of violence in October 2015. An example: on 7 December, the Palestinian Authority's Louay Akka revealed that one prisoner, Wasim Marouf, had 28 cigarette burns on his hands, chest and back when he was visited in Ofer prison in Israel. Marouf, accused of attempting to stab a soldier, suffers from epilepsy and mental illness and had recently had a kidney removed.

According to a joint statement issued on Prisoners' Day, April 2015, by NGOs Adalah, the Al Mezzan Center for Human Rights, Physicians for Human Rights – Israel and the Public Committee Against Torture in Israel, "Impunity for torture also continues; of 860 complaints filed between 2001-2014, no investigations were opened."

> We demand that Israel cease its systematic use of administrative detention as a mechanism of deterrence and punishment against Palestinian society, and interference with political processes. We demand that Israel end the practice of torture and ill-treatment against Palestinian prisoners, and end the severe tactics of arrest and detention of Palestinian minors, including abuse that amounts to torture and CIDT [cruel, inhuman or degrading treatment]. We further demand that Israel revokes all discriminatory legislation that target the rights of Palestinians in Israeli prisons, and that it ensures transparency and accountability of Israeli security and prison authorities.

But violent treatment of prisoners continued. On 5 November, a lawyer from the Palestine Prisoners' Society who visited inmates at Etzion and Ashkelon jails reported that a 19-year-old, Hazem Hadwan had been pushed down a flight of stairs by prison guards and five other prisoners reported being severely beaten. On 24 November, a lawyer found that eight prisoners had been assaulted by guards. Yousef Erekat had been assaulted, forced to strip and then coerced into admitting to a charge of stone throwing. Ismael Muhammad Bader, aged 44, had been beaten around the head with guns and left tied up for five hours. Six others had been similarly assaulted.

Women

Although Israel is a state party to CEDAW (the Convention on the Elimination of all forms of Discrimination Against Women), it has not signed the optional protocol designed to protect their human rights. Women are frequently abused during interrogations and used to influence family members (see page 55, where a wife was deliberately hurt during an army raid while the husband was in jail). Research conducted by the Public Committee Against Torture in Israel in 2013 discovered that 53 per cent of the women experienced physical or verbal abuse during an arrest of a family member. Mothers and wives of detainees thus become victims of secondary traumatization which harms their daily lives and families.

Conditions for women prisoners, as for men, are often appalling. Detained lawyer Shireen al-'Eesawy, arrested in June 2014 and held without trial, was put in solitary confinement in 2015 following an argument with guards at Ha-Sharon prison:

> The cell was too small; its door sealed shut. They even sealed the door with plastic. I couldn't breathe and fell unconscious before they removed the plastic to allow some air through. I had no sheets or covers. I had to sleep on the ground; they even confiscated all of my belongings. The cell has no sink and is completely unfit for human use. Whenever they took me to see my lawyer, or whenever I was shortly allowed into the prison yard, the soldiers always cuffed me, and chained my legs.

When prisoners are transferred to another prison or taken to court for trial, the process is made as unpleasant as possible. Body searches are intrusive and humiliating and take place before and after court hearings and also at night, as a form of punishment. The transfer usually starts very early in the morning – around 2 or 3am. When Khalida Jarrar was taken for trial in early December, she was held inside the freezing prison bus from 2am till 7am, then taken to an unheated room with a concrete floor and over-flowing toilet. All the women were handcuffed and shackled. Following her conviction she was moved to a jail along with abusive Israeli criminal offenders. Due to the inhumane conditions (plus the unlikelihood of receiving justice) many prisoners waive their right to appear in court.

Another female prisoner who suffered solitary confinement in 2015 was 61-year-old Fathiyeh Abd al-Fattah Khanfar, whose crime was to attempt to smuggle a SIM card to her jailed son. Her cell was infested with cockroaches, with no toilet or water, and only a thin mattress to lie on the concrete floor.

Two teenagers, Jihan Erekat, 17, and Nour Istabraq, 15, were held in Ashkelon prison. Perhaps because there is no women's section, they were confined to their bug- and cockroach-infested cell.

Medical negligence

A frequent charge made by human rights groups against the Israeli prison service is that of medical negligence:

- Prisoners are given simple painkillers for serious medical complaints, instead of necessary treatment;

- Medical conditions are ignored and requests for hospital visits denied;

- Transportation to hospital is so painful (shackles, metal seats that are freezing in winter and burning in summer, no toilet facilities, no heating, no water, hours taken on relatively short journeys) that some prisoners prefer to suffer in prison;

- Prisoners are removed from hospital before their treatment is complete.

Prisoners' health is made worse by the poor conditions inside Israeli jails. Cells are often damp, with no form of heating. In January 2015, Issa Qaraqe, head of the Palestinian Prisoners' Committee, confirmed that prisoners were being left without warm clothing and bedcovers in freezing winter conditions. The Israeli authorities had refused to allow the Red Cross to remedy the situation and instead had forced prisoners to buy light, inadequate covers from their prisons' canteens.

When 41-year-old Adnan Mohsin, who is paralysed and suffers from a range of health complications, was arrested, the soldiers at first refused to take his wheel chair and then insisted on handcuffing and blindfolding him. When in prison, where he was held as an administrative detainee, he fell from his chair due to the cramped conditions. He spent most of the time in Ramla prison, which lacks basic medical supplies and equipment. He was finally released in February 2015.

By the time 22-year-old diabetic Jaafar Awad was released from prison on 21 January 2015, he was suffering from pneumonia, heart problems, and thyroid and pancreas complications, due to being administered incorrect insulin shots in Eshel prison. He died in April.

Fadi al-Darabi, aged 30, died from a stroke on 11 October. His family claimed that he had been left in solitary confinement, untreated, after suffering abdominal bleeding two years earlier.

Jalal Al-Sharawneh, aged 17, was treated for a gunshot wound to the leg at Asaf Haroveh, but taken back to prison prematurely, where his leg deteriorated dangerously. Iyas al-Rifai had an operation to remove a tumour in his stomach, but was returned to prison while still needing treatment. Sami Abu Diak and Murad Saad also suffered after being returned to prison prematurely.

Money, money, money...

Israel frequently fines prisoners large sums in addition to their sentences.

When Jaffar Awad was finally released to die, this was only on condition of a fine of 40,000 shekels (£6980/$10,200). Amaal al-Shawish, aged 48, accused of trying to smuggle a mobile phone to her imprisoned son, was released to house arrest on the condition of paying a fine of 15,000 shekels (£2618/$3,800). Khalida Jarrar was fined 10,000 shekels (£1745/$2,582), this in addition to her prison sentence.

In March, the Palestine Authority, which had been paying around 13 million shekels (£2.27/$3.65 million) a year to Israel on behalf of prisoners, warned lawyers to avoid plea bargains that entailed such fines in future. Meanwhile, prisoners continue to be fined sums their families can scarcely afford for minor infractions, and unless they pay they are not released.

The Suffering of Palestinian Children

"Every child has the right to life. Governments must do all they can to ensure that children survive and develop to their full potential."

UN Convention on the rights of the child Article 6 (survival and development)

"Why do Gaza's children have no rights? Why does no one feel our pain? I want one human to come and live in Gaza just for two hours. I don't want him to stay for a day, just two hours to feel what we feel. There is no food, no electricity, no water. Our future is gone. All the children here need psychiatric treatment. And for the children whose families have been killed, how will they live?"

14–year-old boy in Gaza who called the Save the Children-supported helpline

"[In future attacks, Israel is] going to hurt [Lebanese] civilians to include kids of the family. We went through a very long deep discussion... we did it then; we did it in [the] Gaza Strip; we are going to do it in any round of hostilities in the future."

Defence Minister Moshe Ya'alon, May 2015

There has been plenty of evidence that Ya'alon's words should be taken seriously. UN statistics show that during the so-called 'armed conflict' in July/August 2014 in Gaza, 551 children were killed by Israeli airstrikes and ground troops; a further 3,436 were injured, with about a third of the injured sustaining permanent disabilities.[1]

Even without direct 'armed conflict', 2015 has been another year of heartache and horror for Palestinian children, whether they are growing up in impoverished and often highly-dangerous refugee camps in Lebanon, Syria or Jordan, or in the occupied West Bank or Jerusalem, or in Gaza. And in Israel itself, Palestinian children continue to be treated as second-class citizens and denied the excellent educational facilities and funding offered to Jewish children, rather than treated as a cherished part of the state's future.

---

1   See www.unrwa.org/gaza-emergency

In this section we will touch on just some specifics of the abusive, deprived and traumatising circumstances of Palestinian children's lives. It should be remembered, however, that the other sections of this book also apply to children as much as to their parents and older relatives. The following gives therefore only limited insight into their heart-breaking plight.

Trauma, deprivation and fear: the living nightmare of Gaza's children

> **"Tomorrow there's no school in Gaza,**
> **they don't have any children left.**
> **In Gaza there's no studying,**
> **No children are left there,**
> **Olé, olé, olé-olé-olé."**

The racist song above, which celebrates the killing of over 500 children in the 2014 offensive on Gaza, was chanted regularly throughout 2015 by Israeli supporters of the late Meir Kahane. (No arrests.)

Palestinian children generally, and Gaza's children especially, are among the most traumatised in the world. Save the Children CEO Justin Forsyth said in a statement, "Many children in Gaza have now lived through three wars in the past seven years, the last one notable for its brutality. They are emotionally and, in some cases, physically shattered."

But not only have three wars taken their toll, producing the devastating mental, emotional and physical health effects of complex traumatization, many children live with traumatic events which compound those effects, such as violence, raids, deprivation, starvation, homelessness, the inaccessibility of normal healthcare and more on a daily basis.

To understand what ongoing and complex traumatisation does to a child, one needs to imagine stepping into the shoes of a child that has experienced and seen horrors no child should have to endure, and lives in a territory that offers fear, terror, deprivation and insecurity instead of safety and nurturing.

Imagine you are such a Palestinian child in Gaza. Imagine that you are so frightened that you can't sleep, wet your bed at night, wake up screaming from nightmares and often begin to shake uncontrollably or feel your heart racing. Imagine that you hear the sounds of bombs, stun grenades and screams in your head. Imagine that you can't get the images of corpses, maimed people and collapsing houses out of your mind. Imagine that you might have seen your parents or your big brother killed, or your school destroyed, or your friends maimed and wounded or your little baby brother screaming for food that isn't available. Imagine that there was no place you could run to, or hide, because there was a wall around you, whilst the bombs kept coming!

Now imagine you have lived through such a brutal war not only once, but two or even three times during your short life. Imagine how it feels to never ever be able to relax, never feel safe and having to cope on your own with your feelings of terror, fear and sadness the best you can because you know that your mother and father can neither protect you nor console you, and that they cannot re-assure you that this will never happen again. After all, they themselves are traumatised and often grief-stricken and know that they are powerless. Imagine that your teachers, your doctor, your friends cannot help you either, because they are in the same position.

Now imagine that whilst you have to cope with these feelings and memories and the devastation around you, you haven't got enough to eat (Gaza); there is a shortage of water; you experience raids, checkpoints and soldiers on your way to school (West Bank and Jerusalem); there are ruins all around you; work for your parents is scarce, and, most importantly, there is no way out; you can't see a future, and you know that all you and your parents have experienced – and more - could happen again at any moment in time.

The statistics about severe trauma symptoms in Palestinian children, especially in Gaza, are indisputable. They correspond with Post-traumatic Stress Disorder (PTSD) and complex PTSD symptoms listed in the *Diagnostic and Statistical Manual of Mental Disorders* as well as by the World Health Organisation. Symptoms include extreme fear responses, anxiety disorders, phobias, depression, flashbacks, nightmares, hopelessness, isolation and an array of physical and psychosomatic symptoms, such as bedwetting, stomach upsets and headaches.

On 6 July, Save the Children published a report entitled 'A Living Nightmare: Gaza – one year on'. It is based on an assessment in Gaza, completed by their field team in April and May 2015, which looked at the impact of the crisis on the mental health of school-aged children (6 to 15 years) a year after the conflict, with the aim of understanding their evolving needs. One section of the report sums up the effects on children of the current situation. "Unexpectedly high levels of continued severe emotional distress and trauma were reported to us by children and their parents in Gaza":

Nightmares: on average, seven out of ten children in the worst-hit areas of Gaza are suffering from regular nightmares, with the problem so severe in some areas that eight out of ten children suffer from nightmares every single night. One father reported "*My children were in the street [during the war] and saw the body pieces on the street after a shelling. My son is now traumatised, and my daughter has nightmares and wakes up frightened. I don't know how to help them.*"

Bedwetting: 75% of the children interviewed in the worst-hit areas are experiencing unusual bedwetting regularly, with 47% of children in one particularly badly affected area experiencing it every night.

Fear: up to 89% of parents reported that their children suffer consistent feelings of fear, while more than 70% of children in worst-hit areas worry about another war.

School refusal: more than 50% of children in some areas do not want to go to school anymore, or have poor attendance. Some explained that they are afraid to leave their homes; others feel unsafe in school buildings, some of which were damaged or destroyed in the conflict. Some children who have had to move to new areas after their homes were destroyed feel too anxious to try and make new friends.

Listlessness and lack of motivation: three in ten children are demonstrating decreased motivation and listlessness, according to their parents.

Isolation and withdrawal: parents report that two in ten children are showing symptoms of increased isolation and appear withdrawn.

The report goes on to point out that the 2014 ceasefire does not mean that life for Gaza's children is 'normal', as anyone with the good fortune to live in a stable western nation would see it:

Even during times of relative calm, children and their families are exposed to high degrees of violence and deprivation. Drones and F-16s are common in the skies of Gaza and live ammunition is routinely used in the border areas and at sea, making a terrifying environment for children both in Gaza and those close to the border in Israel.

The long-term devastating mental, emotional and physical health consequences of ongoing traumatisation are well documented in medical and psychological literature all over the world. A more recent scientific field of research, namely Epigenetics – the study of changes in organisms by modification of gene expression – has begun to shine some light on the intergenerational consequences of DNA changes brought about by environmental factors. These changes in gene expression – expression of a person's DNA - can be passed down to the next generation. Here I just want to cite two studies, which apply to Gaza's population, especially its children.

An epigenetic study that examines the effects of trauma, published in *Biological Psychiatry* in August 2015, entitled 'Holocaust exposure induced intergenerational effects on FKBP5 methylation' concerns the ongoing effects of the trauma suffered by 32 Holocaust survivors, due to the repeated exposure to glucocorticoid hormones, which can reduce a person's ability to handle stress. This and other studies in this developing field are showing that the effects of repeated exposure to stress factors can cause heightened levels of a whole range of mental illnesses in future generations.

Famine has been another area of epigenetic research. As discussed in the section on the blockade of Gaza, when Israel first set up the siege of Gaza, their officials decided 'to put Gaza on a diet.' There are severe restrictions on the quantities and types of food permitted to enter the enclave. In addition, Gaza's ability to provide the necessary supplements for a healthy diet have been severely restricted by the constant attacks (ceasefire violations) on fishing boats and farmers. Famine has been shown as another epigenetic factor: girls born to Dutch women who suffered from famine at the end of World War II had an increased risk of developing schizophrenia, for example[2].

Gaza's children, of course, suffer from both ongoing trauma and malnutrition.

And even without a full-scale attack going on, home is not necessarily a safe haven in the Gaza enclave: on 24 April, 14-year-old Fadi Abu Mandi had attended a football match and was now dutifully following his father's orders

---

2 www.hongerwinter.nl/item.php?id=32&language=EN

and studying for his exams in the family home in the Maghazi refugee camp. Suddenly he felt an excruciating pain in his back. He had been shot by a bullet fired at farmers in the Gaza strip (an Israeli ceasefire violation). The bullet had passed through an open space in the roof of the house. Months later, it appears that he will never walk again.

Forgotten refugees

And it is not just in Gaza that Palestinian children suffered trauma and malnutrition in 2015. Neglected to the point of being invisible to the entire world (often the fate of the abused child), 2015 proved horrendous for many children in refugee camps in Syria, notably Yarmouk, but also elsewhere in Syria and in Lebanon. These are the grandchildren of people who fled their homes during the highly-successful Zionist terror campaign of 1948. Israel refuses to acknowledge their right to return to their homes (which have of course been stolen and either demolished, sometimes covered with 'parkland' or rebuilt or are now lived in by Jews). Throughout the massive refugee crisis caused by the fighting in Syria, Israel has, true to form, refused to take in any refugees, let alone Palestinian ones.

Palestinian refugee parents, who had themselves grown up in camps, faced enormous problems in trying to maintain some semblance of normality for their children. Armed factions roamed the camps causing havoc and Palestinian families, although as a whole the parents had no wish to take sides, often found themselves caught in the middle. We will never know how many of the children who have drowned in the Mediterranean in 2015 were in fact Palestinians trying to escape this horror.

It was in April that ISIS invaded Yarmouk camp, which is near Damascus. *Aljazeera* quoted one refugee: "They [ISIL] came in from Hajar al-Aswad area, and then not only were they barbaric, but the regime shelling of the camp intensified even more. It was more barrel bombs everywhere…" By August, typhoid had broken out to add to the misery of the starving Palestinians left in the camp. And as the civil war spread its tentacles to neighbouring areas, life for children and their parents also became increasingly hazardous in the Lebanese camps, whence many of those who had lived in Syria had fled.

West Bank and Jerusalem

And children in the occupied West Bank and Jerusalem also faced traumatic events throughout the year. Even before the heightening of tension in October, there were many who lived in constant fear that their home would be demolished, or their father's land would be stolen, or their big brother or sister would be taken by soldiers and imprisoned or injured or killed. And then there are the raids, often by night, which are discussed elsewhere. Children suffer from the effects of high levels of unemployment among grown-ups, from the road blocks, walls and sieges that render impossible the family gatherings that should play such an important part in a happy childhood and are hopefully remembered for a lifetime; they suffer from harassment by settlers or the army and from all the psychological effects of growing up in an all-to-often terrifying situation. It should be pointed out that many Palestinian children in Israel itself, in the Negev, for example, also face the perils of home demolition and dispossession.

Palestinian schoolchildren face harassment in many forms. Below are just a few examples from 2015 of the hazards of life for Palestinian children.

On 26 February, children in the village of Urif, near Nablus, arrived at their school to find that settlers from Yitzhar had sprayed anti-Palestinian graffiti, including 'Death to Arabs' on the walls. On the same day, a team from the (Israeli) Hebron City Administration arrived with the military at the village of Al-Majaz and handed over an order to demolish the village school, formed from caravans donated by a European institution.

In March, children from al-Tira and Beit Ur al-Fuqa villages in western Ramallah, following the closure (to them) of a settlement road, were having to reach school via a 40-minute detour that involved walking through sewage channels filled with rain and waste water in winter and inhabited by snakes in summer. According to a report in *Maan News*, repeated raids on the school by the Israeli army had hampered school maintenance, so classrooms were covered in mould in winter. A student, Ayman Abd al-Fattah, told the reporter that he and his classmates had been repeatedly harassed by Israeli settlers from Beit Horon while on their way to school and were also afraid of the soldiers. On 23 March, after receiving reports of stone throwing along Route 60, soldiers raided the Al-Sawiya girls' school, south of Nablus, where they fired tear-gas and stun grenades at students. Children in the H2 area of Hebron, which is administered by Israel, are regularly tear-gassed on their way to school.

In April, the UN Office for the Coordination of Humanitarian Affairs (OCHA) reported that, for the second time in three weeks, Israeli forces had shot and injured a Palestinian child, on this occasion a 13-year-old girl, with rubber-coated steel bullets as she was making her way back from school close to Shufat checkpoint.

On 25 September, 3-year-old Maram Abed al-Latif al-Qaddumi was standing on a balcony in her home in the village of Kafr Qaddum in Qalqiliya (West Bank) when an Israeli soldier shot at her head with a rubber-coated steel bullet.

On 17 September, Israeli troops in the Ras al-Amud neighborhood of occupied East Jerusalem were deployed metres away from the Silwan junior and primary boys' schools. According to the Wadi Hilweh Information Center the troops fired sound bombs towards the students and detained several, but were prevented from entering the school itself by administrative staff and teachers. In the same month, the army demolished Samra School, which had been built by Jordan Valley Solidarity out of mud bricks.

The dangers of being a schoolchild in occupied territory were highlighted on 5 October, when 13-year-old Abed al-Rahman Obeidallah was shot in the chest while returning home from school. There were clashes going on in Aida refugee camp where he lived, but he was not involved. He was rushed to hospital but was dead on arrival. He was, of course, not the only 13-year-old child (to pick a random group) to be killed or injured in October: other victims include Adham Musallam from Hebron (hospitalised after being attacked by settlers at al-Arrub refugee camp, also 5 October), Ahmad Manasra (took part in a stabbing attack in East Jerusalem and was run over by a car; he lay on the ground and was kicked by a police officer while bystanders shouted "Die, you son of a whore!" 12 October), Ahmad Sharaka (shot in the neck with a live round during clashes in Al-Bireh; he died in hospital, 13 October), another 13-year-old, name unknown (shot in the foot with a rubber-coated steel bullet in Aida refugee camp, 23 October), and another (shot in the cheek and left shoulder during clashes in Hizma village, 24 October). On 31 October, dozens attended the ceremonial 'funeral', in Shuhada Cemetery in Duheisha refugee camp in southern Bethlehem, of 13-year-old Issa Ahmad Adnan al-Muti's lower leg,. An Israeli soldier had shot the child during a protest in northern Bethlehem on 28 September, allegedly with an illegal dum-dum bullet, of the type that expands on impact, causing irreparable damage.

The violence continued to the end of the year. On 6 December, Israeli forces fired tear gas at several schools in Hebron. Dozens of children had to be taken to medical centres for treatment, and one of the centres was then raided. On 7 December, 15-year-old Khalil Mohammed Ahmed Kiswani was shot in the left eye as he left school to return home with his father. On 10 December, a gang of settler thugs, including a well-known extremist named Anat Cohen harassed children on their way to Qurtuba school in Hebron. The children were frightened and returned home. Their school is near the illegal Beit Hadassah settlement in the centre of Hebron, and settlers are trying to close it down. On 22 December, the army tried to force its way into Tuku secondary school, Bethlehem area, but were stopped by teachers. They fired stun and tear gas grenades as they left. The following day, the Zahrat al-Madaim school for girls, in Hebron, was tear gassed.

Education

UN Convention on the rights of the child
Article 28 (right to education)

Every child has the right to an education. Primary education must be free. Secondary education must be available to every child. Discipline in schools must respect children's dignity. Richer countries must help poorer countries achieve this.

Article 29 (goals of education)

Education must develop every child's personality, talents and abilities to the full. It must encourage the child's respect for human rights, as well as respect for their parents, their own and other cultures, and the environment.

In Israel

The education of Palestinian children has suffered in 2015 in many ways. In Israel, one might expect the situation to be good, as Israeli education overall is among the best in the world, with a high percentage of graduates. In fact, however, according to the Follow-Up Committee for Arab Education, Jewish pupils receive at least five times more funding than Arab pupils – $1,100/£718 each compared to \$192/£125. There is a shortage of 6,000 classrooms and 4,000 teachers in Palestinian schools, while Jewish schools have twice as many computers for a given number of students as the Palestinian schools. Small wonder, then, that the drop-out rate is high. According to an article by Meirav Arlosoroff published in 2014 in Israel's liberal newspaper, *Haaretz*, some 32 per cent of Palestinian children drop out of high school compared with 8 per cent of Jewish teenagers, and only 24 per cent achieve a high-quality matriculation certificate, compared with 45 per cent of Jews. The situation becomes even more extreme higher up the system, with only 9 per cent achieving a BA, 4 per cent a doctorate, and only 2 per cent among the academic faculties.

But there is one area of excellence: the 47 Christian schools, mostly run by the Roman Catholic church, which cater for around 33,000 pupils, are some of the finest schools in Israel and have a matriculation rate of 93 per cent, which is higher than most of the Jewish schools. Over 30 per cent of Palestinian MKs (members of the Israeli parliament) and a high proportion of academics, lawyers and other professionals come from these schools, the pupils of which are about 40 per cent Muslim and 60 per cent Christian. Many of the schools predate the foundation of Israel and until fairly recently the state contributed between 60 and 70 per cent of their running costs, with parental contributions making up the rest.

In 2014, however, they were told that the state was cutting its contribution and by 2015 the state's contribution was further cut down to a mere 29 per cent. And, to make the intention clear, the state also capped the parental contribution, so that parents could not make up the shortfall, even if they could afford it. Highly-educated Palestinians, it seems, are not wanted in Israel.

In contrast, Netanyahu's government agreed to pay 100 per cent of the costs of Jewish Haredi/ultra-Orthodox schools in return for their parties joining his coalition. Naftali Bennett, of the settler Jewish Home party is now Minister for Education. The excuse for cutting funding to Christian schools was that they refused to join the public education system. In fact, as the schools' representatives have pointed out, they already teach the core curriculum, whereas the Haredi schools refuse to teach subjects such as maths, English and science.

At the start of the school year (2 September) the Christian schools went on strike after talks with the government had achieved nothing. As the Bishop of Nazareth, Marcuzzo, said: "If Christian schools are threatened, in the long run, it is the very Christian presence in Israel that is threatened." Finally, on 28 September, the pupils returned to school after a temporary compromise was reached with a one-time payment from the government of 50 million shekels. It remains to be seen what will happen in following years.

Another glimmer of hope lies in the Hand in Hand schools, in which about 1,400 pupils, roughly half of them Jewish and the other half Palestinian, learn in both languages and discover each other's cultures. There are five such schools at present; a sixth is planned, though only one mixed school continues up to the highest grade. Only 30 per cent of funding comes from the state and the schools have faced opposition: the kindergarten in Jaffa was criticised by Tel Aviv municipality for not raising the Israeli flag on Independence Day (which would be a bit like asking Scots to celebrate Culloden or Irish Catholics to celebrate the battle of the Boyne); two classrooms in the Jerusalem school were set on fire in November 2014 and anti-Arab hate graffiti sprayed on the walls.

But if the continued existence of excellent church schools is under threat, the Hand in Hand schools only serve a tiny percentage of pupils, while the condition of the state schools for Palestinian children is third rate, there is a sizable number of Palestinian children in Israel whose situation is far worse, for they have no access to education at all. These are the children of Israel's Internally Displaced Persons, or 'Present Absentees' – Palestinians who fled from their homes to avoid the massacres carried out by the nascent IDF in 1948 and were never allowed to return. Under the Israel's 1950 'Absentee Property Law' their homes were confiscated; they remained in Israel, but have no rights to state services. There is more about this group elsewhere, but here we will just note that those services include education and that Israel's IDPs number around 350,000, a large proportion of whom are children.

In Jerusalem

"Every child has the right to learn and use the language, customs and religion of their family, whether or not these are shared by the majority of the people in the country where they live."

UN Convention on the rights of the child, Article 30 (children of minorities)

The children in Jerusalem fall into a bizarre category – or pit – of their own. Jerusalem is occupied territory in the eyes of the world, apart from Israel, which regards it as an integral part of the 'Jewish' state. Here, the infrastructure is in a pitiable condition and the will to improve the situation for Palestinian children appears to be completely lacking. This is hardly surprising, given the government's commitment to creating a Jewish city, a policy backed by extremist settlers (including, as already mentioned, Minister for Education, Naftali Bennett). In the densely-populated Al Tur neighbourhood, for example, an area of land had been set aside for a much-needed girls' school. Instead, it was bought in the early 1990s by the Moskowitz couple, financial backers of the Ateret Kohanim, the racist organisation that buys up housing in order to expel the Arab tenants and replace them with Jewish incomers. The land now houses a Jewish religious school or yeshiva and a Jewish-only settlement. The remaining land reserve has been allocated by the Jewish-controlled municipality of Jerusalem for use as a nature reserve and national park – a familiar ploy to take land away from Palestinians.

Here, as in Israel, students (around half the total) who cannot afford private education, which in any case is expensive and not properly regulated, are offered a Zionist curriculum in which the West Bank is referred to as Judea and Samaria, and the Palestinian flag and Koranic references have been removed from textbooks.

In the West Bank
Children in the West Bank face similar difficulties. The following factsheet[3] from the Ecumenical Accompaniment Programme in Palestine and Israel sums up the situation. Though the facts relate to 2014, nothing had improved by 2015.

SUMMARY:

Palestinian schoolchildren's access to education is greatly restricted due to the following human rights violations that direct results of Israel's military occupation of Palestine:

Attacks: The UN Monitoring and Reporting Mechanism (MRM) noted that in 2014 there were 104 attacks on education in Palestine, which directly affected 15,787 students. These attacks were committed by the Israeli military and Israeli settlers, and included: acts of vandalism, acts of harassment and/or physical violence towards Palestinian students on their commutes to and from school; military raids on schools; usage of

---

3 www.eappi.org/en/resources/factsheets/access-to-education/view

schools as interrogation and/or detention centers; and firing of teargas, stun-grenades, rubber bullets and live ammunition in and around school premises.

Demolitions: Palestinians are largely prohibited by the Israeli Civil Administration [ICA] to build structures in Area C of the West Bank [62% of the WB] and East Jerusalem. Thus, to cope with population growth, communities are forced to build houses and schools without Israeli-issued permits. The ICA, a branch of the Israeli Military renders these structures illegal and frequently demolishes them.[4]

Closures: Everyday, students throughout the West Bank must pass through military checkpoints to get to school. Some of these checkpoints are static in location, while others are randomly setup in front of schools. At these checkpoints Israeli soldiers search students' belongings and often harass them. Many of these children must also cross dangerous settler bypass roads, walk through military zones, and even firing zones to make it to school. In 2014, 63 incidents of denial of access to education were documented in Palestine affecting more than 4854 students.

The problems noted above have resulted in a reduction in time for learning; poorer academic achievements; a lack of attendance; and increased dropout rates. It is also reported that parents are increasingly pulling their children out of school due to the dangers that they face during their commutes. Girls are disproportionally affected, as they are more likely to stop attending school when faced with harassment or physical abuse. Yet, harassment, violence and arrests largely affect boys.

---

4   On 31 August 2015, for example, Israeli forces came to deliver a 'stop work' notice for a school in the Manafer Yatta area (within the infamous Area C) of the Hebron Hills. The school – a collection of caravans, in reality – was to have served a small community of some 4000 inhabitants.

UNRWA schools

The United Nations Relief and Works Agency for Palestine Refugees in the Near East is responsible for the education of 493,000 students in the Gaza strip, the West Bank, Syria, Lebanon and Jordan.

According to their website:

In Gaza, 252 UNRWA schools serve over 240,400 students. These children grow up in bleak conditions, frequently surrounded by poverty and violence. School provides them with one place where they are able to learn the skills for a better future.

Years of underfunding have left the education system in Gaza overstretched, with 94 per cent of schools operating on a double-shift basis, hosting one 'school' of students in the morning and a different group in the afternoon. As a result, children's education is severely truncated. In 2006 examinations, nearly 80 per cent of students failed mathematics, and more than 40 per cent failed Arabic.

In the West Bank, UNRWA provides only preparatory education; secondary students matriculate into national schools. Nonetheless, we operate 97 educational facilities in the field, which reach over 50,000 students. The Agency also operates two vocational training centres, where over 1,000 students are trained in skilled trades and manufacturing.

Young Palestine refugees, many of them students, have been especially vulnerable to the effects of the conflict in Syria. Because the majority of UNRWA schools are located within the Palestine refugee camps themselves – in areas that have suffered serious violence – one of the most pernicious of these effects has been a disruption in their education.

Before the outbreak of the conflict, all of the 118 UNRWA schools in Syria were running on double shifts to provide around 67,300 students with primary and secondary education, following the Syrian curriculum. Violence, damage, closures and other factors, however, have left only 42 of those 118 schools operational as of March 2014. Some of these schools are now operating three shifts. We are also educating some of our students at 43 government schools, which the Ministry of Education has agreed to let UNRWA use in the afternoons.

In total, we have enrolled around 44,000 young Palestine refugees – around 70 per cent of the pre-conflict total.

Lebanon is the only field where we offer secondary education. In total, we serve 38,173 students at 68 schools throughout the country. UNRWA also operates one vocational training centres, which reach 1,143 students.

In Jordan, UNRWA provides basic education to over 118,500 students at

174 UNRWA schools. Students in the fourth, eighth and tenth grades take national quality-control tests in the core subjects – Arabic, English, science and maths – and consistently achieve better results than students from private or government schools.

We are also excited to be able to provide university education in teaching, Arabic and English to about 1,200 students through the Faculty of Educational Sciences and Arts.

From which it can be clearly seen that UNRWA plays a key role in the education of Palestinian children. In 2015, however, the agency faced a severe crisis: in August, as the start of the 2015/2016 school year approached, the agency was $101 million (about £66,600,000) short of the sum needed for its schools to open on time. Parents and teachers organised demonstrations across the occupied territories as the deadline approached. Children feared the genuine possibility that their schools, and with that their already slim chances for the future, would remain shut.

By 19 August, some $80 million had been pledged, mainly from wealthy Arab states, but with $15 million from the US and smaller sums from Switzerland, Britain, Norway, Sweden and the Slovak Republic. The schools could re-open, but with classes of up to 50, and an average of 41 or 42. In an interview with IRIN, UNRWA Commissioner-General Pierre Krähenbühl pointed out,

> I need everybody to understand that this is not just another financial deficit year, it's a year where we came much closer than we ever should have to having the school year delayed – not because of war like last year in Gaza – but a funding shortfall. That should never have happened…

> What we saw with the education program is reducing the services to Palestinian refugees and failing to address their dignity and other aspects of their rights is a risk the world can't take, because not only is there an issue in and of itself of the unresolved conflict here between Israel and Palestine with the occupation and all the rest, but there is also an instability in the Middle East that should lead people to reflect very, very carefully on the costs of reducing the services currently available to Palestinian refugees, who already have very limited prospects in life and a very challenging future.

To which we must add the fact that many of Gaza's schools, like the rest of its infrastructure, remain damaged and unusable after the repeated assaults on the enclave.

Child prisoners

"Who will the judge send to prison? He who demolished the home, seized the land, killed the brother, or the boy who threw a stone?"
Palestinian MK [Member of the Knesset] Jamal Zahalka, on the bill extending the sentence for stone-throwing to a maximum of 20 years

According to Israeli human rights group B'Tselem, between 2005 and 2010, "93 per cent of the minors convicted of stone throwing were given a prison sentence, its length ranging from a few days to 20 months." The current, extremist government of Israel, however, is now contemplating new laws under which there would be a mandatory minimum penalty for stone throwing of four years, and the child's parents would be stripped of social benefits (bear in mind the high levels of unemployment among Palestinians).

Children in the occupied territories live under two separate systems. If they are the children of Jewish illegal settlers, they are subject to Israeli civil and criminal law, with the safeguards and protections that one would expect. (And it is safe to assume that no Jewish child, in Israel or in the occupied territories, will face a four-year sentence for throwing stones at a Palestinian.) Palestinian children are subject to the Palestinian authorities but also, more crucially, they fall under Israeli military law. This means that they are prosecuted in military courts that lack the normal procedures of a fair trial.

They can be imprisoned from the age of 12 (the current Israeli government plans to approve custodial sentences within Israel itself for children of 12 and over who commit 'nationalistically motivated' crimes).

Palestinian children are the most vulnerable detainees and are subject to psychological and physical harm during relatively brief periods of detention. As of February 2015, 182 Palestinian children were being held as 'security prisoners' in Israeli prisons. Between 500 and 700 children are prosecuted in the Israeli military courts each year, most commonly for the 'security offense' of stone throwing. A September 2014 military order to reform court requirements to include use of audio-video recordings and standardize language during interrogations does not apply for security offenses.

The international community has highlighted the serious violations of rights against Palestinian minors in Israeli prisons. The **European Neighborhood Policy** progress report on Israel of March 2015 noted particular concern over reports of "blindfolding, painful hand-ties, physical violence, lack of adequate notification of legal rights, verbal abuse, strip searches and solitary confinement while under interrogation." The **UN Human Rights Committee's** concluding observations in November 2014 that the implementation of reforms by the Israeli government was not effective, and that minors remained exposed to arbitrary arrest and detention and denied full procedural rights.

The international community has repeatedly called on Israel to address these issues faced by Palestinian minors in detention. According to the **UN Special Rapporteur on Torture's** report in March 2015: "the unique vulnerability of children deprived of their liberty requires higher standards and broader safeguards for the prevention of torture and ill-treatment." However, to this day, Israel has no legislation that establishes or prohibits torture as a crime, as obligated in the UN human rights treaties to which Israel is a party.

Recommendations

The four human rights organizations: call upon the international community to demand that Israel incorporate the international recommendations of the UN and EU bodies in order to address the deteriorating human rights conditions of Palestinian prisoners and to end its violations of international law. We demand that Israel cease its systematic use of administrative detention as a mechanism of deterrence and punishment against Palestinian society, and interference with political processes. We demand that Israel end the practice of torture and ill-treatment against Palestinian prisoners, and end the severe tactics of arrest and detention of Palestinian minors, including abuse that amounts to torture and CIDT. We further demand that Israel revokes all discriminatory legislation that target the rights of Palestinians in Israeli prisons, and that it ensures transparency and accountability of Israeli

---

security and prison authorities.

Signing organizations:
Adalah - The Legal Center for Arab Minority Rights in Israel
Al Mezan Center for Human Rights
Physicians for Human Rights-Israel (PHR-I)
Public Committee Against Torture in Israel (PCATI)

PROJECT FUNDED BY THE EUROPEAN UNION -
JOINT PROJECT OF ADALAH, PHYSICIANS FOR HUMAN RIGHTS-ISRAEL
AND AL MEZAN (GAZA)

The contents of this joint statement are the sole responsibility of Adalah, Al Mezan, PHR-I and PCATI and under no circumstances should be regarded as reflecting the position of the European Union

---

To summarise: the basic human rights of Palestinian children are routinely violated in a number of ways.

- They are often simply grabbed off the street by soldiers and arrested without their parents' knowledge.

- The arrest frequently takes the form of a military raid on their home in the small hours of the morning.

- Children continue to be routinely denied the presence of their parents during interrogation.

- They are frequently denied the presence of a lawyer; in fact for many children the first they see of their lawyer is during the trial itself.

- They are often beaten during arrest and/or interrogation; during arrest and transfer, for instance, many children are tied, thrown onto the floor of the vehicle and kicked; they may be blindfolded (78 per cent of cases, according to UNICEF); their hands may be painfully tied (91 per cent); they may be forced into stress positions.

- They are frequently threatened – that their parents or siblings will be made to suffer, for example, or that they will be beaten or tortured (no idle threat) or sexually assaulted.

- They are usually not informed of their rights.

- Interviews are not automatically audio-visually recorded and a copy made available to the defence.

- They may be denied toilet facilities for long periods of time.

- They are bullied and tricked – by being told that others have confessed and accused them, or that they will be freed if they confess and so on.

- Children have been made to sign 'confessions' in Hebrew, which they do not understand.

- Their parents are frequently made to pay substantial fines to secure their release.

- Courts rarely grant bail to Palestinian children.

- They are often imprisoned far from their homes: some 60 per cent, according to Defence for Children International-Palestine are transferred to prisons in Israel, where it is difficult for their parents to obtain permits for them to visit.

- The military judges are either active or reserve army officers and rarely exclude evidence obtained through torture or coercion.

- They may be kept for long periods in solitary confinement.

Most of the arrested children are teenagers, but some are even younger. On 28 April, for example, ten undercover operatives seized 7-year-old Ihab Ahmed Zaatari and his 12-year-old brother Muhammad Mahdi off the street in East Jerusalem (there was nothing happening at the time, so this was a pre-planned arrest). The two were forced into a car and taken to a police station where they were interrogated. Their parents were refused entry into the station, as was their lawyer. According to *Maan News*, their father reported that they were kept without food or water until the younger child was released at around 3am and the elder at 7am.

On 5 October, soldiers arrived at the home of Muhammad Jamal al-Jaabri in the al-Ras neighbourhood of Hebron and accused his son Yousef of stone-throwing. They ransacked the house and threatened to arrest the boy. Eventually, they left without arresting the three-year-old…

Efforts to improve the situation for child prisoners and bring their treatment in line with international law have so far met with little success. For older boys, arrest and detention is a terrifying experience. In October, Hussein al-Sheikh, a lawyer for the PA Committee for Prisoners' Affairs, was allowed to visit detainees in Israel's Etzion detention centre and was appalled by what he found. Muhammad Jamal Khalaf (14), Wadee Nasser al-Jundi (15), Muhammad Salih Ghur (17), Asif Dakhlallah Umour (14) and Abd al-Majid Younis Jaafra (16) bore scars on their hands and faces where they had been bitten by police dogs. Another boy, 16-year-old Asim Muhammad Abu Eisha had bled after being hit on the head, but had not received medical treatment.

In November, a lawyer for the Commission of Prisoners and Freed Prisoners' Affairs in Palestine, Hiba Masalha, revealed terrible accounts of Palestinian minors tortured inside Israeli gaols to Palestinian newspaper *Al-Resalah*. One of the minors, 15-year-old Baraa Mashhour from Abu-Dis, East Jerusalem, was arrested on 19 September. Mashhour says he was arrested in the evening near his house, where there were clashes between Israeli troops and Palestinian youth. Mashhour claims that seven Israeli soldiers assaulted him, beating him with their hands, feet, steel-capped boots and rifle butts. He says one of the soldiers beat his right hand dozens of times with the butt of his rifle while he was on the ground. Then he was lifted up and handcuffed with plastic clips that were tied tightly. Mashhour was made to walk with the troops to a nearby military camp, where he was blindfolded and beaten again.

Three hours later, he was taken to the settlement of Ma'ale Adumim. There, he was interrogated before being taken to another settlement for a medical check. The following day, Mashhour was taken to the hospital and had an X-ray of his right hand that showed multiple fractures from the beatings. Despite the need for a surgical operation, he was initially only supplied with a cast and eventually operated on eight days later. While he was in hospital, Mashhour was chained to the bed and interrogated for three consecutive hours.

Another young Palestinian boy, 15-year-old Mohamed Salahuddin, from the Hezma neighbourhood in North Jerusalem, was arrested by three Israeli policemen on 4 October in the al-Ram neighbourhood. The three policemen, says Salahuddin, assaulted him and beat him harshly with their hands, feet and rifle butts. He says he felt faint and coughed until he vomited. Then, he was shoved against a military Jeep, where he was handcuffed and insulted several times. Salahuddin was taken to an interrogation centre and his father was brought to witness the interrogation, which lasted for one hour. After the interrogation, he was left alone for six hours, blindfolded and with his hands and legs tied, before being taken to a cell, where he remained for nine days. He was then taken to Hasharon Prison, where he was strip-searched before entering the department dealing with minors.

By the end of October, the number of child prisoners had doubled and a new wing was opened to house some 60 children at Givon prison. Lawyers from human rights groups, including the Public Committee Against Torture in Israel, Addameer and Defense for Children International reported that the children said their cells were mouldy and cold, and they were being beaten and inadequately fed.

According to the Israeli Prison Service (IPS), as of 30 November 2015, there were 5,936 Palestinians (West Bank, East Jerusalem and Gaza) held as "security prisoners" in Israeli detention facilities including 407 children. In the case of children there was a 33 per cent increase in the number compared with the previous month and an annual increase of 7 per cent compared with 2014. According to the IPS, 56 per cent of Palestinian children and 88 per cent of adults continue to be detained in facilities inside Israel, in violation of the Fourth Geneva Convention and Rome Statute of the International Criminal Court. A further 27 children were held in IPS detention as "criminal prisoners". Criminal offences include entering Israel without a permit, most frequently in pursuit of work.

The figures do not include minors held for short periods of a few hours or days and then released.

The Israelis have made it clear that they intend to continue the practice of keeping prisoners, including children, in jails in Israel, in contravention of international law.

Growing tension – January to September

"If I'm elected, there will be no Palestinian state."

PM Netanyahu, 16 March 2015

Throughout the first three quarters of 2015, tensions grew steadily. Almost daily incursions into the Al Aqsa mosque compound by extremist religious settlers, accompanied by heavily armed troops, alarmed worshippers, who know that those same settlers wish to demolish the mosques and replace them with a Jewish temple.

In the West Bank and Jerusalem, demolitions, land theft, agricultural and commercial destruction, road blocks, settler attacks and army raids on towns, villages and refugee camps continued to make normal life impossible. In Gaza, the promised easing of restrictions did not happen; instead the blockade continued unabated, Israeli ceasefire violations occurred on an almost daily basis, and much of the aid that had been promised in Cairo the previous year had not materialised. In Israel itself, Palestinians continued to be treated very much as second class citizens: Bedouin in the Negev faced enforced 'resettlement', school children suffered inferior education, unemployment was sky high, and many continued to live without any access to state benefits.

These ongoing causes of tension are covered elsewhere. Together, they combined to ratchet up fear and anger among Palestinians. Below, we will consider two more elements in the toxic brew that was to explode in an outburst of violence – on the part of Israelis and Palestinians – in October.

Israeli elections

This book is not primarily about Israelis, but elections in Israel are of critical importance to Palestinians, whether or not they can take part. On 17 March, elections were held for the twentieth Knesset. On his Facebook page, in a last-minute appeal to voters, Netanyahu stated: "The right-wing government is in danger. The Arabs are going to the polls in droves. Left-wing NGOs are bringing them on buses."

Prior to March, Israel's electoral law had been changed. Israel allocates seats under a system of proportional representation. Formerly, a party had to acquire 2 per cent of the vote in order to be represented. In the previous Knesset, the threshold had been raised to 3.25 per cent. As Palestinians form less than 20 per cent of the electorate, many of them saw this as an attempt to prevent 'Arab' parties from gaining any seats. The move had been pushed for by Yair Lapid (who promotes settlement expansion and the annexation of Jerusalem, claims that the Palestinians are to blame for the failed peace process, and has stated "We're not looking for a happy marriage with the Palestinians, but for a divorce agreement we can live with."). The other chief instigator was then Foreign Minister Avigdor Lieberman (who believes the Palestinians should be expelled from Israel).

In order to ensure seats, therefore, the Palestinians combined to form a Joint List. Lieberman's reaction was to state on Israeli TV: "There is no difference between the Communists, the Islamists and the Nasserists. What unites them is hatred of the State of Israel, and they represent the terrorist organizations in the Knesset." He and his party (Yisrael Beiteinu/ Israel our Home) promptly filed a motion to disqualify the Joint List, and specifically MK Haneen Zoabi, from taking part in the elections. The motion was approved by the Central Elections Committee, but failed when the case was brought to the High Court.

As the election campaign wore on, Palestinians were to witness a barrage of racist comments. One of Leiberman's slogans was "Ariel to Israel, Umm al-Fahm to Palestine" – in other words, settlements such as Ariel should be annexed and become part of Israel and the 1.7 million or so Palestinians of Israel should be expelled to, presumably, some form of Palestinian Bantustan. When, on TV, Ayman Odeh, head of the Joint List, reminded viewers that Palestinians form 20 per cent of the population, Lieberman (born in Russia) replied "For now."

On 3 March, right-wingers threw liquid over Zoabi at a forum on women in politics and one of her consultants was attacked with metal rods on exiting and had to be hospitalised. Extremist Baruch Marzel commented on Facebook: "We promised, we fulfilled, we will continue…" Attempts to disqualify Marzel – "I will encourage their [Palestinians 'disloyal' to a Jewish Israel] emigration… I am sure that it's possible to arrange that a great part of our enemies will not be here. There are ways…" – from standing for the elections had also failed.

As election day drew near, settler militant Sagi Kaisler organised 1,500 settlers, armed with sticks, guns, tear gas and other weapons, to act as volunteers in polling stations in 'Arab' areas. His justification for this was "Wherever there are Arab villages, there is fraud. This is the way they work. They do this in their local elections, they are not doing this against the state, it is in their nature … the [Arab] Joint List united in order to pass the electoral threshold, but primarily because they are evil parties that want to overthrow the rightwing government … We are in a battle for the future of our state, against Arabs, against Europeans and against some American forces."

The outcome, when a coalition government was finally patched together in May, was an extremist government dominated by settler parties, such as Naftali Bennett's Jewish Home (HaBayit HaYehudi). Bennett, who became Minister for Education, has made his position quite clear with remarks like:

> If you catch terrorists, you have to simply kill them … I've **killed lots of Arabs** in my life – and there's no problem with that.

> There is **not going to be** a Palestinian state … It's just not going to happen. A Palestinian state would be a disaster for the next 200 years.

> Building [illegal settlements in the West Bank] **is our answer** to murder.

> (Editorial comment: not building settlements would be a much better answer!)

Bennett's fellow party member, Ayelet Shaked, mentioned elsewhere for advocating the mass killing of civilians in Gaza, became Justice Minister.

Another party member was the new Deputy Minister for Defence, Rabbi Eli Ben-Dahan, who lives in the illegal settlement of Har Homa. According to the rabbi, "[Palestinians] are beasts, they are not human."

Likud's Tzipi Hotovely was to become Deputy Foreign Affairs Minister. Pro-settlement, pro-annexation of the West Bank, Hotovely advocates assassination: "Israel must declare a war of annihilation of Hamas … and return to the assassination policy."

Deaths

Which brings us to the question of those who died in the run up to October's increase in violence. While we are not suggesting that any individual deaths should be laid at Hotovely's door, it should be emphasised that it is highly probable that none of these would have occurred were there any prospect of a just peace, an end to the Israeli military occupation and blockading of Palestinians in Gaza, and the establishment of a state or states in which Palestinians and Israelis enjoyed equal rights, including the right of return and, moreover, if Israel became a state in which racism (including racism masquerading as religion) was banned from public discourse.

Below is a list of those who died as a result of this appalling situation in the first three quarters of 2015.

14 January: Osama Jundiyya, 17 years-old, from Yatta in the West Bank, was walking with a friend near the Gush Etzion Junction between Bethlehem and Hebron. The Israelis claimed that the two were stealing a car from a supermarket car park in a nearby Jewish-only settlement and Osama and his friend were shot while attempting to run away (which appears in their eyes to have justified the killing). Palestinian sources later claimed that Israeli soldiers prevented an ambulance from reaching the seriously-wounded boy before he died.

14 January: 20-year-old Sami al-Ja'aar, a Bedouin citizen of Israel, was shot during clashes between locals and police, who later claimed to be operating against drug dealers in the area. He was taken to hospital but died of his wounds. Sami was standing on the patio of his home at the time he was shot.

19 January: Sami Ibrahim Zayadna, aged 45, was attending Sami al-Ja'aar's funeral in the Bedouin city of Rahat when the police chose to appear in force and attack mourners, despite an earlier agreement that they would stay away. Raed Salah, head of the Islamic Movement in Rahat, was delivering the eulogy when the police appeared, firing tear gas and plastic bullets at mourners. Sami Zayadna died of tear gas inhalation. Over 40 other people were injured. The Negev-Co-existence Forum later stated: "This is part of a pattern of Israeli provocation and escalation. Al Arakib village was recently destroyed for the eightieth

time. The organisation is now calling for Israel's Attorney General to establish an Independent Commission of Inquiry for the Killing of two Bedouin Citizens by the Police." A general strike was called in protest at the two deaths. Bedouin MK Talab Abu Arar called on Palestinians in the army and security services to "take off their uniforms and quit".

31 January: Ahmad Ibrahim Jaber Abu al-Azzah, aged 19, was shot while with a group throwing Molotov cocktails at settler vehicles driving on a bypass road near the village of Burin, Nablus area.

25 February: 19-year-old Jihad Shehada al-Jaafari was standing on the roof of his family's home during a pre-dawn arrest raid on Bethlehem's Duheisha refugee camp. An Israeli spokeswoman later claimed that the soldiers had been met with stones and Molotov cocktails and had opened fire in self defence, killing 'the leader' of the rioters. An autopsy revealed that an M16 bullet had entered through his left shoulder and penetrated his lungs, causing massive internal bleeding. The report claimed that the shot was fired at close range and was "similar to an execution".

7 March: Tawfiq Abu Riyala, aged 37, a Gaza fisherman, was shot dead by the Israeli navy, who alleged that he had strayed outside the permitted limit and was warned before being shot. His brother claimed that he had been building an artificial reef from planks, metal and tyres, well within the limit, in order to attract the fish. (Most of the valuable, fish-attracting underwater rock formations are outside the limit.) He owed money for the loan on his two boats and so had sailed out that day to continue working on his plan, despite escalating Israeli aggression against fisherman.

25 March: Ali Mahmoud Safi, aged 20, was shot on 18 March during a protest in al-Jalazun refugee camp near Ramallah against a separation wall being built to protect the settlers of Beit El. He was hit in the chest with a 22 caliber tutu bullet, which caused massive internal bleeding. A former political prisoner and a member of the Popular Front for the Liberation of Palestine, his funeral was widely attended.

8 April: Muhammad Jasser Ibrahim Karakrah, aged 27, stabbed two soldiers at the Sinjil Junction, which is near the Israeli settlement of

Shilo and was shot dead.

10 April: 22-year-old former prisoner Jaafar Ibrahim Awad, from Hebron, died from severe pneumonia, heart problems, and thyroid and pancreas complications which had been neglected during his time in jail. He had spent a total of three years in prison and, although severely ill, had only been released on payment of a fine of 40,000 shekels (£6,748).

10 April: Ziyad Awad, aged 27, was shot and killed at Jaafer's funeral, which took place the same day. Thirteen others were injured.

15 April: an Israeli, Shalom Sherki, aged 25, was killed when Khaled Koutineh, aged 37, from the West Bank town of Anata, drove his car into group waiting at a bus stop in Jerusalem. His father, Rabbi Uri Sherki, believes that Palestinians should have no political rights but should be declared 'resident aliens'. Prior to his son's death he had declared his support for Bennett's Jewish Home Party.

25 April: Muhammad Abu Ghannam, aged 17, was shot at Za'im checkpoint, east of occupied Jerusalem, just after midnight. The Israelis claimed that he had attempted to stab a soldier and had then tried to run away. The Palestinians admit that he had quarrelled with the soldiers, but his mother stated that he did not have a knife and had gone out to attend a wedding party. Witnesses claimed that Red Crescent medical crews had been prevented from taking him to a nearby hospital and he had bled to death. Clashes ensued in the neighbourhoods of al-Tur and al-Issawiya and some 20 people were injured.

25 April: Muhammad Yihya Yunes Aby Jheishah stabbed a soldier near the Ibrahimi Mosque/the Tomb of the Patriachs, Hebron, where Baruch Goldstein murdered 29 Palestinian worshippers in 1994. The previous week, settlers had raised the Israeli flag above the mosque to provoke the Palestinians.

28 April: Muhammad Yahiya, aged 18, died of a shot in the stomach sustained the previous day. The Israelis claimed he had been trying to breach Israel's 'security fence' in al-Araqa village in western Jenin.

20 May: Omran Omar Abu Dheim, a 41-year-old school bus supervisor with five children –Rasha, 14, Hamza, 11, Raghad, 9, Hala, 6 and Muhammad, 16 months old – had left home and 8.30 and was driving to work. The Israelis claimed that he was attempting to run down border guards, leaving them 'moderately injured', when he was shot. An eyewitness told his brother that Omran was trying to make a U-turn but was blocked by a truck unloading vegetables. An argument broke out between him and the Israeli soldiers on each side of the road and they opened fire. Although he was near two hospitals, eyewitnesses claimed he was pulled out of the truck and left for half an hour with no first aid. The Israelis confiscated surveillance cameras before their shop-keeper owners could check the footage. His wife confirmed that Omran was not interested in politics and his daughter Rasha, who learned of his death on Facebook, said "The soldiers killed my compassionate father. They stole him from us."

•

On 25 May, UN Special Coordinator (UNSCO) for the Middle East peace process issued a statement that the current untenable status quo "will inexorably lead to the continued erosion of living conditions for Palestinians and for Israelis alike and will undermine the security and stability of all." In a report presented to the Ad Hoc Liaison Committee (AHLC) at the bi-annual meeting in Brussels on 27 May, the coordinator called for the new Israeli government to confirm its commitment to the two-state solution and halt settlement expansion. It commented on the lack of building permits in Area C of the West Bank and the financial instability of the Palestinian Authority, and reiterated the call for the blockade of Gaza to be ended. The report also commented on the rise of violence in East Jerusalem and the settlement expansion there. It highlighted "the extent of the frustrations that grips the Palestinian population after almost 50 years of occupation".

•

10 June: 20-year-old Izz al-Din Walid Bani Gharra was shot in the chest during a dawn raid by Israeli army forces on the Jenin refugee camp in the northern West Bank. The Israelis claimed that he had thrown an explosive device at them as they were leaving. He was hailed as

a martyr by Hamas. His mother said, "I lost everything after Izz was killed; it was a shock; my son Izz loves life and he loves Palestine. Israel killed him in cold blood." (*Ma'an News*) By now, some 900 Palestinians had been injured by Israeli forces in 2015, according to UNOCHA, and many more had been injured by settlers.

14 June: at about 4am, 21-year-old Abdullah Iyad Ghanayim was returning from work at his uncle's poultry farm to his home in the West Bank town of Kufr Malik. The army constantly make their presence felt here. The Israeli account claims that he threw a Molotov cocktail at a military vehicle causing it to flip over and crush him. An accident, therefore. An eyewitness, also his cousin, told a journalist from *Electronic Intifada* that "the soldiers were singing and cheering in the jeep while women were crying and trying to get closer to see the body." Abdullah had spent two years in Ofer military prison for stone throwing. While there, he had successfully completed his matriculation. A Palestinian prisoner in the jeep allegedly claimed that the soldiers were shouting "aim at him" when the jeep hit Abdullah. Whatever the truth, he was left screaming in pain, with fuel and oil dripping on his severely-injured body, while the soldiers preventing the locals from lifting the jeep off him until 6.30am. It appears the soldiers kept pointing at his house and asking "Do you have anybody missing?", and his family believe he was targeted directly.

19 June: Danny Gonen, a citizen of Lod in Israel, was shot while driving near the illegal settlement of Dolev in the Ramallah district. A Palestinian called the car over and then shot Danny and his companion with a handgun. By this time, an average of two Israelis per week had been injured in 2015 and Shalom Sherki and Danny killed, in comparison with 39 Palestinians injured per week and 13 killed. Netanyahu commented on Twitter: "We can't let the relative quiet achieved thanks to many successfully prevented attacks mislead us." The following month, the Israeli police arrested the men behind the attack.

27 June: Hammad Jom'a Romanim, aged 27 and a taxi driver from al-'Oja village, was heading towards Nablus. Israeli soldiers claim that he opened fire on them and they shot back, wounding him. He died shortly after of his wounds.

30 June: an Israeli, 27-year-old Moshe Malachi Rosenfeld, from the illegal Kochav Hashahar settlement, died of wounds received the previous day when a gunmen in a passing car opened fire on group near the illegal Shvut Rahel settlement. One of his injured companions later said "We need to be safe in our country, in every place in the country. A Jew needs to feel safe in his country." Naftali Bennett at his funeral stated: "We play by the rules of Jewish morals and they behave like savages. We risk our lives not to hurt the innocent, while they risk their lives to hurt the innocent. Our enemy is not like us, they are not a member of the family of nations… If there is such a thing as a settler, then we are all settlers."

3 July: 17-year-old Muhammad Hani al-Kasbah was shot twice and killed after allegedly throwing stones at a military vehicle Qalandiya checkpoint, south of Ramallah, and damaging the windscreen. The vehicle contained General Yisrael Shomer, the commander of the Binyamin Brigade, who got out and shot the teenager. Witnesses claimed that he had not been among the stone throwers, but was intending to climb the annexation wall in order to attend prayers at Al Aqsa mosque. An Israeli spokesperson initially said that Muhammad had approached the vehicle and started throwing rocks; warning shots had been fired, but he had then continued to approach and had been shot. An officer in Central Command told Israeli newspaper *Haaretz* that Shomer "did what he had to do due to threat to his life." As the dead boy's father said "The youth throw rocks every day. They throw rocks and the soldiers keep driving. But on this day? An Israeli general gets out of his jeep and shoots my son. Why?" Later, a video emerged which shows Kasbah running away from the vehicle, though it does not show the final shots. Medical examination confirmed that he was shot in the side and the back. His two brothers, Yasser and Samer, had been killed by the Israeli army in the Qalandiya refugee camp in May 2002 during the Second Intifada.

22 July: Muhammad Ahmad Alawneh, 21, died in hospital after being shot with a live bullet in his chest. It happened during an arrest raid in Birqin town, west of Jenin in the occupied West Bank. The Palestinian youths had responded with stones, Molotov cocktails and burning tyres. The Israelis claimed that they had used tear gas and rubber-coated bullets, but no live ammunition. Either way, he was dead.

23 July: 53-year-old Falah Hammad Abu Maria died in hospital after being shot twice in the chest in his own home in the town of Beit Ummar in northern Hebron after soldiers broke in and shot his 22-year-old son, Muhammad, twice in the pelvis. His other son, Ahmad, aged 25, was also injured with schrapnel. His wife claimed that Falah was shot in cold blood when he had run to an upstairs balcony to call for an ambulance. He may have thrown a pottery jar at the Israelis, but had no dangerous weapon. Having killed him and injured his sons, the soldiers left without making an arrest. Eight more people were injured when troops attacked with rubber-coated bullets and tear gas at his funeral, which took place the same day.

27 July: Muhammad Abu Latifa, aged 18, was shot on the roof of his house while he was attempting to run away during an arrest raid in the Qalandiya refugee camp near Ramallah. Muhammad, a Fatah supporter, had served six months in Israeli detention in 2013, charged with firing a gun in the air during a funeral. He had frequently joined other youths in defending the camp against incursions by Israeli troops. The Israelis claimed that a paramedic had attempted to save him, but his father claimed that he was deliberately left to bleed to death. At his funeral, 14 Palestinians were injured by the Israelis, 6 of them with live fire.

31 July: Ali Saad Dawabsha, just 18 months old, was burned alive after Israeli settlers set fire to his home in Duma.

31 July: 17-year-old Laith al-Khaldi from the Jalazone refugee camp near Ramallah was shot in the chest during clashes near the Atara checkpoint. Israeli sources claimed he had thrown a Molotov cocktail at soldiers who had fired in response. He later died at the Palestine Medical Complex near Ramallah.

31 July: 17-year-old Mohammad Hamid al-Masri was walking with a friend near the buffer zone near Beit Lahiya in northern Gaza when soldiers opened fire on them. He died instantly. The Israelis later claimed that warning shots had been fired and the soldiers had fired at "their lower extremities" after which they had walked away.

8 August: Saad Dawabsha, father of little Ali, who died on 31 July, also

died of his burns.

9 August: 20-year-old Anas Muntaser Taha was shot dead after he allegedly stabbed a 26-year-old Israeli settler who was filling his car at a petrol station near Ofer checkpoint on Route 443, southwest of Ramallah in the occupied West Bank.

15 August: Rafeeq Kamil Rafeeq al-Taj, aged 21, was shot five times after he stabbed a Border Police officer near Beita in southern Nablus. Red Crescent medics tried to save him, but he died of his injuries. The officer was lightly wounded. Two days earlier, another Palestinian had allegedly tried to stab an Israeli soldier.

17 August: Mohammed Amsha Atrash, aged 24, according to the Israelis, approached a Border Police Officer at Zaatara military checkpoint asking for a drink of water, then pulled out a knife and attempted to stab the officer, who was lightly injured. Atrash was shot dead. His family vehemently denied the Israeli account. Mohammed and his twin brother were building houses together and planned to get married on the same day. Mahmoud claimed "Mohammed didn't carry a knife. I would know if he had a knife and Mohammed didn't." Mohammed was not political but was apparently the family jester, and the one who took the blame when the two got into scrapes. He had dropped out of school to help his father, who had heart trouble, and was paying to put his younger sister through college. His mother pointed out that since the army had changed the rules of engagement to say that soldiers could only shoot if their life was threatened, there had been a spate of stabbing attack allegations, giving soldiers the excuse to shoot.

6 September: Riham Dawabsha also died from her burns.

13 September: an Israeli, Alexander Levlovitch, aged 64, a resident of Jerusalem, died of injuries sustained when his car crashed after stones were thrown at it and he lost control. Five teenagers were later charged with manslaughter.

21 September: Diyaa Abdul-Halim Talahmah, aged 21, died during an Israeli raid near the village of Khursa, in southern Hebron. The

Israelis claim he was killed when an IED he was carrying exploded. The Palestinians claim he was shot.

22 September: 18-year-old Hadeel al-Hashlamon, a student, was passing through a checkpoint in Hebron when, according to the Israeli version of events, a metal detector went off, a soldier called on her to stop and fired warning shots on the ground but she continued. The Israeli account claims that he then fired at her legs, but she raised a knife and the soldier shot her in self defence. Not so, according to Israeli rights group B'Tselem and Amnesty International. Even if she was, or may have been, carrying a knife (Palestinian witnesses say she was not), at the time she was shot a metal barrier separated Hadeel and the soldier. The soldier, it seems, was shouting at her in Hebrew, which the frightened girl did not understand, and Fawaz Abu Aisha, a local resident who was also there, tried to intervene to translate and calm the situation but was told to leave. After being shot in the legs, she fell, and it was then, when she was completely incapacitated, that the soldier fired at her torso. Video footage shows that she was then left to bleed for some 30 minutes before being dragged away by the feet as soldiers and settlers looked on. Amnesty concluded: "…the killing… was an extrajudicial execution… Pictures of the stand-off that led to her death and accounts by eyewitnesses interviewed by Amnesty International show that she at no time posed a sufficient threat to the soldiers to make their use of deliberate lethal force permissible."

Two days later, Netanyahu's office made an announcement:

> The security cabinet has decided to authorize police to use live ammunition against people throwing stones and Molotov cocktails when the life of a third person is threatened and no longer only when the police officer is threatened. We have decided to penalize more severely adult stone-throwers with a minimum sentence of four years in prison and also to authorize larger fines for minors and their parents. These sanctions apply to all Israeli citizens and residents of Israel [including residents of occupied East Jerusalem].

25 September: Ahmad Izzat Khatatbeh, aged 26, from Beit Furik village, died from wounds received during clashes at the Beit Furik checkpoint, near Nablus.

On Thursday 1 October, Eitam and Na'ama Henkin, an ultra-Orthodox Jewish couple were shot dead in the West Bank, and settlers, the IDF and Israel's extremist government responded with fury. Some 200 settlers, backed by the army, attempted to raid the town of Huwwara, Nablus area. Other towns and villages that came under attack included the village of Sinjil north of Ramallah, where settlers blocked the entrance to the village, attacked a home and smashed a car; armed settlers, with army support, stormed the northern entrance to Taquo, firing on residents and throwing stones, and the army occupied homes and set up sniper positions; at Al-Fanduq, armed settlers fired on and stoned several homes and vehicles; settlers stormed Burin village, stoning homes and vehicles, damaging an ambulance and setting fire to and destroying olive trees in the east of the village. The Israeli Army, firing stun and tear gas grenades at residents, took part in the attack. Other settler attacks took place at Far'ata, Kafr Laqif, Izbit Shufa, Awarta, al-Labban al-Sharqiya, Beit Anoun and near al-Faradis village. Ten Palestinians were injured by stone-throwing settlers near the Huwwara checkpoint and had to be hospitalised. The editor is not aware of any arrests of settlers. By Thursday night, the West Bank was under a virtual lock down

Hamas, while not claiming responsibility, stated "This operation [the murder of the Henkins] was in response to the crimes of the Zionists." The Popular Resistance Committees referred to the burning of the Dawabsha family and the killing of Hadeel (see above) and said the Israelis "needed a painful response to settlers to stop their terrorism against our people in the West Bank." Another Palestinian commentator referred to the incursions at Al Aqsa.

Israeli PM Netanyahu claimed the killing were "the effects of Palestinian incitement". In his funeral speech for the Henkins, President Rivlin re-affirmed Israel's claim to the West Bank and assured mourners that settlement construction would continue.

Lives and Deaths – a case study

"Revenge… Long live the Messiah King"
>   Words spray-painted on the house where Ali Dawabsha was burnt alive

In this section, we will look at two tragic events in which a total of five – three Palestinians and two Israelis – were murdered. We will consider the lives of the victims, the murderer of the Israelis and those who have been detained following the murder of the Palestinians. We will consider the background and motives behind these horrors and look at the outcomes: the contrasting reactions of the Israeli government in the two cases and the events that unfolded after the murders.

Settler attack

Duma is a small village – around 2,200 inhabitants in 2006 – in the Nablus region of the West Bank. It used to be largely agricultural, but now a sizable proportion of its workers are engaged in the construction industry. Most of the villagers have grown up under Israeli occupation. The chief threat hanging over Duma is the presence nearby of a cluster of so-called 'outposts'. Theoretically considered illegal, even under Israeli law, the outposts are generally established by religious extremists, determined to extend the Jewish hold over the West Bank by seizing Palestinian land and establishing new settlements. The young inhabitants of the outposts are responsible for a significant proportion of the violence against Palestinians. The track record shows, however, that the outposts are first declared illegal; feeble measures are sometimes taken against them, but they are provided with utilities by the Israeli government and are not demolished. After a while, they are then declared legal; Palestinian land is formally taken over, and full-scale settlement development begins.

The presence of the illegal settlers means that what should be a hard, simple, but in some ways idyllic life, of the sort the inhabitants of Duma and other small villages all around the Mediterranean have led for millennia, is continually under threat. On 24 April, for example, settler militants forced several shepherds off Duma land. Israeli soldiers, meanwhile, terrorised a 14-year-old boy, Mohammad Musalim, holding him captive for over three hours.

Worse was to come. In the early hours of Friday 31 July, the Dawabsha family, poor farmers, were asleep on mattresses on the floor in their humble single-storey home on the outskirts of the village. It was very hot, and they may have left the windows open. As they slept, Israeli settlers crept up to the house and threw in Molotov cocktails and flammable liquids. They left, having set fire to another house and scrawled 'Vengeance' and 'Long live the Messiah' on the walls of both houses. The mother, Riham Dawabsha, woke to find her husband, Saad, on fire. She and Saad managed to escape from the house with their four-year old son, Ahmad. Villagers rushed to help them, but their baby, Ali Saad Dawabsha, one-and-a-half years old, was trapped in the house and burned alive. Saad suffered burns on 80 per cent of his body; Riham had burns on over 90 per cent of her body and Ahmad 60 per cent.

A witness, Musallem Dawabsha, 23, told *Ma'an News*: "We saw four settlers running away keeping distance between each other. We tried to chase them but they fled to the nearby Maale Efrayim settlement."

What were the feelings of the arsonists as they approached Duma? Excitement? Fear? Perhaps not fear, for they surely believed that there was very little chance that, even if they were caught, they would be punished with any severity. When, on 27 July, a Palestinian bus driver suffered severe burns to his eyes and upper body after being pepper-sprayed by two settlers, Israeli rights group B'Tselem reported "rather than restricting violent settlers, Israeli security forces impose restrictions on the Palestinian… The undeclared policy of the Israeli authorities in response to these attacks is lenient and conciliatory."

Two days before, Shin Bet, Israel's internal security service, had announced the discovery of a manual in the car of a known extremist, Moshe Orbach, who is accused of being its author. Entitled *Kingdom of Evil*, it gives advice on how to attack churches, mosques and Palestinian homes, as well as beating up Palestinians. The manual also includes instructions for setting fire to a Palestinian house: "Stock up with a petrol bomb, preferably of a litre and a half; a lighter; gloves; a mask; a crowbar/hammer; a bag to carry it all. When you get to the village, search for a house with an open door or window without bars."

Orbach was under house arrest at the time of the Duma attack, but the Israel Religious Action Centre, part of the Israel Movement for Progressive Judaism, has been trying since 2012 to persuade the Attorney General to prosecute the rabbis who produced a similar volume, *The King's Torah*, which condones the killing of non-Jews, including babies.[1]

Speaking of Duma, Israeli Prime Minister Netanhayu promised to find the perpetrators of this 'terrorist act', while UN Secretary General Ban Ki-moon called for them to be brought swiftly to justice.

On 8 August, 30-year-old Saad Dawabsha died of his injuries. The morning of the same day, extremist settlers hurled two firebombs at the home of one Mahmoud Fazza al-Kaabna in Duma and threw stones at his house.

Riham lingered on, hovering between life and death while her mother stroked her and urged her to live. Sadly, she too died on Sunday, 6 September. She was just 27. On the following Tuesday, settlers attacked and injured Burhan Mustafa Amsha, 34, Muhammad Hussein al-Atrash, 23, and Tayseer Rashid al-Atrash, 78, as they were returning from visiting her grave.

The aftermath

Following such a horrific murder, one might have expected a full-blown enquiry and a crack-down on the illegal outposts close to Duma village. Prime Minister Netanyahu expressed horror, but could not resist proclaiming: "What distinguishes us from our neighbors is that we denounce and condemn murderers in our midst and pursue them until the end, while they name public squares after child murderers."[2]

On 5 August, the authorities arrested a Jewish extremist, Mordechai Meyer, aged 18. He was to be held under administrative detention for six months. He is not suspected of carrying out the Duma arson, but of involvement in the arson attack mentioned earlier on the Church of Loaves and Fishes on the shores of the Sea of Galilee.

The following week, two more extremists, Meir Ettinger, grandson of terrorist

---

1   "There is a reason to kill babies [on the enemy side] even if they have not transgressed the seven Noahide Laws because of the future danger they may present, since it is assumed that they will grow up to be evil like their parents."

2   Not exactly true, of course: Israel's international airport is named after David Ben Gurion, who helped plan and carry out the ethnic cleansing of Palestine; Netanyahu himself officiated at the ceremony to name a highway in Jerusalem after Yitzhak Shamir, responsible for the massacre of villagers at Deir Yassin, and in Tel Aviv, there's a park named after Ariel Sharon, who, among other things, carried out massacres in Al-Bureij refugee camp, in Gaza, and Qibya, in Jordan. All three men became Prime Ministers of Israel.

Rabbi Meir Kahane, and Eviatar Slonim, were also detained. Ettinger was believed to have been connected to groups carrying out so-called 'price tag' attacks on Palestinians. (In response to any move by the government against settlers, they attack Palestinian targets, leaving the message 'price tag' scrawled at the scene.) However, Ettinger has allegedly moved on to advocating full-scale revolt against the state with the aim of replacing it with a religious Jewish kingdom (shades of ISIS here) and with murder as a legitimate weapon. According the *Ynet News*, Slonim's American-born ultra-Orthodox parents were outraged at his arrest: "Mordechai studied Torah, liked all living beings, lives outdoors in Samaria [West Bank]… they had to arrest someone. According to what I know my son people believed in beauty, the idea of settling the land [ignoring the fact that it has been settled for thousands of years] and the infusion of God into his life." Honenu, the Zionist legal aid organisation representing him, states: "We firmly object to the use of administrative detention against Jews [sic]."

In response to media attention, Shin Bet also dutifully arrested seven suspects from the Baladim outpost and two more from the notorious Adei Ad on 9 August. The following day they were released.

And meanwhile what of Duma: have the residents been protected since the attack? The following day, 1 August, Israeli troops positioned at the entrance to the village fired rubber-coated bullets and stun and tear gas grenades at Palestinian protesters, injuring one Mohammad Bakr Dawabsheh. On 3 August, a settler mob attacked and overturned a vehicle near the Duma village road junction. On 5 August, along with several other houses and shops in Duma, the burnt house was raided by troops allegedly looking for evidence.

On 7 September, as Riham was buried, Palestinian spokeswomen, Hanan Ashrawi, accused the Israeli authorities of protecting rather than arresting the arsonists. On 7 and 11 September, the village was again raided by troops, who fired stun and tear gas grenades.

On 10 September, Israeli newspaper *Haaretz* reported that Israel's Defence Minister, Moshe Ya'alon, had now admitted that the establishment knows who carried out the attacks "but has chosen to prevent legal recourse in order to protect the identity of their sources."

Pressure on Israel to find and prosecute the perpetrators continued. Within

Israeli power echelons, a conflict began to emerge between ministers who support the ultra-religious settlers, such as the Minister for Justice, and the security service, Shin Bet. The latter clearly sees the extremists as a danger, their aim being the violent overthrow of the secular government.

Meanwhile, throughout the year, another murder case dragged on: three suspects were accused of murdering 16-year-old Mohammed Abu Khdeir in July 2014 by beating and choking him, pouring lighter fuel over him and down his throat and burning him alive. In July 2015, his father said that the Israeli authorities had forced the family to take down a large poster of their murdered son, which they had put outside their house. They had been told they would be fined 2,000 shekels (about £350) for every day they left it up. On 30 November, two minors and 31-year-old Yosef Haim Ben-David were found guilty. Ben-David's lawyers immediately claimed that he was insane at the time and therefore cannot be held responsible. The court, which had earlier found him fit to plead, agreed to consider this last-minute claim.

On 29 December, five Israelis, including a soldier, were arrested after a video of a wedding between two extremists 'went viral' on the internet. In the video, wedding guests are seen dancing, waving guns and knives and singing a revenge (against Palestinians) song. One guest waves a firebomb. A screen shows pictures of the Dawabsha family and another of the guests stabs the photo of the dead baby with a knife.

Finally, two suspects, one a minor, were charged with murder. There were immediate outcries from settler supporters that the suspects had been tortured by Shin Bet. It remains to be seen whether they will receive, and serve, an appropriate sentence. (The grandfather, Yitzhak Ganiram, of one suspect arrested during the course of the investigations was sentenced to seven years for offences back in the 1980s but was pardoned after serving three months.) If it turns out that they were tortured, it is quite possible that the evidence against them will be dismissed; they will not, of course, be tried, like Palestinians, in a military court where such evidence is admissible.

On 1 October, in response to a legal challenge by Israeli rights group Yesh Din, the government finally admitted that it is considering legalising five outposts, including the notorious Adei Ad, covering 2.4 square miles of Palestinian land; these are the very outposts which almost undoubtedly harbour the murderers. Yesh Din had argued that Adei Ad should be removed "not only because it is constructed illegally, in part on land owned privately by Palestinians, but also because it serves as a hub for criminal activities and grave violence, leading to systematic human rights violations of the Palestinian residents in its vicinity."

Two Israelis murdered

The second tragedy occurred on 3 October near the Lion's Gate in Jerusalem when a 19-year-old Palestinian, Mohanned Shafiq Halabi, from al-Bireh town, near Ramallah, attacked an Orthodox Jewish couple, killing the man, Aharon Bennett, aged 24 and injuring his wife Adele. Rabbi Nehemia Lavi, 41, who courageously came to their aid, also died in the attack after Halabi grabbed his gun. The Bennett's two-year-old was also injured, though lightly. Israeli soldiers shot Halabi dead on the spot.

The attack followed the double murder on 1 October, when two ultra-religious settlers were shot dead in a drive-by shooting when they were driving between Itamar and Elon Moreh settlements, near Nablus.

Rabbi Aharon Bennett, killed two days' later, was born in France but emigrated to Israel, which means that he had dual nationality, in contrast to Palestinian exiles living in refugee camps in Lebanon, for example, who have never been allowed to return to their homeland, modern Israel, but are not accepted as citizens where they live. Unlike some of the Orthodox, who choose not to serve in the army, he was an IDF soldier, promoted posthumously to corporal. He and his wife lived in Beitar Illit, an Haredi (ultra-Orthodox) settlement, founded in 1985, with the fastest growing birth rate in Israel and the occupied territories. (Haredi take the biblical injunction to 'go forth and multiply' very seriously. They are regarded as Israel's answer to the politely-named 'demographic threat': that Palestinians will in time out-number them.) The Haredi Jews have a history of clashing with secular Jews over such things as Sabbath opening hours and the segregation of men and women. In Beitar Illit, the buses are segregated and boys and girls are discouraged from being seen together in public. Haredi newspapers blot out pictures of women (notably, Merkel was erased from a photo taken after the Charlie Hebdo massacre).

Beitar Illit is one of those settlements that pollutes Palestinian farmland in the surrounding area with its sewage. Since the settlement was established, farmers in nearby Wadi Fukin also allege that 11 wells have dried up. On 11 June, the Israeli army arrived with bulldozers and vehicles levelled 35 dunams

(4 acres) of land belonging to Palestinian farmer Sabri Rashad Manasra from Wadi Fukin. The local council head, Ahmad Sukkar, believed that this had been done so the Israeli authorities could create an industrial and commercial zone in the area on private lands confiscated from Wadi Fukin and the nearby village of Husan. The Israelis claimed that the farmer had been violating state lands. Locals had been told back in August 2014 that the state was expropriating some 1000 acres of private land belonging to Wadi Fukin and the neighbouring village of Jaba. Either way, we may be sure that the illegal residents of Beitar Illit will benefit from the land theft.

Rabbi Nehemia Lavi, the second murder victim, originally came from Beit El settlement, but moved to become a rabbi at the Yeshivat Ateret Kohanim in Jerusalem. He, too, was an IDF soldier, having volunteered in the summer of 2014 to take an officer's course as part of his IDF reserve duty. The website of his yeshiva makes it clear that the yeshiva's mission is to turn the Muslim quarter of the old city into the 'Renewed Jewish Quarter'. To this end, backed by donations from Americans Irving and Cherna Moskowitz, the organisation buys up property in the Muslim quarter, expels the Muslim tenants and installs Jewish religious extremists. On 27 August 2015, for example, settlers took over a building in the Batn al-Hawa area in Silwan, East Jerusalem, claiming the building had been sold to the yeshiva. Escorted by Israeli troops, the settlers stormed in at 2.30am, barring the windows and raising an Israeli flag on the roof.

Earlier in the month, a lawyer working for the yeshiva issued evacuation notices for three Palestinian buildings owned by the Sarhan family in Batn al-Hawa, claiming that the land on which the homes are built belong to three Jewish men from Yemen who lived there before 1948 (*Maan News*). The move was condemned by Peace Now as a deliberate part of a campaign "to alter the character of the neighborhood and change the status quo in Jerusalem".

According to the PLO Negotiations Affairs Department, settlers had taken over some 39 homes in Silwan, which now house around 400 settlers. They are not there to be good neighbours. On 11 September, a gang of settlers entered Silwan and assaulted 8-year-old Ziyad Abu Qweidir. More attackers poured out of one of the occupied buildings. The Wadi Hilweh Centre, which monitors such activities, reported that at least 15 Palestinians were injured, including children ranging from 5 to 16 years of age, as well as a pregnant woman and a 75-year-old man. Two, a 60-year-old and a 14-year-old, were admitted to hospital; Zaid Abu Qweidir (8), Adam al-Rajabi (9), Rahaf Abu Qweidir (5), Udayy al-Rajabi (12), Hamza al-Rajabi (12), Yazan al-Rajabi (14) and Walid al-Shaer (16) received treatment for injuries at the scene. Settler security guards and IDF troops arrived to support the settlers, firing tear gas and stun grenades at Palestinians (a tear gas grenade landed inside a house where there were five young children).

The murderer of the two rabbis, Mohanned Shafiq Halabi, was a law student at al-Quds University. Like them, he was deeply religious and his family later referred to him as a martyr for the Al Aqsa mosque (see pages 111-120) where Israeli forces have stepped up incursions to escort Jewish religious extremists around the site, blocking entrances and banning young Muslims of both sexes on a daily varying basis. Mohanned came from Surda village, about three miles from the town of the town of al-Bireh, West Bank. In order to understand why this young man, with all his life ahead of him, should have committed these murders, knowing as he must have done that he himself would almost certainly also die, it is interesting to consider the atmosphere he grew up.

Al-Bireh

Al-Bireh is one of the most threatened towns in the occupied territories. The Israeli army targeted and raided al-Bireh numerous times in 2015, starting from early January. A city of some 60,000 people, many of them refugees, al-Bireh, according to its website, dates from 4,500BC, and lies just 16km from Jerusalem. Nearby are the illegal settlements of Psagot and Beit El, which also houses a military base.

4 January: 02:25-03:30, the Israeli Army raided al-Bireh, invaded a home and beat up a resident, Eyad Al-Fazi'. The injured man was admitted to hospital.

5 January: 08:35 the army raided with stun and tear gas grenades

6 January: 14:10 as above, and again at 14.10 on 13 January (also with rubber coated bullets), 15.00 on 16 January (stun and tear gas grenades), and at 15.30 on 20 January.

On 25 January, troops raided the al-Amari refugee camp in al-Bireh and ordered two residents, Ahmad Rumanah and Mohammad Rumanah (a special needs patient), to report for interrogation at Israeli Military Intelligence.

The following day, it was stun and tear gas grenades at 14.00, and the next day the raid occurred between 00.35 and 02.25. On 29 and 30 January there was a raid at 9.00.

There were army raids on the 3, 4, 5, 6 and 10 February. On 5 February, a 14-year-old boy, Dajanah Anbar, from the al-Jalazoun refugee camp was wounded and the following day an apartment block in the city was raided and CCTV recordings were confiscated. More of the same in March, with raids on 7 (militants from Beit El settlement also stoned passing residents and vehicles that day), 8, 10, 13, 16, 19, 22, 23 and 24 March (on which day troops abducted two 15-year-old boys).

Also, on 28 March, Laila Ghannam, the governor of the Ramallah and al-Bireh district, was briefly detained by troops stationed at the entrance of Nabi Saleh village in the northern Ramallah district. She had come to attend the weekly march to protest against the illegal separation wall and land seizures that affect the village. Soldiers allegedly threatened her with 'direct targeting' if she continued her support for the village, but she refused to be brow-beaten, saying "we will not be frightened of detention even if we are directly targeted; we will take part in the weekly march and will not be prevented from exercising our rights on our land."

On 2nd April, Palestinian lawmaker and member of the Popular Front for the Liberation of Palestine, Khalida Jarrar, was sentenced to six months' administrative detention (imprisonment without trial). Her alleged offences were belonging to a terror organisation and unspecified 'terror activities'. An articulate supporter of women's rights and involved in prisoner issues, Jarrar is one of 15 Palestinian legislators and 23 female political prisoners detained by Israeli occupation forces, according to Addameer (Arabic for conscience), the Palestinian Prisoner Support and Human Rights Association. She had continued living in al-Bireh, defying an occupation order banishing her to Jericho.

The army raids continued through April: on 3, 7, 10 (Israeli forces in the city fired live ammunition and rubber-coated bullets and stun and tear gas grenades, wounding and hospitalising three residents: Mohammad Matariya, Mohammad Shalabi and Mohammad Hamoudeh), 14, 15, 16 (a 17-year-old, Sufiyan Maqdadi, is taken) and 26 April.

May is very busy, with army raids on 8 (a mob from the Psagot settlement also invaded al-Bireh farmland), 9 (Psagot thugs stoned several homes in the city), 10 (the army opened fire towards children in the city), 11 (a 16-year-old, Ra'fat Abu Libdeh was wounded in the day's raid), 12, 13, 14 (two children, Bassil Qur'an, aged 14, and Majed Karakra, aged 15, were wounded by Israeli troops firing live ammunition, rubber-coated bullets and stun and tear gas grenades), 15, 19 (a mob from Psagot settlement attacked several people at a picnic near the al-Hashimiya School in al-Bireh), 21, 23, 24, 25 and 27 May.

In June, there were raids on 1, 8, 9, 11, and 20, when the army came to support settlers from the Psagot settlement. A local boy Islam Sarsour (15) was wounded, being hit twice in the leg by bullets apparently fired by one of the settlers. According to an eyewitness, there were four settlers near the gate to the settlement, close to Palestinian houses. The boy was some 60 metres away from them.

July was blessedly quiet, with only three raids recorded. In August, there were raids on 3, 12, 18, 19 (the army came to demolish a workers' living accommodation block in the Sateh Marhaba area), 24 and the 31 August, when the army arrived at 02.15 and assaulted and abducted a 16-year-old boy, Ma'moun Mujahid, after having abducted another youngster, Abdel-Fattah Al-Arouri (16). They returned at 08.45 and 11.30 that day.

September started with an army raid with stun and tear gas grenades and another the next day. On 6 September, between 01:20 and 04:30, the Israeli Army raided the al-Amari refugee camp in Al-Bireh, searching several homes and injuring two residents, one of whom, Loai Rajab, was admitted to hospital after being beaten up by Israeli soldiers. The Israeli army ordered three other people to report for interrogation at Israeli Military Intelligence. Early the following day, Israeli forces detained Najwan Odeh after ransacking her home in a southern suburb of the city. Odeh works at Qatar Charity and is a presenter at Women FM Radio in Ramallah.

More raids followed on 16, 18, 21, 23, and 29 September, when six people were wounded, one of whom was taken prisoner. On 30 September the army again came to al-Bireh and took prisoner a talented al-Bireh Youth Foundation soccer player.

It was three days later that Halabi attacked his victims.

Aftermath

Up to 30 September, 26 Palestinians had been killed by Israeli forces since the start of 2015, according to UN documentation. (This does not include the three members of the Dawabsha family, as they were killed by settlers. Nor did it include the infants who died of cold in Gaza, following the destruction of their homes the previous summer.) In the same time period, three Israelis had been killed by Palestinians. What followed after the murder of four more Israelis on 1 and 3 October was an outbreak of violence in which settlers, largely supported (though occasionally checked) by Israeli police and army, went on the rampage and the government vowed vengeance.

The murderer was already dead (though not those who shot Eitam and Naama Henkin, the two ultra-Orthodox settlers mentioned earlier; their alleged attackers were arrested later in the month), but the following days were to see the numbers of deaths and injuries spiralling.

4 October 2015

Settler attacks

> **Jerusalem** – 10:15, settlers in the al-Sheikh Jarrah neighbourhood stoned residents and vehicles, damaging three vehicles.
>
> 11:15, a man, Taysir Abu Ramouz, was admitted to hospital with knife wounds after being assaulted by a settler gang.
>
> 12:15, Ahmad Al-Malahi, was admitted to hospital after being beaten up by settlers.
>
> 20:55, Ibrahim Aliyan (a resident of Beit Safafa village) was admitted to hospital after being beaten up.
>
> 22:50, Abu Tawfiq Dandis (a resident of the Ras al-Amud neighbourhood) was admitted to hospital after being beaten up.
>
> **Ramallah** – 01:00, an Israeli mob raided Beit Illo village and attacked several homes.

09:50, Aysar Abu Arra and Mahmoud Abu Arra, were injured and their vehicle damaged by stone-throwing settlers.

11:05, Israeli settlers raided Deir Nathim village, while the Israeli Army fired stun and tear gas grenades in support.

16:00, a gang of Israelis from the Psagout stone a Palestinian home in east al-Bireh city.

19:35, a Zionist mob from the Nili Occupation settlement stoned Deir Qadis residents and vehicles.

Qalqiliya – 09:40, settlers from the Karni Shomron stoned passing residents and vehicles.

Nablus – 13:20, mobs from the Shilo and Eli settlements stoned residents and vehicles between Nablus and Ramallah.

19:30, Settlers stoned residents and vehicles passing through the Huwara checkpoint.

Salfit – 09:40, a gang from the Emanuel Occupation settlement in Wadi Qana stoned passing residents and vehicles. One person, Nael Zahran, was injured.

Bethlehem – 11:30, a gang from the Kafr Itsiyon Occupation settlement junction beat up and hospitalised a resident of Bani Na'im, Mohammad Tariya.

12:10, a group of Israeli settlers raided Khilat Sakariya village and attempted to set fire to a resident, Jamal Assad. The settlers withdrew, accompanied by occupation forces.

21:40, settlers raided al-Walaja village.

Hebron – morning, a settler mob raided al-Manazil village in South Yatta, damaged several solar panels and stoned vehicles and residents.

11:55, a mob from the Haji Occupation settlement, supported by the

Israeli Army, assaulted residents and closed the main road.

19:15, louts from the Susiya Occupation settlement in south-east Yatta closed the main road leading to Bi'ir al-Ad village.

Army actions

Jerusalem – 08:00, settler militants, escorted by Israeli troops and police, invaded the Al-Aqsa Mosque compound and molested worshippers.

10:00, Bab Hata Gate (Al-Aqsa Mosque compound) stun and tear gas grenades

11:30 and again at 21:50, Abu Dis: rubber-coated bullets and stun and tear gas grenades

13:20, Ras Al-Kabsa area in Abu Dis: rubber-coated bullets and stun and tear gas grenades

15:00 and again at 18:00, al-Ram: stun and tear gas grenades

15:30 and again at 21:00, Qalandiya checkpoint: rubber-coated bullets and stun and tear gas grenades; eight wounded – Abdel-Rahman Al-Araj (15), Samih Hamad, Tuhdi Al-Toukhi, Ahmad Zahar, Ibrahim Al-Rashid, Mohammad Abu Qwiek, Ahmad Wahdan and Anas Shadim

17:00, Anata and Shu'fat checkpoint: rubber-coated bullets and stun and tear gas grenades

19:20, Bab Al-Majlis Gate, al-Sa'yada, al-Tur and Ras al-Amud: rubber-coated bullets and stun and tear gas grenades

19:25, Israeli forces near the Bab Al-Sahara Gate assaulted a resident, Ameer Farahat.

20:00, al-Issawiya village: rubber-coated bullets and stun and tear gas grenades; one unidentified person wounded

21:00, al-Thuri neighbourhood and Shuafat refugee camp: rubber-coated bullets and stun and tear gas grenades; one person, Mohammad Burqan, hospitalised with critical head wound.

Ramallah – 19:40, in al-Bireh, six Palestinian residents – Ali Badr, Mohammad Dar Zied, Musa Sabah, Mohammad Hammad, Mohammad Abu Qwiek and Hamdallah Tal'at Al-Taweel – were wounded when the Israeli Army opened live fire and fired rubber-coated bullets and stun and tear gas grenades.

02:00, Israeli troops raided Surda village, searched a home and assaulted family members, hospitalising one of them.

12:50, Silwad: rubber coated bullets and stun and tear gas grenades

21:35, al-Nabi Saleh village and simultaneously north Bir Zeit: rubber-coated bullets and stun and tear gas grenades

Qalqiliya – 20:00, rubber-coated bullets and stun and tear gas grenades; one person taken prisoner

20:00, Jayus: stun and tear gas grenades

14:40, Salfit: stun and tear gas grenades

Tulkarem – 21:20, Hufaytha Suliman, was killed and three other residents, Ahmad Jallad, Mohammad Al-Shouli and Omar Jadbah, were wounded when Israeli troops opened up with live fire, rubber-coated bullets and stun and tear gas grenades at people in west Tulkarem. Five other people were detained.

11:10, the Israeli Army raided Quffin, occupied and searched a home and set up a sniper post on the roof.

Nablus – 12:25, during a raid by a mob from the Yitzhar Occupation settlement, eight people, including three youngsters – Khaled Al-Safadi (16), Sultan Al-Safadi (16) and Mohammad Al-Safadi (17) – were wounded when the Israeli Army opened fire with live ammunition, rubber-coated steel bullets and stun and tear gas grenades in support of the settlers. The wounded adults were identified as Yusef Al-Safadi, Ammar Falah Ammar, Ahmad Al-Safadi, Abdallah Al-Safadi and Mahmoud Al-Safadi. The Israeli Army was intent upon preventing the villagers from rescuing their crops, which had been set on fire by a settler arson attack.

05:30, occupation forces raided Yatma village, searched a home, assaulted a resident, Eman Othman, and made off with personal property.

Salfit – 14:40, stun and tear gas grenades and 15:30, indiscriminate fire

Bethlehem – 13:00, Israeli soldiers seized a 14-year-old, Yazen Al-Sir, and held him captive for over three hours.

17:45, north Bethlehem: rubber-coated bullets and stun and tear gas grenades

22:10, Israeli forces, firing rubber-coated bullets and stun and tear gas grenades, abducted a 16-year-old youth, Mohammad Abu Shusheh.

Hebron – 13:10, Israeli troops, positioned in Bab al-Zawiya and close to the Tarik Bin Zayid School, opened live fire as well as stun and tear gas grenades, wounding three minors, Muhammad Al-Natsheh (13), Ma'moun Mujahid (17) and Ragheb Masoudah (17), as well as an adult, Mohammad A'mmar.

18:05, Assi Al-Ja'bari, was wounded when the Israeli Army fired live ammunition and stun and tear gas grenades towards several residents in Bab Al-Zawiya.

07:05 and again at 18:20, al-Urub refugee camp: stun and tear gas grenades.

07:05, al-Tabaqa village road junction: rubber-coated bullets and stun and tear gas grenades.

17:10, Bani Na'im: stun and tear gas grenades

18:20, Beit Ummar: stun and tear gas grenades

18:20, Khursa village and the al-Fawar refugee camp road junctions: rubber-coated bullets and stun and tear gas grenades

Jericho – 15:40, stun and tear gas grenades

In addition to the incidents detailed above, early on Sunday morning, Israeli police near the Damascus Gate of Jerusalem's Old City shot and killed Fadi Samir Mustafa Alloun, 19, who came from the occupied East Jerusalem village of al-Issawiya. As so often, accounts of the death vary hugely. The police alleged that Alloun was 'neutralised' in the course of a knife attack on a 16-year-old settler. Following his death, they descended on his home in force, reportedly assaulting women with rods and tasers and damaging furniture, and arrested his father and uncle.

Alloun's family and friends deny that he was involved in the stabbing. They claim that he was a gentle young man with a beautiful singing voice. His mother and brother Mohammad had long been separated from Fadi and his father: she had travelled to Jordan 18 years earlier to nurse her dying father and had subsequently been refused a permit to return. Thereafter, Fadi had only been able to communicate with his mother and brother through Skype. (She was not allowed to return for her son's funeral.)

Later, videos[3] emerged making it clear that at the time of his death, Fadi posed no threat, but was being pursued by a mob of settlers, shouting "Shoot him! He's a terrorist! Shoot him!" and "Don't wait! Shoot him!" Only after Fadi lies dead do the police ask "Where are the injured" and "Did he stab anyone?" Even later, a further video came to light which suggests that Fadi was not carrying a knife, but was attacked by a gang of settlers and was trying to escape when shot. Whether he had attacked the settler who was wounded or whether he was himself attacked and had simply tried to defend himself, the videos make it clear that he posed no threat at the time of his killing but was hunted down and shot.

Overnight on the same Sunday, Huthayfa Othman Suleiman, aged 18, was shot in the chest by live fire from the Israeli army during clashes in the village

---

3 www.electronicintifada.net/blogs/ali-abunimah/
video-death-chanting-israeli-mob-rejoices-palestinian-teen-executed

of Bana, east of Tulkarem and died in the operating theatre. Snipers deployed from rooftops also shot one Omar Jabda in the abdomen and thigh and wounded two others in the legs. Six people were wounded by rubber bullets. On Monday, 13-year-old Abed al-Rahman Shadi Obeidallah died after being shot in the heart by Israeli soldiers when he was on his way home from school.

Also on Monday, the Red Crescent, which is affiliated to the Red Cross, announced that at least 499 Palestinians had been wounded since Saturday, 41 of these by live rounds. By Tuesday, Errab Foqaha, speaking for the Red Crescent, told *Ma'an News* that Israeli forces had carried out 13 attacks on Red Crescent ambulance crews since Sunday. She added that the latest attacks on their emergency relief teams brought the total number to 27 since Friday, and had left 17 staff members injured and 10 ambulances damaged.

In the wake of the Palestinian attacks, Prime Minister Netanyahu announced that the demolition of homes belonging to attackers would be speeded up. Halabi's home was demolished overnight 8/9 January 2016.

Shoot to kill

"Don't hesitate, even when an incident just starts, shooting to kill is the right thing to do."

Yair Lapid, former Israeli minister and leader of the 'centrist' party Yesh Atid

"We need to prosecute police officers and soldiers that leave terrorists alive after an attack."

Shmuel Eliyahu, chief rabbi of Safed

"Israel must declare a war of annihilation of Hamas ... and return to the assassination policy."

Tzipi Hotovely, deputy foreign affairs minister, Likud party

"Every terrorist should know that he will not survive the attack he is about to commit."

Police Minister Gilad Erdan

"Israel must clarify with actions (not with words) that in the face of the widespread terror, all the rules have changed. Whoever raises a knife over a Jew in the Land of Israel will be the one to lose his privilege to breathe air on the globe – and should be killed on the spot - without any doubt."

Moshe Feiglin, columnist and former Deputy Speaker of the Knesset

The first three quarters of 2015 had witnessed much violence against Palestinians, accompanied by demolitions, land theft, agricultural destruction and all the other means of establishing 'Greater Israel' at the expense of its Palestinian inhabitants. There was also a relatively small number of Palestinian attacks on Israelis, some four of whom had died, compared with some 32 Palestinians, many of whom had been killed in circumstances where they appear to have been either completely innocent of any offence against the Israelis or, at the least, offered no danger to their killers.

In October, the toxic brew boiled over, as UN officials and other observers had long warned it would. The murder of the Henkins, rapidly followed by that of rabbis Aharon Bennett and Nehemia Lavi, resulted in a huge increase in the number of settler attacks on Palestinians, often backed by the armed forces, while gangs of young Israeli racists roamed Jerusalem asking drivers, pedestrians and rail travellers"Are you Arab?", with predictable consequences if the answer were "Yes." On the Palestinian side, there was an increase in knife attacks on soldiers, police and settlers, mainly carried out by youngsters (the youngest being only 13). By the end of the month, some 72 Palestinians had been killed in October alone and eight Israelis. (According to Palestinian sources, two more, who were initially thought to have been killed by Palestinians, had actually died as a result of car accidents).

The official response was predictable: as we have already seen, the Minister for Education has no problem with killing Palestinians; the Justice Minister believes in the wholesale massacre of [Palestinian] civilians; the Deputy Minister for Defence thinks Palestinians are not human; the Minister for Agriculture, like the Minister for Education, wants to flatten the Al Aqsa site and build a Jewish Temple in its place, and the Prime Minister and his cabinet have made it abundantly clear that they regard the West Bank and Jerusalem as part of Israel and will never agree to a two-state solution.

Instead of seeking to calm the situation and reassure both sides, the government imposed a virtual lockdown on Palestinian areas of Jerusalem, ordered a wave of army raids on villages, towns and refugee camps in the West Bank, authorised the use of live fire in place of less fatal riot control methods, and relaxed the gun permit laws.

Various officials warned Israeli citizens to arm themselves and be prepared to take lethal action at any sign of trouble. Some 8,000 gun permit requests were made on 11 October, within 24 hours of the gun laws being relaxed.

Undoubtedly, some of those wounded or killed were knife attackers, but many more were not and there was an increase in the number of cases that could justifiably be called extrajudicial execution or just plain murder, or attempted murder. By 10 October, 15 Palestinians had already been killed that month by Israeli forces and a further 1,000 injured. The dead included 7 Gazans shot with live fire at a demonstration near the border fence, several others killed in clashes with the army in the West Bank, among them, 13-year-old Abed al-Rahman Shadi Obeidallah, who was shot in the chest during clashes in Aida refugee camp, and 16-year-old Ishaq Badran, killed, according to the Israelis after a stabbing attack, though Palestinian witnesses claim he did not attack anyone and was shot for no reason.

The injured included Shuroq Salah Dwayat, from East Jerusalem, who was shot four times in the upper body from close range by a 35-year-old settler, who claimed she attempted to stab him. Palestinian witnesses tell a very different story: he was harassing the 18-year-old girl and then attempted to assault her. Another survivor was 29-year-old Israa Abed, an Israeli citizen and the mother of three children, who was shot in the bus station at Afula. Initial Israeli reports claimed that she was shot while attacking a security guard. Later, video footage emerged showing a terrified woman, her hands held up in the air, standing motionless as several soldiers approach her. She appears to be holding something in one hand, but is certainly not threatening anyone when one of the heavily armed men fires several shots at point blank range. A still picture appears to show that what she was holding was a pair of sunglasses. Later still, it was announced that Israa, who is a student of genetic engineering, was not guilty of intending to stab anyone, but no-one will be charged with her shooting.

On Sunday 11 October, Kenneth Roth, Human Rights Watch's executive director, warned that "Indiscriminate or deliberate firing on observers and demonstrators who pose no imminent threat violates the international standards that bind Israeli security forces. It is particularly troubling when those seeking to monitor the security forces' conduct are among the casualties." He was referring to the shooting of a HRW research assistant, who was also a journalist and was wearing a jacket clearly labelled 'PRESS'. She had been watching a peaceful demonstration of Palestinians, including families with young children, when the soldiers opened fire "without warning", wounding her and seven others.

On the 14 October, a group of nine human rights organisations called for a more moderate response to the Palestinian attacks:

Human Rights Organizations in Israel: Politicians' calls to police and soldiers to shoot rather than arrest endorse the killing of Palestinians

No-one disputes the serious nature of the recent events. However, it seems that too often, police officers and soldiers are quick to shoot to kill.

Since the beginning of the current wave of violence, there has been a worrying trend to use firearms to kill Palestinians who have attacked Israelis or are suspected of such attacks. Several incidents have been documented and reported, raising concern that the chosen response to such persons is the harshest possible, with lethal or – at the very least – unnecessary consequences. In instances when Jews have been suspected of attacks, none of the suspects has been shot.

Politicians and senior police officers have not only failed to act to calm the public climate of incitement, but on the contrary have openly called for the extrajudicial killing of suspects. They have also urged civilians to carry weapons. For example, Jerusalem District Police Commander Moshe Edri was quoted as saying: "Anyone who stabs Jews or hurts innocent people is due to be killed." Interior Security Minister Gilad Arden declared that "every terrorist should know that he will not survive the attack he is about to commit." MK Yair Lapid stated that "you have to shoot to kill anyone who pulls out a knife or screwdriver." Much of the media joined in and encouraged a similar approach. The bodies responsible for supervising police operations – the State Attorney's Office and the Department for the Investigation of Police – remained silent in the face of these comments.

No-one disputes the serious nature of the events of recent days, nor the need to protect the public against stabbing and other attacks. However, it seems that too often, instead of acting in a manner consistent with the nature of each incident, police officers and soldiers are quick to shoot to kill. The political and public support for such actions endorses the killing of Palestinians in the Territories and in Israel.

Rather than imposing collective punishment on Palestinians in the West Bank (including East Jerusalem) and the Gaza Strip, the Israeli government should act to end the reality of ongoing and daily oppression faced by some four million people who live without hope of any change in the situation, without any horizon for the end of occupation, and without prospects for a life of liberty and dignity. The statement is signed by the following organizations:

Association for Civil Rights in Israel
Amnesty International – Israel Branch
B'Tselem
Gisha
Public Committee Against Torture in Israel
HaMoked – Center for the Defence of the Individual
Yesh Din – Volunteers for Human Rights
Adalah – The Legal Center for the Rights of the Arab Minority in Israel
Physicians for Human Rights – Israel

The appeal had no effect and the death toll continued to mount as the month wore on.

ISRAELI FORCES IN OCCUPIED PALESTINIAN TERRITORIES MUST END PATTERN OF UNLAWFUL KILLINGS

27 October 2015, 18:50 UTC Amnesty Press release

Israeli forces have carried out a series of unlawful killings of Palestinians using intentional lethal force without justification, said Amnesty International today, based on the findings of an ongoing research trip to the West Bank, including East Jerusalem.

The organization has documented in depth at least four incidents in which Palestinians were deliberately shot dead by Israeli forces when they posed no imminent threat to life, in what appear to have been extrajudicial executions.

In some cases, the person shot was left bleeding to death on the ground and was not given prompt medical assistance, in violation of the prohibition of torture and other ill-treatment. Since 1 October, Israeli forces have killed more than 30 Palestinians in the occupied West Bank and Israel either after stabbings were carried out or the Israeli authorities allege stabbing attacks were intended.

"A clear pattern has emerged of lethal force being used unlawfully by Israeli forces following a wave of recent stabbing attacks by Palestinians against Israeli civilians and military or police forces in Israel and the occupied West Bank," said Philip Luther, Director of the Middle East and North Africa Programme at Amnesty International.

"There is mounting evidence that, as tensions have risen dramatically, in some cases Israeli forces appear to have ripped up the rulebook and resorted to extreme and unlawful measures. They seem increasingly prone to using lethal force against anyone they perceive as posing a threat, without ensuring that the threat is real.

"Intentional lethal force should only be used when absolutely necessary to protect life. Instead we are increasingly seeing Israeli forces recklessly flouting international standards by shooting to kill in situations where it is completely unjustified. Israeli forces must end this pattern of unlawful killings and bring all those *responsible to justice.*"

In an especially egregious case, Israeli forces shot dead 19-year-old Sa'ad Muhammad Youssef al-Atrash in the Old City of Hebron as he attempted to retrieve an ID card at an Israeli soldier's request on 26 October. The Israeli police labelled the incident an "attempted stabbing" but an eyewitness watching the events unfold from her balcony said he had posed no threat when he was shot. One of the soldiers had asked him for ID, and as he reached into his pocket to grab his card another soldier standing behind him shot him on his right side, she told Amnesty International. The eyewitness said he was shot six or seven times and bled profusely as he lay on the ground for about 40 minutes afterwards, while soldiers failed to provide medical treatment. She also reported seeing soldiers bring a knife and place it in the dying man's hand.

"Then they put him on a stretcher and pushed him towards an ambulance but didn't put him in. By this time he looked extremely yellow and I thought that he was dead at that point. He remained in front of the ambulance for another 20 minutes before he was put inside it and taken away," the witness said.

On 25 October, a short distance from where al-Atrash was killed, Israeli border police shot dead Dania Jihad Hussein Ershied, 17. Shortly before she was killed, she had passed through a checkpoint equipped with a metal detector and two revolving gates, between which Israeli forces frequently lock people they deem suspicious.[1] At a second checkpoint in front of

---

1   Witnesses pointed out that had she been carrying a knife, this would have been detected at the first checkpoint.

Hebron's Ibrahimi Mosque she was called for a second inspection by more than five border police officers, who began searching her bag and yelling at her to show her knife.

Warning shots were fired at her feet, prompting her to step back and raise her hands in the air. She was shouting at the police that she did not have a knife and still had her arms raised when police again opened fire, shooting her six or seven times.

A photo of Ershied's body shows a knife lying near the body, and the Israeli police spokesperson stated that she attempted to stab a border policeman. However, even if Dania Jihad Hussein Ershied had a knife in her possession, eyewitness accounts indicate she was not posing a threat to Israeli forces when she was shot, and her killing is therefore absolutely unjustified.

Amnesty International has gathered evidence of other recent shootings in which Israeli forces used unwarranted lethal force in what were likely extrajudicial executions.

[The statement goes on to discuss the killing of Fadi Alloun on 4 October and Hadeel al-Hashlamoun on 22 September, both of whom are discussed earlier, then continues as below.]

As Philip Luther, Director of Amnesty's Middle East and North Africa Programme put it: Israeli forces and civilians have faced genuine attacks and threats to their lives over the past weeks. But heavily armed soldiers and police wearing body armour facing a possible knife attack have a duty to use proportionate and graduated force and attempt to arrest suspects before resorting to the use of lethal force.

Unfortunately, Israel's investigation systems have long served to perpetuate impunity for unlawful killings of Palestinians by Israeli military and police forces. While we urge the Israeli authorities to conduct independent, impartial investigations into all these incidents, wilful killings of Palestinians in the Occupied Palestinian Territories are grave breaches of the Fourth Geneva Convention, over which all states can exercise universal jurisdiction.

On 5 November, the results of a peace index survey, conducted by telephone on 28/29 October, were announced. The survey covered a representative sample numbering some 600 individuals. It revealed that some 80 per cent of Jewish Israelis believed that the homes of Palestinian attackers should be demolished (but only 53 per cent if the attacker were Jewish). Some 53 per cent agreed that "any Palestinian who has perpetrated a terror attack against Jews should be killed on the spot."

On the same day, 73-year-old Thawarat al-Sharawi was driving to have lunch with her sister. As she approached a petrol station in Halhul, West Bank, she may have been driving a little faster than usual to get away from clashes in the area and from the accompanying tear gas. According to the Israeli account, she aimed her car at soldiers and they shot her dead – in fact she was shot at 15 times. Israeli sources made much of the fact that her husband had been killed by tear gas in 1988. Her family pointed out that it was hardly likely she would have waited so long to take revenge. Later, a video showed that, as so often, the military were lying. Her car was not aiming at them at all when they opened fire and they had never been in any danger. Her picture shows a sweet, cuddly little apple-faced granny.

The following day, 22-year-old Muhammad al-Bhaisy was shot with live fire simply for placing a Palestinian flag on Gaza's boundary fence[2]. For a while, soldiers fired on those who tried to come near to carry him away, but he was eventually taken to hospital.

On 22 November, a settler leader from Elon Moreh called Gershon Mesika rammed 16-year-old Ashraqat Taha Qatanany with his car, later claiming she had a knife and was about to attack pedestrians. Accounts of what happened after varied: either he then exited his vehicle and shot her dead himself, or the settler in the car behind him shot her or, in a later account by Gershon, soldiers shot her. Palestinian witnesses say she did not have a knife and was not about to harm anyone. A knife appears to have been tossed by her side later. Israel's right-wing, ultra-religious Arutz Sheva called Gershon 'a hero'. This praise must have been timely for Gershon, as, at the time he killed the girl, he had been suspended as head of the Samaria Regional Council for corruption.

---

2   See www.facebook.com/ExposingIsraelsAgenda/videos/623837001089728/?pnref=story

Free press?

"One day the nightmare will be over"

Razi Nabulsi, Palestinian journalist and activist, spent 11 days in prison in 2014 for incitement after quoting this song title on his Facebook page

On 7 January, two brothers, Saïd and Chérif Kouachi, later identified as belonging to Al Quaeda's Yemen branch, broke into the offices of French satirical magazine *Charlie Hebdo* and killed 11 members of staff. An outraged world responded with massive demonstrations in support of press freedom. Some 2 million marched in Paris in a show of national unity. Included were some 40 national leaders, among them Israel's Netanyahu, who pushed his way to the front and later called on France's Jews to emigrate to the 'safety' of Israel.

Throughout the remainder of the year, Palestinian journalists and news outlets continued to be attacked by the Israeli government and military. On 18 January, Israeli soldiers raided Beitunya, Ramallah area, invaded an apartment building, took prisoner a journalist, after searching his vehicle, and took his laptop computer. Journalists covering peaceful demonstrations were routinely targeted. At Bil'in, on 6 February, for example, nine activists and a journalist, Issam al-Rimani, a photographer for the newspaper al-Hayat were pepper-sprayed at the weekly protest march. On 27 February, Reuters photojournalist Abd al-Rahman al-Qussini was hit in the neck by a tear gas grenade at a protest at Kafr Qaddum. On 30 March, at a march of 2,000 people at Huwwara, near Nablus, to commemorate Land Day[1], journalists were targeted by troops firing tear gas, stun grenades and rubber-coated steel bullets (the elementary school, with the little ones inside, was also targeted).

Journalists were again among those at the receiving end of rubber-coated steel bullets and tear gas canisters at the funeral of Muhammad Karakra, on 12 April. (Karakra had stabbed two Israeli soldiers at the Sinjil junction near the Shilo settlement before being shot.) Three days later, Israeli forces raided the home of Amin Abdul Aziz Abu Wardeh, general manager of the Asda news website at 2am. They seized three laptops and a mobile and then arrested him,

---

1 The Day of the Land commemorates a mass protest in 1976 against land theft and plans to Judaize Galilee, northern Israel. Six Palestinians were killed, many more were wounded, and hundreds arrested when the Israeli police and army attacked the marchers.

bringing the number of Palestinian journalists in Israeli prisons to 20, six of whom had been arrested in 2015. At the weekly protest against the separation wall and settlement land theft in Nabi Saleh, on 24 April, an Israeli journalist and human rights activist and a Palestinian photojournalist from AFP were attacked by soldiers who were preventing journalists from covering the march. They were kicked, insulted in Hebrew and stones were thrown at them. The scene was caught on camera.[2] An IDF spokesman later said: "the behaviour seen in the video is reprehensible and isn't in line with the guidelines issued by the commanders in the region... The IDF guidelines allow for free press coverage in the territory under control of the Central Command in general, and specifically during demonstrations."

On Saturday, 2 May, journalists had organised a peaceful march in Bethlehem to celebrate World Press Freedom Day. Israeli forces fired tear-gas canisters and stun grenades into the crowd, injuring, among others, the head of the Union of Palestinian Journalists Abd al-Nasser al-Najjar, member of the union's general committee Muhammad al-Laham, and Reuters photographer Muhammad Abu Ghaniyyeh. Al-Najjar later commented that the march was to proclaim "our refusal to systematic Israeli suppression policies against journalists even as they express their right of coverage and freedom of expression."

On 25 May, the Palestinian Centre for Development and Media Freedoms (MADA) announced that violations against female journalists (a third of all Palestinian journalists) had tripled since 2010, with journalists caught in the crossfire between rival factions.

On 16 May, a protest was held near Huwwara checkpoint to commemorate the Nakba, the Jewish terror campaign carried out in 1948 in which hundreds of Palestinian men, women and children were murdered and thousands driven from their homes. Nidal Shtayyeh, working for Chinese news agency Xinhua was shot: "The march was peaceful and no stones were thrown... I raised my camera to my right eye to take a picture, but a soldier shot me in my left eye with his rifle, and the rubber bullet went through my gas mask's glass eye cover and into my eye." He was taken to a hospital in Nablus but was later referred to St John's eye hospital in occupied East Jerusalem. The Israeli authorities, however, refused to give him a permit to enter the city, despite appeals from the Red Crescent and a private lawyer.

---

2 www.rt.com/news/254065-israel-soldiers-journalists-assault/

The following month, MADA again reported rising numbers of violations of press freedom. The 21 violations carried out by the Israelis included detention, physical assault, travel bans and forced censorship.

On 18 June, Palestine 48 TV Station was due to open in Nazareth. Funded by the West Bank's Palestinian Authority, it would have been the first Palestinian Arabic-language station broadcasting in Israel and intended to highlight the lives of Palestinians in Galilee, the Triangle Area, and the Negev. That same day, Netanyahu, acting Communications Minister, ordered it to be shut down on the grounds of its 'foreign funding'. In July, the Public Security Minister signed an order banning the station for six months on the grounds that it harmed Israeli sovereignty.

The following day, Israel's new Culture Minister, Miri Regev, former general and chief army censor, castigated people protesting at her threat to cut funding for a children's theatre after its Palestinian director, Norman Issa, refused to participate in plays in illegal settlements in the West Bank. She told a magazine she hadn't wanted the ministerial job: "I say to myself, who am I working for? For a group of ungrateful people who think they know everything, some of them petty bores, hypocrites."

On 5 August, freelance cameraman Amjad Arafeh was summoned to the Russian compound in Jerusalem and informed that he had been banned from travelling for three months. British authorities joined in the clampdown on press freedom when West Bank photographer, Hamde Abu Rahma, from Bil'in, was refused a visa by the UK Border Agency to travel to Britain and be present at an exhibition of his photographs as part of Scotland's Edinburgh Fringe events. (He had previously visited Germany, Switzerland, Italy and Holland, where he had been allowed to speak freely about the Palestinian experience.)

As Palestinians continued to be banned from the Al Aqsa mosque while Jewish religious extremists were escorted around by Israeli forces, journalists again came under attack. On 26 August, two schoolgirls were stopped at the Chain Gate by soldiers, who tore up the birth certificates that proved their ID. Journalist Liwa Abu Rmeila was attacked by soldiers for attempting to report the scene and two cameramen were fined on the spot for 'causing an obstruction'. There were 20 Israeli violations of press freedom in August, according to the Union of Palestinian Radio and Television Journalists.

Detainees now included 46-year-old Nidal Abu Aker, the director of Bethlehem's Al-Wehda Radio and presenter of a programme called "In Their Cells". On 7 September, Najwan Odeh, from al-Bireh, a presenter at Women FM Radio in Ramallah, joined the detainees after troops invaded and ransacked her home. On 10 September, the detention order (without trial) was renewed against Nidal Abu Aker, who had been on hunger strike against his imprisonment since 20 August.

On 9 September, three more journalists were stopped from entering Al Aqsa and told they were on a blacklist. More trouble at Al Aqsa on 14 September, when cameraman Ayman Abu Rumouz was assaulted while taking refuge in a shop near the mosque and another cameraman was injured and detained.

On 25 September, Italian video journalist Andrea Bernardi and his Palestinian colleague Abbas Momani, working for AFP, were attacked by soldiers at the funeral of Ahmed Khatatbeh. Bernadi was pinned to the ground, two cameras were smashed and another camera and a mobile were taken. Both men were wearing jackets clearly marked PRESS. The incident was caught on camera by Palmedia[3] and the Israelis sentenced one officer to 14 days' imprisonment and the other was confined to barracks for 30 days. The Foreign Press Association pointed out that no action would have been taken had the incident not been filmed.

On 2 October, freelance photo-journalist Ahmad Hasan was shot in the right leg by a sniper while covering the weekly march at Kafr Qaddum. The next day, Ahmad Bahahme of Awda TV was shot in the leg by a tear gas canister while covering clashes near the illegal Beit El settlement. And the following day, Hana Mahamid of Al-Mayadeen TV channel (Lebanon) was shot in the face with a stun grenade while filming clashes between Palestinian youths and Israeli troops in Jerusalem's al-Issawiya neighborhood. She had been wearing a flak jacket, clearly marked PRESS and claimed that her team had been deliberately targeted.

On 10 October, Daliya Al Namari of the Russia Today Arabic news channel was at the scene when soldiers shot dead 16-year-old Ishaq Badran, claiming he had attacked settlers, a claim denied by witnesses. The troops attacked her and forced her away while she was still live on camera.

---

3 www.rt.com/news/254065-israel-soldiers-journalists-assault/

On 20 October, the Government Media Office (Ministry of Information) announced that it had documented 62 violations of press freedom in the October upsurge of violence. The possibility of taking the issue to the ICC was raised. On 23 October, it was reported by locals that Palestine TV reporter and cameraman Sira Sarhan and Hadi al-Dibs had been used as human shields by troops who had forced them to stand in front of their Jeep to prevent youths throwing rocks.

Meanwhile journalists in Gaza, where some 17 journalists had been killed in the previous year's Israeli assault, were also being targeted by troops as they tried to cover clashes near the border fence, according to deputy speaker of the Union of Gaza Journalists, Tahsin al-Astal.

On 3 November, Israeli forces broke into the offices of Manbar al-Hurriyya (Freedom Tribune) radio station in Hebron, where they destroyed some equipment and confiscated the rest, telling employees that the station was now closed. The station was accused of making "false and malicious claims of security forces executing and kidnapping Palestinians in order to provoke violence." At dawn on 11 November, in occupied Beit Sahour, Israeli troops broke into[4] the (closed) offices of the independent English-language International Middle East Media Centre (IMEMC) and its founding organisation, the Palestinian Centre for Rapprochement. The media centre had been suffering from cyber attacks since 14 September and now troops smashed equipment. The centre had publicised the killing of Fadi Alloun on 4 October, captured on camera in a video[5] that contradicted Israeli claims that he had posed a threat at the time.

On 20 November, Al-Khalil Radio, Hebron, was stormed and shut down, with equipment confiscated and the offices damaged. Again, the Israelis accused the station of incitement.

The following Friday, Palestinian activist and cameraman, Hamdi Abu Rahma was shot with a rubber-coated steel bullet while covering the weekly protest march at Bil'in.

On Sunday, 6 December, Israeli troops raided the Infinity and Lamasat print shops in Hebron, accusing them of incitement and supporting Hamas. (At the same time, troops raided Tabban, also in the Hebron district, where they

4 www.imemc.org/article/73364

5 www.youtube.com/watch?v=nj8gXqGh2Vo#t=22

removed doors and windows from tin dwellings provided by Operation Dove (Association Community Pope John XXIII).

On 13 December, the non-violent activists of Youth Against Settlements, in Hebron, were told that their offices might be closed. They had offended the Israeli authorities by releasing photos showing the extra-judicial execution of Hadeel Hashlamoun, shot by soldiers who falsely claimed that they were defending themselves against a knife attack. The following day, they were told that the offices were now within a closed military zone, within which only local residents would be allowed. The area is one where aggressive settler groups frequently abuse and threaten Palestinians and foreign volunteers attached to the group had often documented such cases. Locals now faced the threat of being left without the protection offered by those able to spread the details of their sufferings to a worldwide audience.

On 16 December, Bara Abdullah Hamdan, a Bethlehem radio journalist, was handcuffed and taken to a military base, where his mobile was seized and all photos deleted. He was later released.

No news is good news

As the year progressed, the authorities in Israel became increasingly alarmed by the progress of the boycott movement and the growing online availability of photos and videos showing the daily abuses suffered by Palestinians. The mainstream media coverage of the situation, in which the Israeli authorities' version of events was essentially given credence over Palestinian claims, was now being challenged by online evidence. Whereas all foreign journalists in the occupied territories must register with the Israeli military and submit any film footage to them for censorship, ordinary Palestinians were now able to post their version online.

And time and again, the Israeli version was shown to be incorrect: the general who claimed he had shot an unarmed teenager in self-defence was shown to have shot him in the back as he ran away; the young mother who was shot in Afula bus station was not threatening her heavily-armed attacker with a knife; Fadi Alloun was running away when killed, while settlers urged soldiers to kill him; 13-year-old Ahmed Manasra was shown being kicked as he lay bleeding on the ground while by-standing settlers yelled "Die! Son of a bitch." Many others were shown being deliberately left to bleed to death instead of being given life-saving medical help.

Attempts to boost the hasbara industry – the dissemination of pro-Israel propaganda and 'good news' stories – were being countered by a tidal wave of reality, available through online sources.

As we have seen, Palestinian news outlets and reporters were increasingly accused of incitement as the year wore on and violence escalated. While NGOs put the blame for the violence on the ongoing occupation, land grabbing, settlement building, the growing campaign to demolish Al Aqsa and replace it with a synagogue and the total failure of any prospect of a just peace, the Israeli authorities thus put the blame on journalists and others who posted these films and pictures.

In late November Israeli Deputy Foreign Minister Tzipi Hotovely held meetings with YouTube CEO Susan Wojcicki and Google's Director of Public Policy, Jennifer Oztzistzki, at Google's Silicon Valley Offices to elicit their cooperation in censoring the social networks: "The attacks daily in Israel are the result of youths and children incited by the education system and the social networks, this is a daily war of incitement."

According to Hotovely (denied by Google), the companies agreed to cooperate with Israel on joint censorship.

Appendix I

Israel/Palestine: a brief timeline

70 AD: the Romans sack Jerusalem and destroy the temple built by King Herod. Wealthy Jerusalemites, rabbis and rebels flee the city and some end up in Jewish communities in other parts of the Roman Empire. In time, many intermarry with Europeans (we now know this from Ashkenazi DNA); those who retain or are converted to the Jewish faith become the ancestors of the Ashkenazi Jews. The poorer and less well connected – country dwellers, herdsmen, fishermen and small traders in towns throughout Palestine – remain; they are the ancestors of the Palestinians.

313 AD: the Emperor Constantine decriminalises Christianity; 326/8 Empress Helena, wife of Roman Emperor Constantius Chlorus and mother of Constantine visits Palestine; by 400 AD Christianity is the official religion of the empire.

634 AD: Muslim armies defeat the Byzantine and Persian armies, gaining control of the Levant, Mesopotamia and Persia. They offer peace and protection to all inhabitants of the conquered areas.

1096: the first crusade; Jews in Germany are massacred as crusaders pass through Europe; 15 July 1099, crusaders take Jerusalem and massacre Christians and Muslims; 1187 Saladin retakes Jerusalem; 1229 crusaders regain Jerusalem but lose it finally in 1244.

1453: Constantinople falls to the Ottoman Turks.

1516: the Ottomans capture Palestine and the long period of Ottoman rule begins; Jews and Christians are tolerated so long as they pay additional tax (this charge is removed with the Ottoman reforms of the mid-19th century).

1897: the first Zionist Congress is held in Vienna. Zionism's declared aim becomes to establish a home for the Jews in Palestine. Theodor Herzl writes in his diary: "We shall have to spirit the penniless population [the Palestinians] across the border … while denying it any employment in our own country." Jews start arriving in Palestine.

1916: The British and French sign the secret Sykes-Picot agreement, to divide the Middle East between these two imperial powers.

1917: the British issue the Balfour Declaration in a letter written by Foreign Secretary Lord Balfour to Lord Rothschild –"His Majesty's Government view with favour the establishment in Palestine of a national home for the Jewish people, and will use their best endeavors to facilitate the achievement of this object, it being clearly understood that nothing shall be done which may prejudice the civil and religious rights of existing non-Jewish communities in Palestine, or the rights and political status enjoyed by Jews in any other country."This is when the Palestinians, who had been hoping to achieve their own independent state, first realise they have been betrayed by Imperial Britain.

1919: the American King-Crane Commission reach the following conclusion,"If [the] principle [of self-determination] is to rule, and so the wishes of Palestine's population are to be decisive as to what is to be done with Palestine, then it is to be remembered that the non-Jewish population of Palestine — nearly nine-tenths of the whole — are emphatically against the entire Zionist program.. To subject a people so minded to unlimited Jewish immigration, and to steady financial and social pressure to surrender the land, would be a gross violation of the principle just quoted...No British officers, consulted by the Commissioners, believed that the Zionist program could be carried out except by force of arms. The officers generally thought that a force of not less than fifty thousand soldiers would be required even to initiate the program. That of itself is evidence of a strong sense of the injustice of the Zionist program...The initial claim, often submitted by Zionist representatives, that they have a 'right' to Palestine based on occupation of two thousand years ago, can barely be seriously considered."

1922: the League of Nations (which contained not a single Middle Eastern state) gives the British a 'Mandate' over Palestine.

1936-9: the Palestinians revolt against British rule and the Zionist take over; the revolt is crushed with considerable brutality and the Palestinians are left virtually unarmed; David Ben-Gurion comments "politically we are the aggressors and they defend themselves... The country is theirs, because they inhabit it, whereas we want to come here and settle down, and in their view we want to take away from them their country, while we are still outside"; the Jewish terrorist Irgun group carry out 60 attacks against the Palestinians and the British army.

1939-45: Jewish underground terrorist groups continue to arm themselves; the Palestinians are now virtually unarmed.

1947: on 29 November, the United Nations passes resolution 182, approving a plan to partition historical Palestine into two states. Under the partition plan 56.47 per cent of the land (excluding Jerusalem) is to be given to the Jews, who form only 33 per cent of the population; the remainder would be a Palestinian ('Arab') state, but Jerusalem would be an open city under UN control.

1948: David Ben-Gurion and the Jewish terrorist groups unleash a terror campaign on the Palestinians. There are massacres at Tantura, Deir Yassin, Dawameh, Lydd (modern Lod, not in the area designated to be part of Israel) and other places; the aim is to capture a much greater area than that envisaged by the UN partition programme and in this it is successful; the refugees who flee the murderous Jewish terror gangs are never allowed to return; the terror campaign becomes known to Palestinians as the Nakba/the catastrophe; at the end of the campaign, Israeli forces have taken 78 per cent of historic Palestine.

1949: the Palestinian state never materialises; instead, Jordan annexes the West Bank, while Egypt administers the Gaza strip, until 1967.

1964: Nasser of Egypt and other Arab leaders agree to set up the Palestinian Liberation Organisation (PLO) as the representative of the Palestinian people. Three years later, Fatah, the largest resistance group, along with several others, joins the PLO, which becomes dominated by the armed resistance groups.

1967: June brings the Six-Day War; although this is billed as Israel defending itself, Menachen Begin, when PM in 1982, admits: "In June 1967, we had a choice. The Egyptian army concentration in the Sinai approaches did not prove that Nasser was really about to attack us. We must be honest with ourselves. We decided to attack him." The Israeli forces capture the West Bank and Gaza and annex Jerusalem and the Golan Heights.

December 1987 to 1993: the first Intifada, in which Palestinians rise up against the occupying army

1993 and 1995: Oslo accords I and II, signed by Israel and the PLO, are supposed to establish a 'road map' to peace.

4 November 1995: the assassination of Yitzhak Rabin by a Jewish extremist, thought by many to signal the end of hope for the peace process; from this time onwards the peace process stalls, settlement building continues and Palestinians begin to lose hope.

January 1996: the first Palestinian general election for president and members of the legislative council; despite Israeli attempts to sabotage it, the election is noted by international observers as being well conducted – free, open and democratic; the PNA (Palestine National Authority) is established and Palestinians look forward to the end of occupation, liberation, and the chance to set up their long-awaited state.

September 2000 to February 2005: disillusion spreads among Palestinians as the peace process is stalled, while the occupation and settlement building continues; the second Intifada starts, triggered by Ariel Sharon's visit to Al Aqsa on 28 September 2000.

12 March 2002: UN Security Council Resolution 1397 reaffirms a two-state solution and lays the groundwork for a road map for peace. Arab leaders set out a comprehensive Arab Peace Initiative. Arafat endorses the proposal, but Israel virtually ignores it.

16 June 2002: Israel starts construction of the illegal Separation Wall, annexing yet more Palestinian land into Israel.

March 2002: the Israelis lay siege to Yasser Arafat's headquarters, the Muqatah; on 29 March Israel launches Operation Defensive Shield, lasting until 3 May. UN estimates that 497 Palestinians killed and 1,447 wounded, mostly members of the Palestinian security forces and militant groups.

19 September 2002: Israelis again lay siege to the Muqatah, destroying most of the buildings and ignoring a UN demand to desist. UN Under-Secretary-General Terje Rød-Larsen, one of the architects of the Oslo accords, comments on 27 September, "The Israeli army's siege of Yasser Arafat amid the ruins of his bulldozed presidential compound could mean 'the death' of hopes for a Palestinian state and a peace agreement… We're moving in the direction of state destruction and not state-building."

October 2004: Yasser Arafat is transferred to a hospital in France, where he dies on 11 November, possibly murdered with polonium by Israeli security and with the consent of top Israeli officials.

Summer 2005: Israel withdraws from Gaza, while retaining control of Gaza's airspace, coast and borders; this is done with the aim of annexing Jerusalem, the Jordan valley and large areas of the West Bank; according to Dov Weissglass, PM Ariel Sharon's senior adviser, "The significance of the disengagement plan is the freezing of the peace process, and when you freeze that process, you prevent the establishment of a Palestinian state, and you prevent a discussion on the refugees, the borders and Jerusalem. Effectively, this whole package called the Palestinian state, with all that it entails, has been removed indefinitely from our agenda."

January 2006: tensions start to appear among Palestinians, due to the lack of progress with peace talks; Hamas win elections to the Palestinian legislative council; efforts to create a unity government fail; Israel arrests Hamas members while the Quartet (US, Russia, UN and European Union) demand that Hamas recognise Israel, which they refuse; foreign assistance is halted and economic sanctions imposed.

2007: Hamas ends up in control of Gaza and Fatah in control of the West Bank; in September, Israel starts the blockade of the Gaza strip.

29 February 2007: Israel launches ground and air offensive against Gaza; in June, Hamas takes over full control of the Gaza strip.

19 December 2008-18 January 2009: Israel attacks Gaza in Operation Cast Lead; an estimated 1,166-1,417 Palestinians and 13 Israelis die.

14-21 November 2012: Operation Pillar of Defence, the Israelis again attack Gaza; they claim this is in response to rocket attacks; 158 Gazans, overwhelmingly civilians, are killed and 6 Israelis.

8 July-26 August 2014: Operation Protective Edge; over 2,000 Gazans, mainly civilians, are killed and more than 10,000 wounded; 66 Israeli soldiers are killed and 6 civilians (including one Thai).

Appendix II

Gaza ceasefire violations January and February

2 January: Northern Gaza – evening, an Israeli Army position behind the Green Line opened fire on east Jabalya, wounding a 25-year-old resident in both feet. The Israel spokeswomen claimed the soldiers were dispersing a riot.

Central Gaza – evening, an Israeli Army position behind the Green Line opened fire on the al-Bureij refugee camp.

Khan Yunis – afternoon, an Israeli Army position behind the Green Line opened fire on people in the al-Farahin area of Abasan al-Kabireh as they were hunting birds near the border.

3: Northern Gaza – morning, the Israeli Army shot its way onto Beit Lahiya farmland and bulldozed crops.

Rafah – dawn, the Israeli Navy opened fire with machine guns and on Palestinian fishing boats, wounding one fisherman, Jamal Nu'man, and destroying his boat with a shell. The Israeli spokeswoman claimed they were smuggling.

5: Khan Yunis – morning, an Israeli Army position behind the Green Line opened fire on al-Qarara farmland.

Central Gaza – afternoon, an Israeli Army position behind the Green Line fired stun and tear gas grenades at goatherds in the east al-Bureij refugee camp.

8: Khan Yunis – evening, an Israeli Army position behind the Green Line opened live fire and fired tear gas grenades at al-Qarara farmland.

10: Rafah – morning, an Israeli Army position behind the Green Line opened fire on shepherds and several other residents near the Sufa Crossing.

13: Northern Gaza – evening, the Israeli Army, equipped with bulldozers, opened fire while making an incursion onto east Jabalya farmland.

Khan Yunis – afternoon, an Israeli Army position behind the Green Line opened fire on several farmers in east al-Fukhari.

14: Khan Yunis – morning, an Israeli Army position behind the Green Line opened fire on farmers and farm workers on farmland in east al-Qarara, Khaza'a and the al-Farahin area of Abasan al-Kabira.

16: Northern Gaza – evening, one person was wounded when an Israeli Army position behind the Green Line opened fire on people in east Jabalya.

Khan Yunis – afternoon, an Israeli Army position behind the Green Line opened fire on several farmers and shepherds in east al-Qarara.

17: Rafah – dawn, the Israeli Navy opened fire on Palestinian fishing boats off Rafah.

18: Rafah – an Israeli Army position behind the Green Line opened fire on east Rafah farmland.

19: Northern Gaza – dawn, the Israeli Navy opened fire on Palestinian fishing boats off al-Sudaniya.

Khan Yunis – afternoon, an Israeli Army position behind the Green Line opened fire on shepherds at work in al-Qarara and in the al-Farahin area in east Abasan al-Kabira.

Rafah – evening, an Israeli Army position behind the Green Line opened fire on east Rafah farmland.

21: Gaza – 09:30, the Israeli Navy opened fire on Palestinian fishing boats off al-Sudaniya, wounding a fisherman, Atef Bakr, and damaging his fishing boat.

Gaza – dawn, Israeli Navy again opened fire on Palestinian fishing boats off al-Sudaniya.

Khan Yunis – evening, the Israeli Navy opened fire on Palestinian fishing boats off al-Shateh.

23: Northern Gaza – evening, one person was wounded when an Israeli Army position behind the Green Line opened fire on residents in east Jabalya.

Northern Gaza – dawn, the Israeli Navy opened fire on Palestinian fishing boats off al-Sudaniya.

Central Gaza – evening, an Israeli Army position behind the Green Line opened fire on Deir al-Balah agricultural land.

Central Gaza – dawn, the Israeli Navy opened fire on Palestinian fishing boats off Deir al-Balah.

Khan Yunis – dawn, the Israeli Navy opened fire on Palestinian fishing boats off Khan Yunis.

Rafah – dawn, the Israeli Navy opened fire on Palestinian fishing boats off Rafah.

24: Central Gaza – evening, an Israeli Army position behind the Green Line opened fire on al-Maghazi refugee camp farmland.

25: Northern Gaza – morning, the Israeli Navy opened fire on Palestinian fishing boats off al-Sudaniya.

Northern Gaza – evening, an Israeli Army position behind the Green Line opened fire on agricultural land in the east al-Farahin area of Abasan al-Kabira.

28: Khan Yunis – morning, an Israeli Army position behind the Green Line opened fire on farmers in east al-Fajjari.

29: Northern Gaza – morning, an Israeli Army position on the Green Line opened fire on east Beit Hanun.

Northern Gaza – evening, the Israeli Navy opened fire on fishing boats off al-Sudaniya.

Northern Gaza – evening, the Israeli Navy opened fire on fishing boats off Rafah.

30: Northern Gaza – morning, the Israeli Navy opened fire on fishing boats off al-Sudaniya.

Khan Yunis – an Israeli Army position opened fire on Khan Yunis.

1 February: Northern Gaza – 05:00, the Israeli Navy opened fire on Palestinian fishing boats off al-Waha in Beit Lahiya.

Northern Gaza – 07:00, the Israeli Navy again opened fire on Palestinian fishing boats off al-Waha in Beit Lahiya.

Northern Gaza – 09:00, the Israeli Navy yet again opened fire on Palestinian fishing boats off al-Waha in Beit Lahiya.

Khan Yunis – afternoon, an Israeli Army position behind the Green Line opened fire on local residents.

2: Northern Gaza – 10:00, the Israeli Navy opened fire on Palestinian fishing boats off the al-Waha district in Beit Lahiya.

Northern Gaza – morning, Israeli gunboats again opened fire on Palestinian fishing boats off al-Waha.

Central Gaza – afternoon, an Israeli Army position behind the Green Line opened fire on farmers trying to work their farmland in the east of the al-Maghazi refugee camp.

3: Gaza – 21:30, the Israeli Navy opened fire on Palestinian fishing boats off the Gaza City al-Shat'a refugee camp.

4: Northern Gaza – 09:30, the Israeli Navy opened fire on Palestinian fishing boats off al-Sudaniya.

5: Northern Gaza – dawn, the Israeli Navy opened fire towards Palestinian fishing boats off al-Sudaniya in west Beit Lahiya.

Northern Gaza – evening, an Israeli Army position behind the Green Line opened fire on al-Qarara farmland.

6: Northern Gaza – afternoon, an Israeli Army position behind the Green Line opened fire on east Jabalya.

Central Gaza – morning, Israeli forces positioned behind the Green Line opened fire on several farmers at work on their land in east Deir al-Balah.

Khan Yunis – afternoon, an Israeli Army position behind the Green Line opened fire on farmland in east Khan Yunis.

Rafah – afternoon, Israeli forces positioned behind the Green Line opened fire on agricultural land in east Rafah.

Northern Gaza – morning, the Israeli Navy opened fire on Palestinian fishing boats off al-Sudaniya beach in west Beit Lahiya.

Northern Gaza – morning, Israeli gunboats again opened fire on Palestinian fishing boats off al-Sudaniya.

Central Gaza – morning, an Israeli Army position behind the Green Line opened fire on farmers in the al-Bureij refugee camp.

Central Gaza – morning, an Israeli Army position behind the Green Line opened fire on farmers in the al-Maghazi refugee camp.

8: Northern Gaza – morning, the Israeli Army shot its way onto Beit Hanun farmland and bulldozed crops.

Northern Gaza – morning, the Israeli Navy opened fire on Palestinian fishing boats off al-Sudaniya in west Beit Lahiya.

9: Northern Gaza – 11:40, an Israeli Army position behind the Green Line opened fire on residents in east Jabalya.

Central Gaza – afternoon, Israeli forces positioned behind the Green Line opened fire on east al-Bureij refugee camp farmland.

10: Central Gaza – an Israeli Army position behind the Green Line opened fire on the al-Maghazi refugee camp, wounding a resident.

13: Gaza – morning, an Israeli Army position behind the Green Line opened fire with live bullets on farmers and farmworkers on north Gaza City farmland.

Khan Yunis – morning, several homes were damaged when an Israeli Army position behind the Green Line opened fire on residents in east Khan Yunis.

14: Khan Yunis – morning, the Israeli Navy opened fire on Palestinian fishing boats off Khan Yunis.

Morning, an Israeli Army position behind the Green Line opened fire on farmers in the al-Sanati area of Abasan al-Kabireh.

15: Central Gaza – 10:15, the Israeli Army stormed into the north-east quarter of the Maghazi refugee camp, opening fire on and wounding a resident, Ahmad Salaah, before taking him prisoner.

16: Central Gaza – afternoon, an Israeli Army position behind the Green Line opened fire on shepherds herding sheep on al-Maghazi refugee camp land.

Khan Yunis – afternoon, Israeli forces positioned behind the Green Line opened fire on several shepherds herding sheep in east Khan Yunis.

17: Northern Gaza – 09:00, an Israeli Army position behind the Green Line opened fire on shepherds near east Jabaliya.

18: Central Gaza – evening, an Israeli Army position behind the Green Line opened fire on people in the al-Maghazi refugee camp.

22: Rafah – morning, an Israeli Army position behind the Green Line opened fire on local farmers to the north-east of the city.

23: Northern Gaza – evening, one person was wounded when an Israeli Army position behind the Green Line opened fire on Beit Lahiya.

Northern Gaza – evening, the Israeli Navy opened fire on Palestinian fishing boats off west Beit Lahiya. One fishing boat was damaged in the attack.

Gaza – afternoon, Israeli forces stormed Juhur al-Dik farmland in south-east Gaza, opening fire and bulldozing crops.

Central Gaza – evening, the Israeli Navy opened fire on Palestinian fishing boats off Deir al-Balah.

Central Gaza – evening, Israeli gunboats opened fire on Palestinian fishing boats off the al-Maghazi refugee camp.

Khan Yunis – morning, an Israeli Army position behind the Green Line launched flares and opened fire on farmers on east Khan Yunis agricultural land.

25: Central Gaza – evening, an Israeli Army position behind the Green Line opened fire on farmers on Deir al-Balah farmland.

26: Northern Gaza – an Israeli Army position behind the Green Line opened fire on farmland in east Jabaliya.

Central Gaza – afternoon, Israeli forces positioned behind the Green Line opened fire on east Deir al-Balah farmland.

27: Northern Gaza – evening, the Israeli Navy opened fire on Palestinian fishing boats off al-Sudaniya.

Khan Yunis – morning, an Israeli Army position behind the Green Line opened fire on farmers on east Khazar village farmland.

28: Northern Gaza – morning, the Israeli Navy opened fire on Palestinian fishing boats off Beit Lahiya.

Northern Gaza – 06:00, Israeli gunboats opened fire on Palestinian fishing boats off al-Sudaniya.

Northern Gaza – morning, an Israeli Army position behind the Green Line opened fire on farmers in east Jabaliya.

Gaza – morning, Israeli forces positioned behind the Green Line opened fire on farmers in east Juhur al-Dik.

Gaza – morning, an Israeli Army position behind the Green Line opened fire on farmers in east Gaza.

Central Gaza – morning, the Israeli Navy opened fire on Palestinian fishing boats off Deir al-Balah.

Khan Yunis – morning, Israeli forces positioned behind the Green Line opened fire on farmers in east Abasan al-Qabireh.

For updates on ceasefire violations and other Israeli actions in the West Bank and Gaza, please contact Leslie Bravery, lorca@clear.net.nz, and ask to be put on the mailing list.

Appendix III

Attacks on Gazan farmland in April

1.4. Central Gaza – morning, an Israeli Army position behind the Green Line opened fire on people working agricultural land in the al-Bureij refugee camp.

Central Gaza – morning, Israeli Army forces positioned behind the Green Line opened fire on people working on al-Maghazi refugee camp farmland.

2.4. Khan Yunis – afternoon, an Israeli Army position behind the Green Line opened fire on agricultural land in the al-Fara'ien area in the east Abasan al-Kabeerah.

3.4. Gaza – morning, an Israeli Army position behind the Green Line opened fire on, and Israeli tanks shelled, al-Zaytoun farmland in south-east Gaza City.

5.4. Central Gaza – morning, an Israeli Army position behind the Green Line opened fire on agricultural land in east Deir al-Balah.

Khan Yunis – morning, Israeli forces shot their way onto farmland near Khazar and al-Fakhari towns and bulldozed crops.

6.4. Central Gaza – morning, soldiers behind the Green Line opened fire on al-Bureij refugee camp farmland.

Khan Yunis – morning, Israeli forces positioned behind the Green Line opened fire on east Khan Yunis agricultural land.

Khan Yunis – morning, an Israeli Army position behind the Green Line opened fire on al-Qarara farmland.

8.4. Central Gaza – evening, Israeli tanks positioned behind the Green Line shelled Deir al-Balah farmland.

Khan Yunis – morning, an Israeli Army position behind the Green Line opened fire on Palestinian farmers on east Abasan al-Kabera and Khuza'a agricultural land.

11.4. Khan Yunis – morning, an Israeli Army position behind the Green Line opened fire on agricultural land in Abasan al-Kabira.

Khan Yunis – afternoon, soldiers behind the Green Line opened fire on al-Fakhari farmland.

Rafah – an Israeli Army position behind the Green Line opened fire on agricultural land in east Rafah.

14.4. Northern Gaza – morning, soldiers behind the Green Line opened fire on Abu Samarah farmland in north Beit Lahiya.

Gaza – morning, Israeli forces opened fire from behind the Green Line towards agricultural land in south-east Gaza.

Khan Yunis – morning, the Israeli Army shot its way onto al-Fakhari agricultural land and bulldozed crops.

Khan Yunis – morning, soldiers behind the Green Line opened fire on farmland in east al-Khaz'a.

Rafah – morning, Israeli forces stormed agricultural land in the al-Nahda neighbourhood and opened fire while bulldozing crops.

15.4. Gaza – evening, an Israeli Army position behind the Green Line opened fire on Juhor al-Dik agricultural land in south-east Gaza.

Khan Yunis – afternoon, Israeli troops positioned behind the Green Line opened fire on farmland in east al-Khaz'a.

18.4. Northern Gaza – morning, an Israeli Army position behind the Green Line opened fire on Beit Lahiya agricultural land in Bu'rat Aby Samarah.

Gaza – morning, an Israeli Army position behind the Green Line opened fire on south-east Gaza farmland.

At 08:00, Israeli forces positioned behind the Green Line opened fire on agricultural land in east al-Khaz'aa.

19.4. Northern Gaza – 10:00, Israeli forces positioned behind the Green Line opened fire on several farmers on agricultural land in east Jabaliya.

Northern Gaza – 12:10, soldiers behind the Green Line opened fire on people on farmland in east Jabaliya.

Northern Gaza – 13:40, soldiers behind the Green Line again opened fire on farmers and farm workers in east Jabaliya.

Northern Gaza – 15:20, yet again, farmers and farm workers on agricultural land in east Jabaliya came under fire from Israeli forces.

Gaza – 14:30, soldiers behind the Green Line opened fire on farmers and workers on Jaher al-Dik farmland.

Khan Yunis – morning, soldiers behind the Green Line opened fire on people at work on al-Fakhari farmland.

20.4. Northern Gaza – 09:10, soldiers behind the Green Line opened fire on people working east Jabaliya farmland.

Central Gaza – morning, the Israeli Army stormed the Wadi Salqa area of Deir al-Balah, opening fire and bulldozing crops.

Khan Yunis – morning, the Israeli Army shot its way onto al-Qarara farmland and bulldozed crops.

Khan Yunis – 16:30, soldiers behind the Green Line opened fire on farmers in east Khan Yunis.

22.4. Central Gaza – 11:30, soldiers behind the Green Line opened fire on Deir al-Balah farmland.

Rafah – 17:10, soldiers behind the Green Line opened fire on agricultural land in east Rafah.

23.4. Northern Gaza – Israeli fighter jets attacked northern Gaza farms, destroying crops and causing widespread damage (this followed the first rocket fired from Gaza in 2015, which landed in an open field, causing no injuries or damage).

Northern Gaza – 23:50, Israeli tanks positioned behind the Green Line shelled and opened fire on agricultural land in east Beit Hanun.

Khan Yunis – 12:00, soldiers behind the Green Line opened fire on al-Fakhari farmland.

24.4. Gaza – 18:00, soldiers behind the Green Line opened fire on agricultural land in Jaher al-Dik.

Central Gaza – 18:15, soldiers behind the Green Line opened fire on Deir al-Balah farmland.

Khan Yunis – 18:15, a child was wounded when an Israeli Army position behind the Green Line opened fire on people in Abasan al-Kabira.

Rafah – 13:25, soldiers the Green Line opened fire on agricultural land in east Rafah.

25.4. Gaza – 10:00, soldiers behind the Green Line opened fire on agricultural land in east Gaza.

Gaza – 19:30, Israeli forces again opened fire from their positions behind the Green Line on east Gaza farmland.

Central Gaza – 17:00, soldiers behind the Green Line opened fire on agricultural land in the al-Bureij refugee camp.

Khan Yunis – 09:30, soldiers behind the Green Line opened fire on farms in Abasan al-Kabireh.

26.4. Northern Gaza – 12:30, a Palestinian farmer, Rami Matar, was wounded when an Israeli Army position behind the Green Line opened fire on farmers in the Abu Safiya area of east Jabaliya.

27.4. Khan Yunis – dawn, soldiers behind the Green Line opened fire on al-Khaz'a farmland.

28.4. Northern Gaza – 18:10, soldiers behind the Green Line opened fire on farmers and farm workers on land in east Jabaliya.

Central Gaza – 09:15, soldiers the Green Line opened fire on Deir al-Balah agricultural land.

30.4. Gaza – 11:50, soldiers behind the Green Line opened fire on agricultural land in east al-Shuja'iya.

Appendix IV

United Nations draft resolution

Consideration of draft resolution A/C.2/70/L.21

At the 31st meeting, on 12 November, the representative of South Africa, on behalf of the Group of 77 and China, made a statement.

Subsequently, Turkey joined in sponsoring the draft resolution.

At the same meeting, the Committee was informed that the draft resolution had no programme budget implications.

Also at the same meeting, the Committee adopted draft resolution A/C.2/70/L.21 by a recorded vote of 156 to 7, with 9 abstentions (see para. 12). The voting was as follows:

In favour:

Afghanistan, Albania, Algeria, Andorra, Angola, Antigua and Barbuda, Argentina, Armenia, Austria, Azerbaijan, Bahamas, Bahrain, Bangladesh, Barbados, Belarus, Belgium, Belize, Benin, Bhutan, Bolivia (Plurinational State of), Bosnia and Herzegovina, Botswana, Brazil, Brunei Darussalam, Bulgaria, Burundi, Cabo Verde, Cambodia, Chile, China, Colombia, Congo, Costa Rica, Croatia, Cuba, Cyprus, Czech Republic, Democratic People's Republic of Korea, Denmark, Djibouti, Dominican Republic, Ecuador, Egypt, El Salvador, Eritrea, Estonia, Ethiopia, Fiji, Finland, France, Gabon, Georgia, Germany, Ghana, Greece, Grenada, Guatemala, Guinea, Guinea-Bissau, Guyana, Haiti, Hungary, Iceland, India, Indonesia, Iran (Islamic Republic of), Iraq, Ireland, Italy, Jamaica, Japan, Jordan, Kazakhstan, Kenya, Kuwait, Kyrgyzstan, Lao People's Democratic Republic, Latvia, Lebanon, Libya, Liechtenstein, Lithuania, Luxembourg, Madagascar, Malawi, Malaysia, Maldives, Mali, Malta, Mauritania, Mauritius, Mexico, Monaco, Mongolia, Montenegro, Morocco, Mozambique, Myanmar, Namibia, Nepal, Netherlands, New Zealand, Nicaragua, Niger, Nigeria, Norway, Oman, Pakistan, Panama, Peru, Philippines, Poland, Portugal, Qatar, Republic of Korea, Republic of Moldova, Romania, Russian Federation, Saint Kitts and Nevis, Samoa, San Marino, Saudi Arabia, Senegal, Serbia, Sierra Leone, Singapore, Slovakia, Slovenia, Solomon Islands, Somalia, South Africa, Spain, Sri Lanka, Sudan, Suriname, Sweden, Switzerland, Syrian Arab Republic, Tajikistan, Thailand, the former Yugoslav Republic of Macedonia, Timor-Leste, Trinidad and Tobago, Tunisia, Turkey, Turkmenistan, Ukraine, United Arab Emirates, United Kingdom of Great Britain and Northern Ireland, Uruguay, Uzbekistan, Venezuela (Bolivarian Republic of), Viet Nam, Yemen, Zambia, Zimbabwe.

Against:

Canada, Israel, Marshall Islands, Micronesia (Federated States of), Nauru, Palau, United States of America.

Abstaining:

Australia, Cameroon, Central African Republic, Côte d'Ivoire, Honduras, Papua New Guinea, Paraguay, Togo, Tonga.

Permanent sovereignty of the Palestinian people in the Occupied Palestinian Territory, including East Jerusalem, and of the Arab population in the occupied Syrian Golan over their natural resources

The General Assembly,

Recalling its resolution 69/241 of 19 December 2014, and taking note of Economic and Social Council resolution 2015/17 of 20 July 2015,

Recalling also its resolutions 58/292 of 6 May 2004 and 59/251 of 22 December 2004,

Reaffirming the principle of the permanent sovereignty of peoples under foreign occupation over their natural resources,

Guided by the principles of the Charter of the United Nations, affirming the inadmissibility of the acquisition of territory by force, and recalling relevant Security Council resolutions, including resolutions 242 (1967) of 22 November 1967, 465 (1980) of 1 March 1980 and 497 (1981) of 17 December 1981,

Recalling its resolution 2625 (XXV) of 24 October 1970,

Reaffirming the applicability of the Geneva Convention relative to the Protection of Civilian Persons in Time of War, of 12 August 1949, to the Occupied Palestinian Territory, including East Jerusalem, and other Arab territories occupied by Israel since 1967,

Recalling, in this regard, the International Covenant on Civil and Political Rights and the International Covenant on Economic, Social and Cultural Rights, and affirming that these human rights instruments must be respected in the Occupied Palestinian Territory, including East Jerusalem, as well as in the occupied Syrian Golan,

Recalling also the advisory opinion rendered on 9 July 2004 by the International Court of Justice on the legal consequences of the construction of a wall in the Occupied Palestinian Territory, and recalling further its resolutions ES-10/15 of 20 July 2004 and ES-10/17 of 15 December 2006,

Recalling further its resolution 67/19 of 29 November 2012,

Taking note of the accession by Palestine to several human rights treaties and the core humanitarian law treaties, as well as to other international treaties,

Expressing its concern about the exploitation by Israel, the occupying Power, of the natural resources of the Occupied Palestinian Territory, including East Jerusalem, and other Arab territories occupied by Israel since 1967,

Expressing its grave concern about the extensive destruction by Israel, the occupying Power, of agricultural land and orchards in the Occupied Palestinian Territory, including the uprooting of a vast number of fruit-bearing trees and the destruction of farms and greenhouses, and the grave environmental and economic impact in this regard,

Expressing its grave concern also about the widespread destruction caused by Israel, the occupying Power, to vital infrastructure, including water pipelines, sewage networks and electricity networks, in the Occupied Palestinian Territory, in particular in the Gaza Strip during the military operations of July and August 2014, which, inter alia, has polluted the environment and negatively affect the functioning of water and sanitation systems and the water supply and other natural resources of the Palestinian people, and stressing the urgency of the reconstruction and development of water and other vital civilian infrastructure, including the project for the desalination facility for the Gaza Strip,

Expressing its grave concern further about the negative impact on the environment and on reconstruction and development efforts of the thousands of items of unexploded ordnance that remain in the Gaza Strip as a result of the conflict in July and August 2014,

Recalling the 2009 report by the United Nations Environment Programme regarding the grave environmental situation in the Gaza Strip, and the 2012 report, "Gaza in 2020: A liveable place?", by the United Nations country team in the Occupied alestinian Territory, and stressing the need for follow-up to the recommendations contained therein,

Deploring the detrimental impact of the Israeli settlements on Palestinian and other Arab natural resources, especially as a result of the confiscation of land and the forced diversion of water resources, including the destruction of orchards and crops and the seizure of water well by Israeli settlers, and of the dire socioeconomic consequences in this regard,

Recalling the report of the independent international fact-finding mission to investigate the implications of the Israeli settlements on the civil, political, economic, social and cultural rights of the Palestinian people throughout the Occupied Palestinian Territory, including East Jerusalem,

Aware of the detrimental impact on Palestinian natural resources being caused by the unlawful construction of the wall by Israel, the occupying Power, in the Occupied Palestinian Territory, including in and around East Jerusalem, and of its grave effect as well on the economic and social conditions of the Palestinian people,

Stressing the urgency of achieving without delay an end to the Israeli occupation that began in 1967 and a just, lasting and comprehensive peace settlement on all tracks, on the basis of Security Council resolutions 242 (1967), 338 (1973) of 22 October 1973, 425 (1978) of 19 March 1978 and 1397 (2002) of 12 March 2002, the principle of land for peace, the Arab Peace Initiative and the Quartet performance-based road map to a permanent two-State solution to the Israeli-Palestinian conflict, as endorsed by the Security Council in its resolution 1515 (2003) of 19 November 2003 and supported by the Council in its resolution 1850 (2008) of 16 December 2008,

Stressing also, in this regard, the need for respect for the obligation upon Israel under the road map to freeze settlement activity, including so-called "natural growth", and to dismantle all settlement outposts erected since March 2001,

Stressing further the need for respect and preservation of the territorial unity, contiguity and integrity of all of the Occupied Palestinian Territory, including East Jerusalem,

Recalling the need to end all acts of violence, including acts of terror, provocation, incitement and destruction,

Taking note of the report prepared by the Economic and Social Commission for Western Asia on the economic and social repercussions of the Israeli occupation on the living conditions of the Palestinian people in the Occupied Palestinian Territory, including East Jerusalem, and of the Arab population in the occupied Syrian Golan, as transmitted by the Secretary-General,

Reaffirms the inalienable rights of the Palestinian people and of the population of the occupied Syrian Golan over their natural resources, including land, water and energy resources;

Demands that Israel, the occupying Power, cease the exploitation, damage, cause of loss or depletion and endangerment of the natural resources in the Occupied Palestinian Territory, including East Jerusalem, and in the occupied Syrian Golan;

Recognizes the right of the Palestinian people to claim restitution as a result of any exploitation, damage, loss or depletion or endangerment of their natural resources resulting from illegal measures taken by Israel, the occupying Power, and Israeli settlers in the Occupied Palestinian Territory, including East Jerusalem, and expresses the hope that this issue will be dealt with within the framework of the final status negotiations between the Palestinian and Israeli sides;

Stresses that the wall and settlements being constructed by Israel in the Occupied Palestinian Territory, including in and around East Jerusalem, are contrary to international law and are seriously depriving the Palestinian people of their natural resources, and calls in this regard for full compliance with the legal obligations affirmed in the 9 July 2004 advisory opinion of the International Court of Justice and in relevant United Nations resolutions, including General Assembly resolution ES-10/15;

Calls upon Israel, the occupying Power, to comply strictly with its obligations under international law, including international humanitarian law, and to cease immediately and completely all policies and measures aimed at the alteration of the character and status of the Occupied Palestinian Territory, including East Jerusalem;

Also calls upon Israel, the occupying Power, to bring a halt to all actions, including those perpetrated by Israeli settlers, harming the environment, including the dumping of all kinds of waste materials, in the Occupied Palestinian Territory, including East Jerusalem, and in the occupied Syrian Golan, which gravely threaten their natural resources, namely water and land resources, and which pose an environmental, sanitation and health threat to the civilian populations;

Further calls upon Israel to cease its destruction of vital infrastructure, including water pipelines, sewage networks and electricity networks, which, inter alia, has a negative impact on the natural resources of the Palestinian people, stresses the urgent need to advance reconstruction and development projects in this regard, including in the Gaza Strip, and calls for support for the necessary efforts in this regard, in line with the commitments made at, inter alia, the Cairo International Conference on Palestine: Reconstructing Gaza, held on 12 October 2014;

Calls upon Israel, the occupying Power, to remove all obstacles to the implementation of critical environmental projects, including sewage treatment plants in the Gaza Strip and the reconstruction and development of water infrastructure, including the project for the desalination facility for the Gaza Strip;

Calls for the immediate and safe removal of all unexploded ordnance in the Gaza Strip and for support for the efforts of the United Nations Mine Action Service in this regard, and welcomes the efforts exerted by the Service to date;

Encourages all States and international organizations to continue to actively pursue policies to ensure respect for their obligations under international law with regard to all illegal Israeli practices and measures in the Occupied Palestinian Territory, including East Jerusalem, particularly Israeli settlement activities and the exploitation of natural resources;

Requests the Secretary-General to report to the General Assembly at its seventy-first session on the implementation of the present resolution, including with regard to the cumulative impact of the exploitation, damage and depletion by Israel of natural resources in the Occupied Palestinian Territory, including East Jerusalem, and in the occupied Syrian Golan, and decides to include in the provisional agenda of its seventy-first session the item entitled"Permanent sovereignty of the Palestinian people in the Occupied Palestinian Territory, including East Jerusalem, and of the Arab population in the occupied Syrian Golan over their natural resources".